ALIEN
ABDUCTIONS

ALIEN
ABDUCTIONS

Creating a Modern Phenomenon

TERRY MATHESON

Prometheus Books

59 John Glenn Drive
Amherst, New York 14228-2197

Published 1998 by Prometheus Books

02 01 00 99 98   5 4 3 2 1

Library of Congress Cataloging-in-Publication Data

Matheson, Terry.
    Alien abductions : creating a modern phenomenon : focusing on the popular works of Budd Hopkins, John Fuller, Whitley Strieber, David Jacobs, John Mack, and others / Terry Matheson.
        p.   cm.
    Includes bibliographical references and index.
    ISBN 1–57392–244–7 (cloth : alk. paper)
    1. Alien abduction. I. Title.
BF2050.M36   1998
398'.4—dc21   98–30816
                                                                                    CIP

Printed by Quinn-Woodbine, Inc., in the United States of America on acid-free paper

ACKNOWLEDGMENTS

I would like to thank the following institutions and individuals for all their help and assistance: the University of Saskatchewan and the College of Arts and Science, for approving this project and granting me the sabbatical leave to complete it; the always helpful and friendly people at the Information and Reference Desk, Frances Morrison Library, Saskatoon, for answering my obscure and innumerable questions; Bernadette Heitmar of the University of Saskatchewan Bookstore; the Greenfield Bookstore, Winnipeg, Manitoba; my sister-in-law, Karen Lopez, of Los Angeles, California, as well as Tyler Maschino of Cedar Falls, Iowa, for their help in finding rare and out-of-print abduction material; Dave and Shirley Weary of Saskatoon, Saskatchewan; John Olson of Ottawa, Ontario; Doug Millington of Charlottetown, Prince Edward Island; Dr. Georgina Hogg, M. Beth Clark, and my mother, Mrs. Ruth Matheson, all of Winnipeg, Manitoba, for reading the manuscript and providing many helpful suggestions; Dr. Isobel Findlay, Department of English, University of Saskatchewan, for editing the original manuscript and, together with her husband, Professor Len Findlay, for offering much-needed ongoing encouragement; Rita Terry and Jayson Brown, also of the English Department, for compiling the index; Kathy Deyell, Steven L. Mitchell, and everyone else at Prometheus Books, for preparing the final version for publication; and most of all my wife, Pat, and my daughters, Suzanne and Lesley, for providing a domestic atmosphere of loving support, which was as unwavering as it was necessary.

"There are people in the world today whose imagination is so vivid that when they have an idea it comes to them as an audible voice, sometimes uttered by a visible figure."

George Bernard Shaw, preface to *Saint Joan*

To the women and men whose extraordinary experiences occasioned the writing of this book.

CONTENTS

PREFACE

It is probably safe to say that there are very few people in North America today who have never heard of the UFO abduction phenomenon. Most of us have at least some knowledge of the frightening stories told by people who claim to have been taken from homes, beds, or even their moving automobiles, and subjected to a series of often unpleasant and painful tests by strange-looking little creatures with large, hairless heads and enormous, dark, "wrap-around" eyes. Rarely a week goes by, it seems, without an appearance by an abductee on television or in a magazine, and each season appears to bring with it a new book or film on the subject. Whatever the actual cause of these experiences, one thing is certain: from their first appearance, alien abduction stories have fascinated the North American public to an unparalleled degree.

Initially, I was struck by the extent of the American public's interest in this subject, to say nothing of its readiness to accept more or less at face value the stories the abductees were telling. This degree of public acceptance is itself surprising when we recall that our century has been replete with visionaries whose claims of having encountered unearthly beings were ignored or otherwise summarily dismissed by all but a few devoted followers. Indeed, it is fair to say that only these particular accounts of contact with extraterrestrial beings have been taken seriously on any kind of scale (if the popularity of abduction books is any indication), even though stories of encounters with otherworldly beings have been in circulation literally for ages. This book grew out of my attempt to find out why the abduction accounts, unlike previous claims made, have not been dismissed as the others were, but have been embraced with considerable enthusiasm.

In my initial examination of abduction literature, I made two discoveries regarding these narratives and their crucial role in determining how they were being received. By and large, authors of most abduction chronicles favored one interpretive possibility—that the experiences were taking place more or less as the abductees claimed—and relentlessly privileged that possibility even when the evidence pointed in other directions, as it frequently did. I also noticed that the original evidence itself—the actual information provided by the abductees—was often far less precise and coherent than was the material the public received. In fact, readers of such books were being manipulated to a significant extent, the writers having employed various strategies designed to enhance coherence and lessen the likelihood that alternative conclusions would be reached.

There are many possible reasons for these authors presenting their material as they did. Obviously, such stories were far more dramatic and gripping (and saleable!) when stated as true events than they would have been if the authors presented them simply as unusual but otherwise inconsequential psychological aberrations peculiar to the persons involved. Nevertheless, the favoring of the extraterrestrial explanation did not seem entirely sufficient to account for the appeal of this version of the stories. From their first appearance, abduction narratives were obviously touching responsive chords far more successfully than their predecessors had been able to do.

It was also obvious that the narratives' popularity was on some level linked to social conditions, which were now presumably ripe for the favorable reception of such stories where they had not been before, and that the public was now seeing a thematic relevance where none had been previously discerned. This relevance of the stories suggested to me that they might be speaking to people much in the way the myths of old had spoken to our ancestors, and that viewing them from a mythological perspective might prove a profitable line of inquiry. I began to suspect that what was occurring was the creation of a modern, secular myth that we were fortunate enough to be able to observe in the process of being formed and refined; and that all the people involved—abductees, authors, and the reading public as well—were working together, however unconsciously, to produce this myth for our time. Simply put, authors were rearranging the raw material provided by the abductees in a manner that appealed to the public, and in doing so fulfilled a function similar to those that classical myths served. What follows is my attempt to investigate the various aspects of this process: first, to demonstrate the various ways the raw material has been reconfigured by the authors of these abduction narratives and second, to show that such manipulation of evidence is an inevitable part of myth-making basic to all societies, for it is regulated by the need to create a narrative that will explain an aspect or aspects of a culture to itself.

Concerning my own relationship to the material, my particular experience as an interpreter of texts (I have been teaching English, and American literature in particular, for over twenty-five years) puts me in a good position to approach these works. For one thing, I have some familiarity with narrative strategies as well as dominant American cultural values; for another, I have no particular scientific predispositions concerning the nature of the material itself. That is to say, I consider myself to be in a good position to bring to these books some experience of how writers of any narrative can influence their readers into forming certain conclusions. At the same time, having no axe to grind as far as the abduction experiences themselves were concerned, I hope I can also bring a reasonably open mind to the subject.

One cautionary note: Readers looking for a definitive explanation of particular UFO abduction experiences will not find it here. Because the book's primary preoccupation is with the general phenomenon in the United States and the way abduction material is conveyed to the public in narrative form, questions concerning what may be actually happening to the persons involved are not our main concern. This is not to say that the question of what exactly *is* originally behind the production of the narratives in question is not important. What is happening to these individuals is of great importance both to them and to society, no matter what the cause of these experiences will eventually prove to be. But it is not the purpose of the present study.

One final note: To many it may appear that I am tacitly implying the authors of the books, together with the abductees, are simply "making it up." But my analysis of the relationship that exists among authors, abductees, and audiences is not intended to suggest fraud but rather fabrication, a form of "making things up" that is basic to *all* storytelling and writing (including my own), as this book's later sections on narrative and myth will illustrate. What is of primary importance is the fact that we in the late twentieth century may well be in the exciting position of being able to observe and study a myth in the process of being created.

1

INTRODUCTION

Both believers and skeptics alike will probably agree that the UFO abduction experience has become an ingrained and accepted part of contemporary North American popular culture. Today, few could disagree with psychologist Robert A. Baker's statement in an issue of the *Skeptical Inquirer* that "the now universally familiar UFO-abduction fable . . . [is] a fable known to every man, woman, and child newspaper reader or moviegoer in the nation."[1] The question is, why this should be the case? One of the purposes of this book is to suggest a possible answer.

The abduction phenomenon is, of course, closely linked with the appearance of unidentified flying objects that for all intents and purposes began to be seen in the years immediately following the Second World War. Of course, sightings of unidentifiable lights in the sky had been taking place for centuries, but only after Kenneth Arnold's "flying saucer" sighting on June 24, 1947, near Mt. Rainier, Washington, were they explicitly theorized to be extraterrestrial in origin. (The so-called foo-fighters sighted during the war, mysterious lights that tailed Allied and German pilots, were thought to be secret enemy craft, interestingly enough, by both sides!)

Knowing something about the public's reaction to that phenomenon can be of help in understanding why alien abduction accounts came to be taken so seriously. Even though the vast majority of early UFO sightings consisted merely of visual observations of bright lights in the sky, the belief that they were intelligently controlled objects from another planet quickly took hold. There are many reasons that the public has been so receptive to this particular explanation; some of these are easy to grasp, others less so. First, some of the reports did specify that apparently solid and metallic objects had been seen. UFOs also began to be sighted at rest, standing in fields or other areas, or in the process of taking off. Furthermore, many of the people claiming such experiences were, to all intents and purposes, highly credible individuals, such as commercial or air force pilots, whose reported encounters with UFOs that gave every appearance of being intelligently controlled craft were difficult to dismiss.

Obviously, society's interest in the subject of UFOs and its increasing readiness to acknowledge the possible existence of alien beings loosely paralleled our own growing awareness after World War II that the exploration of space by human beings was feasible, at least in theory. As we came to realize our own technological potential, it took little imagination to conceive that beings from other planets (if they indeed existed) likely could have developed similar, or even superior, abilities in this regard. Furthermore, if UFOs were manufactured craft, the implications were sobering to say the least, for as they were evidently capable of a maneuverability far beyond the limits of human technological accomplishment, they were undeniably consciousness-raising insofar as they forced us to look at our own accomplishments from a new and humbling perspective.

For our purposes, the importance of the countless UFO sightings that began in the late 1940s and continue to this day cannot be overestimated. For one, it legitimized the notion of extraterrestrial life as a real possibility. Today, for example, most of us might agree that the likelihood we are alone in the universe is very small, but prior to the first modern sightings of UFOs, few people openly embraced such notions. The gradual acceptance of the reality of UFOs by the public was an essential prerequisite, for it increased the public's readiness to accept the possibility that what the abductees were claiming could also be true. Since a large number of people in North America came quickly to believe that UFOs could be extraterrestrial craft from another solar system, the possibility of alien beings abducting humans, on the face of it, is not in itself much more difficult to entertain.[2] Indeed, to those already convinced of the reality of UFOs, the abduction of human beings by extraterrestrials for presumably scientific purposes could even be said to provide a kind of rationale for their presence in our skies in the first place.

Still, although accounts of contact with the occupants of UFOs could be traced almost to the first modern appearance of so-called flying saucers in 1947,[3] the public only began to take abduction accounts seriously in recent years. The British UFO researcher Jenny Randles, for example, discussing the range of observed alien activities in 1979, commented that "Nothing [in alien behavior] seems to indicate a planned campaign of surveillance."[4] Importantly, she made only passing reference to people being abducted, and had no trouble remarking that such cases "are very rare."[5] Yet nine years later in 1988 this same researcher would publish a book devoted to the subject (appropriately titled *Abduction*), where she investigated over two hundred "documented" UFO kidnappings around the world, and where clear patterns from case to case could be seen.

Whatever the reason for the popularity of these stories, the number of declared abductees has grown from a trickle to a torrent, to the point where some UFO researchers have recently speculated that as many as 3.7 million persons in the United States alone may believe that they have been abducted.[6] Exactly why the number of reported abductions should have grown so dramatically in the last few decades is hard to determine. For one thing, similar stories had been circulating throughout society for many years without attracting large numbers of believers. In order to understand the change it is necessary to take a brief look at these earlier encounter-type claims, the so-called contactee occurrences of the 1950s, because the very failure of these stories to capture the public's imagination may suggest why the abduction narratives have been so successful in this regard.

1947: The Modern Era

A decisive moment in the history of UFOs was signaled by a 1947 press release issued by the U.S. Air Force (only to be immediately retracted) stating that a UFO had crashed near Roswell, New Mexico, in the process scattering debris over a large area. Debate continues over the so-called Roswell Incident, many people maintaining not simply that a saucer crashed (and not a weather or spy balloon, as the "official" version maintains), but also that alien occupants were found and retrieved by the military. Some have even questioned if all the aliens aboard *were* dead (rumors persist that at least one or more survived for some years). Other observers claimed to have encountered beings when UFOs had been seen taking off or landing on the ground.[7] UFO occupants continued to be reported, and their appearance and activities were described in various ways. For the most part, the aliens throughout the 1950s seemed preoccupied with taking soil and other samples and showed little or no interest in human beings. When these aliens recognized that they had been observed, witnesses claimed that they usually returned immediately to their craft, although the occasional story surfaced of such beings making unsuccessful attempts to force a person aboard their UFO. As far as the physical appearance of the aliens was concerned, the initial reports from the 1950s varied considerably. A very few were described as ugly, fearsome, nonhuman monsters. Some were small (three to four feet), but many were of average or above-average height (six to seven feet), conspicuously good-looking, and indistinguishable in appearance from humans. Interestingly, descriptions of beings such as this dominated accounts of the earliest close encounters; these aliens offered them exotic food and drink, and spoke about the dangers of nuclear war. George Adamski, the best-known of the "contactees" (as such people came to be called), wrote several books with provocative titles such as *The Flying Saucers Have Landed* (1953) and *Inside the Space Ships* (1955) describing his experiences. In these books he attested to having met beautiful beings of both sexes who hailed from various planets throughout our solar system. Adamski even buttressed his published accounts (which included, among other exotica, descriptions of cities and rivers on the far side of the moon) with photographs of the UFOs on which he had been a passenger. Unfortunately, the resemblance these spaceships bore to pith helmets and canister vacuum cleaners was so striking that the photos were not taken very seriously, at least not by many.

In fact, there were many reasons that the contactees managed to attract only minimal support. First, the tales Adamski and others told were quite literally beyond belief. It seemed preposterous that beings would travel such distances merely to dispense platitudinous and self-evident warnings about war to a number of socially obscure human beings when they could just as easily have made such announcements to the leaders of the world. For this reason alone the contactees were very difficult to believe. But the stories were rejected not simply because they were bizarre or seemed an affront to common sense, or flew in the face of everyday experience; it was also because of the accompanying details they contained.

Strictly speaking, the only way one can come to any decision concerning a claim's credibility is indirectly, first, by examining those details that amplify and flesh out the story and second, by assessing the narrator's character for signs of emotional and intellectual stability. Obviously, if a well-respected individual whose stability we have no reason to question tells us a bizarre story, our readiness to accept that person's account—or at least, not to dismiss it out of hand—will be increased. If that information is lacking, we will try to determine the believability of a story by assessing how believable are the story's accompanying details. In the case of the contactees, it was soon seen that their stories lacked any degree of indirect or secondary verifiability. The tales they told were full of statements none of which could withstand critical scrutiny. That beings could evolve elsewhere in the galaxy and visit our planet could be accepted, at least as a possibility. However, that forests could grow on the far side of the moon *can* be successfully repudiated, because although we have no certain knowledge of other solar systems, we do have certain knowledge of what conditions are like on the airless and inhospitable moon. Scientists were quick to point this out, and they observed as well that the odds of any life evolving on a planet such as Venus—as Adamski had said some of his hosts were from—were highly unlikely, given that planet's lack of water, to say nothing of the extremely high temperatures that were suspected to exist on its surface.[8] That sentient beings could evolve on scorching Venus or frigid Saturn seemed next to impossible. That they would evolve in a manner that made them *all* indistinguishable in appearance from ourselves (as the contactees also claimed) was even harder to accept. Finally, that such beings would be speaking flawless English strained the public's credulity beyond the breaking point. Yet Adamski claimed to have encountered humanlike, English-speaking beings from both of those worlds.

Not only did the stories of the contactees fail to pass muster; the storytellers themselves were also revealed to be highly dubious individuals. Many were found to have had extensive involvement in paranormal groups and eccentric religious movements long before they had made their claims. Adamski, for example, had been associated with the occult world since the 1930s.[9] Finally, their open courting and enjoyment of publicity did little to enhance their credibility. But the most important single reason the contactees were not taken seriously was that the strongest critics often came from within the ranks of UFO believers. Major Donald J. Keyhoe was the founder of NICAP (the National Investigations Committee on Aerial Phenomena), an organization formed in the 1950s that soon came to be one of the largest and most respectable of its kind in America, and one that boasted many scientists and professionals among its membership and executive. While NICAP maintained that UFOs were very likely manufactured craft of extraterrestrial origin, Keyhoe and the majority of his executive officers had no patience with the claims of the contactees, and routinely discounted them. The main reason was simply pragmatic: The contactees threatened to cast the entire UFO phenomenon into disrepute. Keyhoe and others reasoned that if the obviously outlandish experiences of the contactees were lumped together with the less dramatic sightings reported by respectable witnesses, the entire phenomenon could be dismissed as nonsense, thus thwarting NICAP's ultimate goal to force a full-scale government investigation of UFOs. All in all, the repudiation of the contactees by people such as Keyhoe was damning indeed. Since the most virulent criticism was coming from people who were perceived by the general public as being on the same side, it was not surprising that few took anything the contactees said very seriously. As a result, although contactees have continued to surface from time to time, most enjoy at best a brief vogue, only to fade into obscurity soon after their stories have appeared.

The Abductions Begin

There the matter appeared to rest for some years, with UFOs being regarded by a few as a phenomenon worthy of serious study, while contactees were regarded by virtually everyone as harmless, delusional eccentrics. But all this changed in the 1960s when a new element appeared. John Fuller, a writer of considerable experience, published *The Interrupted Journey* in 1966, a thorough investigation into the now-famous Betty and Barney Hill case (discussed in detail in chapter 3 of this book).[10] Although the Hill case was not the first of its kind, it was the first both to be extensively studied by medical and other professionals, and to receive publicity throughout the world.[11] Other individuals soon began to surface who told basically similar stories of having undergone experiences that, if anything, were even more bizarre than the Hills'.

What distinguished the new generation of alien contact accounts from their earlier counterparts of the 1950s was their relative sophistication and subtlety, which enabled them to enjoy immediately a more favorable reception from the public than anything that had been extended to the contactees. At first glance this might seem strange, since on the face of it the basic events the abductees were describing were just as odd as anything that had previously appeared in the contactee literature. But certain things were taking place which had not been present before. First, what was happening—the forcible abduction of *reluctant* human beings—was decidedly more unsettling, and just as assuredly more involving to the reader. Previously, about the only disturbing aspect of the UFO phenomenon concerned the mysterious Men in Black, those sinister figures who, in the 1950s, allegedly appeared at the homes of people who had reportedly seen UFOs, and in vaguely threatening language, told them to "keep quiet" about their experience. Furthermore, the individuals reporting such experiences seemed to be well-adjusted persons whose stories, though undeniably bizarre, did not contain easily refutable or otherwise ridiculous statements such as those made previously. Finally, much of these stories' success was directly traceable to the manner in which the events were being put together for public consumption, as later chapters of this book will demonstrate. Abduction authors learned a great deal, though not necessarily consciously, from the mistakes made by the contactees and from audience responses. Abduction narratives are without question far better written than those of the 1950s, and in consequence far less susceptible to the criticisms that had been leveled against the contactees.

Few of the weaknesses so conspicuous in contactee stories could be seen in the abduction narratives. For one thing, the authors made every attempt to minimize evidence that suggested the abductees were anything other than perfectly normal men and women; any arguably unusual or abnormal aspects of an abductee's life were glossed over or otherwise disregarded. Even more significant, in most abduction narratives very little precise information was obtained about the aliens, making the stories less susceptible to authentication. Usually, alien abductors reveal next to nothing about themselves or their planet of origin, and rarely say anything about their purpose in being here.[12] On those infrequent occasions when an abductee travels in a UFO, the destination is never specified.

This is not to say that abduction narratives are deficient in detail, but only in verifiable detail. Indeed, in some cases the sheer amount of ancillary detail can be quite daunting, if not over-whelming, to the reader. Many abduction authors have used this very feature to argue that, as it is difficult to imagine that such a wealth of detail could be the product of fabrication or fantasy on the abductee's part, so the stories must be true descriptions of real experiences. In fact, this richness, as I will demonstrate, is not nec-essarily an indication that a given abduction account is true. Alter-nate explanations *are* possible, even though authors of abduction narratives rarely mention them.

The Scope of the Present Study

Although it is virtually impossible to subject an abduction narra-tive to a test of its truth, it will probably come as no surprise to learn that, with rare exceptions, most who have personally inves-tigated UFO abductees and published their results appear con-vinced that the abductees' claims are probably true. This study investigates the most important American writers in this group and discusses in considerable detail the writings of journalist John Fuller, artist Budd Hopkins, abductees Travis Walton and the science fiction and horror novelist Whitley Strieber, UFO researchers Ann Druffel and Raymond Fowler, historian David Jacobs, and (most recently) psychiatrist and Harvard professor John Mack. All have produced accounts that have proved compelling and make distinctive contributions to the basic narrative and developing myth. Most importantly, these authors can be positioned quite precisely in relation to where they stand on the question of the events' truth or falsity. All seem basically convinced of the abductees' sincerity and veracity, and appear to believe, for the most part, in the claims the abductees make. Raymond Fowler could be speaking for everyone when quoting a colleague on one abductee's story: " 'It is so unbelievable that it *is* believable!' "[13]

Obviously, not everyone who has written about the abduction phenomenon believes that the abductees are undergoing the same kind of objectively verifiable experiences. Even within the ranks of believers there are differences of opinion concerning the exact nature of the reality to which the abductees are exposed. Budd Hopkins and David Jacobs, for instance, appear convinced that the events described are basically of a physical nature, involving real aliens and equally physical UFOs, and are predominantly negative experiences for the abductees. Whitley Strieber and John Mack, in contrast, believe that what is occurring is in many respects beyond the boundaries of present notions of what constitutes reality, but generally involves a process of growth and spiritual enlightenment on the abductee's part.[14] This significant disagreement (addressed in later chapters) concerning the ethical natures and purposes of the aliens is a most important one that remains as yet unresolved.

Of course, at the other extreme are many individuals (such as Robert A. Baker) who are openly skeptical of the claim that alien abductions are taking place at all. The most prominent organ of UFO skeptics in America is the aptly named *Skeptical Inquirer*, the journal of the Committee for the Scientific Investigation of Claims of the Paranormal (CSICOP). The abduction skeptics' most persistent spokesperson is Philip J. Klass, a former senior editor with *Aviation Week and Space Technology*, who in his books, articles, and television appearances has spent decades in a relentless attempt to refute not only the claims of abductees, but the extraterrestrial hypothesis as an explanation of UFOs as well. In *UFO Abductions: A Dangerous*

Game (1989), Klass argued that a misuse of hypnosis by untrained, often amateur practitioners such as artist and sculptor Hopkins or historian Jacobs (neither of whom had training in medicine or psychology) has resulted in the instilling of false memories into the abductees' minds. According to this argument, hypnotized abductees are being encouraged to regard fantasized abductions as real events, and may also be put under pressure by the hypnotists, most of whom are already confirmed believers in the phenomenon, to "produce" accounts of experiences with aliens.

Although they may occupy positions anywhere from pure skepticism to total belief, these investigators regard the question of the truth or falsity of the claims to be not simply central, but virtually the only one worth asking. This is unfortunate, because such a single-minded preoccupation has unquestionably resulted in other features of the issue being ignored. Psychologist Kenneth Ring put it well when he observed regretfully that to many people, "it may seem obvious that there are just two basic possibilities concerning what to make of [UFOs and abduction claims]: Either they are the products of fantasy, delusion, hoax, or hallucination—or they are real. Such thinking, though it may appeal to our 'common sense,' may nevertheless end by fostering a facile form of reductionism."[15]

Ring added that it is not only intellectually restricting, but it does a disservice to the study of our culture to imply that one has a choice only of declaring oneself either a debunker or a believer in the literal existence of UFOs or abductions. The truth of this observation is hard to deny. Skeptics such as Baker, for example, implicitly deny that there is *any* significance for society in the abduction experience, simply because in his opinion there is nothing recounted in any of the abduction works he discusses "that cannot be easily explained in terms of normal, though somewhat unusual, psychological behavior we now term *anomalous*."[16] The accounts themselves are nothing more than the products of "fantasy-prone" individuals. The so-called missing time element frequently encountered in abduction cases can happen to everyone, and is simply a period of time during which little of any importance occurred, and as such is not registered by the brain, for instance. But Baker's dismissal of abduction claims to the level of "amusing" science fiction does little to advance our understanding of why so many people would find something that is merely "amusing" persistently fascinating, a fact which becomes even more perplexing if Baker is correct. Frankly, Baker appears to have no sensitivity to the possibility that such narratives could ever say anything of relevance to society, because he equates myth with fiction, and fiction with simple falsehood.

The present study is based on the premise that the line of reasoning espoused by Baker and others is too limiting; and that how and why a narrative such as this comes to be created is an area just as worthy of investigation as is the question of what is actually behind the claims the abductees are making. To this end, this book initially examines how the various devices and strategies employed by the authors encourage a specific response in readers. On many occasions, however, these strategies can backfire, creating a response quite different from the one the authors intended. Nevertheless, as the narrative is repeated over time, its basic constituent parts come to be ingrained in the collective consciousness.

Viewed as a modern myth, the UFO abduction narrative can be appreciated as a reflection of American society in the late decades of the twentieth century, and deserves study for this reason alone. Later chapters will discuss the various features of, and functions served by, myths in a society, and consider the abduction narrative, however conflicted and contradictory, as a secular myth responsive to contemporary social conditions.

Because this study is interested in the emergence and evolution of a narrative over time, the accounts are examined in relation to when they were first published, rather than when the various abductions allegedly occurred. It will be found that more recent accounts tend both to respond to problems and answer questions created by older narratives, and also insert new elements, as if such elements are being tested for appropriateness. Conversely, aspects of previous narratives that do not somehow strike a chord with the public are often discarded. Further, earlier accounts tend to be comparatively simple and down-to-earth, while more recent ones (those of the 1990s) are more detailed and involve other areas of the paranormal similar to those frequently encountered in so-called New Age writings.*

---

*In some of these accounts, the aliens are virtually indistinguishable from spirit guides, and elements such as past-life experiences come into play.

Related to this is the steady movement away from what might be termed a "realistic" scenario to increasingly bizarre circumstances surrounding the abductions. For example, in early cases, once one has accepted the basic fact of the abduction, very few events occur that violate physical laws as we know them. Scenes are fundamentally realistic rather than dreamlike, with the aliens acting more or less as we would expect human scientists to behave under such circumstances. By this I mean that most early abductees encounter neither supernatural nor obviously omnipotent beings, but physical entities that seem as bound by the restrictions and limits of the material and temporal environment as we are. Doors usually have to be opened, stairs have to be climbed, halls have to be walked down, and experiments have to be completed within a certain time period. The beings themselves are also recognizably similar to ourselves, at least in certain respects. They are capable of—and indeed, seem to have no proscription against—communicating with us, and they even answer the occasional question. Like us, they possess emotions and demonstrate humor, the capacity to disagree, and even mild annoyance. Though their hypnotic power over humans may be frightening, they themselves are not entirely so, and their purposes, while difficult to discern, are not completely beyond our comprehension. Their experiments, for example, centered as most of them are on the taking of skin and other samples, appear to be motivated by a curiosity about our physical natures with which we can surely identify. Some concern with human sexuality is present in early accounts, but it is only one manifestation of a more general curiosity.

As fresh accounts surface, new developments can be observed. By the time we reach the late 1970s and '80s, accounts begin to surface of aliens who are far less friendly and are often depicted as coldly indifferent to the effects of their experiments on human well-being; in a few instances they appear frankly malevolent.[17] We also start to see more emphasis on the incredible and virtually supernatural powers of the aliens, combined with decreased manifestations of human traits. Most importantly, the power to defy and transcend the limitations of the physical world comes to be more commonly ascribed to them, physical barriers such as windows and doors now appearing to provide no deterrent. Similarly, they appear to have developed an uncanny ability to follow the lives of the abductees, possibly as a result of the implanting of location or tagging devices in the heads and nasal cavities of those they have chosen for a lifetime of experimentation and observation. Early abductees believed they had been chosen randomly, but this soon gives way to a general belief among abductees that they have been picked deliberately. Although why these individuals have been chosen is not made clear, in many cases abductees claim to have been experimented on since their childhood.

Just as the aliens' power appears to increase, so does their ability to escape detection by other human beings. Where early abductees experienced their encounters in remote areas (presumably because the aliens could only avoid detection in this way), now abductions are taking place in urban centers (one, allegedly, even in downtown Manhattan!), frequently in the presence of witnesses who are mysteriously (and, some might say, conveniently) put into trances that in virtually all cases prevents such corroboration of abductees' stories, even when such individuals are in the same house or room.

Increasingly, different types of beings are reported as being aboard the UFOs: The actual experimenters are usually short, gray-skinned, large-headed, and large-eyed humanoids, but they are often directed by slightly taller beings, and are sometimes seen in the company of entities more or less identical in appearance to ourselves. The genetic nature of the experiments performed becomes more pronounced, as is their interest in our sexuality; much physical probing and touching occurs. Eventually, some abductees report that they feel they are being used, not simply as guinea pigs, but as breeders in some vast and inscrutable genetic experiment, on occasion involving hundreds of human beings in huge rooms being experimented on simultaneously. Some female abductees report mysterious pregnancies that just as mysteriously cease for no apparent reason. Other women have been shown children, usually (but not always) wan and sickly looking, whom they intuitively feel are their own offspring. Many of these individuals have been asked, and in some cases are forced against their wills, to hold and cuddle the children who are presumably in need of human nurturing. A few women, in recent accounts, even report having had unpleasant sexual experiences with nonhuman aliens.

But just as frequently some of the more recent abductees emerge from their experiences feeling spiritually ennobled or otherwise sensitized to environmental issues and the welfare of our planet. Some are grateful for their experiences and occasionally bond with their abductors. Here can be seen the emergence of two distinct thematic strains as regards the aliens' characteristics. On the one hand, the aliens continue to behave as cold-blooded scientists employing still-painful methods. But inconsistent though it may seem, in other abduction narratives a spiritual dimension comes to play an increasingly important role. Some abduction narratives even present the abductee as a messenger or prophet bringing warnings of impending catastrophe to humankind. From the outset these two strains have vied for prominence within the developing narrative, neither one dominating and both existing uneasily in a relationship which remains largely unresolved.

As the following chapters will demonstrate, abduction stories are the creative product of abductees and authors (and audiences), working together to produce a narrative that is serving an important social function, and is speaking to us today much as the myths of bygone ages spoke to ancient cultures.

Notes

1. Robert A. Baker, "The Aliens among Us: Hypnotic Regression Revisited," *Skeptical Inquirer* 12, no. 2 (Winter 1987–88): 147–62.

2. Jenny Randles cites Gallup survey figures indicating "fifty-three per cent [in the US] accepting their [i.e., UFOs] reality (with only twenty-nine per cent not accepting it, the rest being unsure)." See Jenny Randles, *Abduction* (London: Robert Hale, 1988), 178. As far back as August 19, 1947, barely two months after the first "modern" sighting, a Gallup poll indicated that nine out of ten Americans "knew about the flying saucers," and there is no reason to suspect that this figure has declined in recent years.

3. The term "flying saucer" was the product of an anonymous headline writer who, to my knowledge, has never been identified. See Keith Thompson, *Angels and Aliens: UFOs and the Mythic Imagination* (New York: Fawcett Columbine, 1991), 4.

4. Jenny Randles and Peter Warrington, *UFOs: A British Viewpoint* (London: Robert Hale Ltd., 1979), 145–46.

5. Ibid., 160.

6. This number was recently established by two of the authors

examined in this book, Budd Hopkins and David Jacobs, who, together with sociology professor Ron Westrum, conducted a questionnaire-type survey. The results appeared in a booklet sponsored by the Roper Organization, *Unusual Personal Experiences: An Analysis of the Data from Three National Surveys* (Las Vegas: Bigelow Holding Corporation, 1992).

7. The most famous of these "landed" UFOs complete with occupants is probably the Socorro, New Mexico, sighting of patrolman Lonnie Zamora, that took place on April 24, 1964. Of course, others have maintained just as vehemently that nothing of an extraterrestrial nature landed at all. See Kal Korff, *The Roswell UFO Crash: What They Don't Want You to Know* (Amherst, N.Y.: Prometheus Books, 1997), and Philip J. Klass, *The Real Roswell Crashed-Saucer Coverup* (Amherst, N.Y.: Prometheus Books, 1997).

8. Jenny Randles is clearly incorrect when she says, in defense of Adamski, that "in 1953 it was considered scientifically possible that there might be life on Venus and rivers on the moon" (*Abduction*, 15). It had been known for centuries that the moon lacked both an atmosphere and water, and the possibility that life could have evolved on Venus was regarded as highly unlikely by most astronomers. Cf. Dinsmore Alter and Clarence Cleminshaw, *Pictorial Astronomy* (New York: Thomas Y. Crowell, 1956): "The lack of free oxygen on Venus is strong evidence against the existence of animal life there" (119).

9. See Thompson, *Angels and Aliens*, 28–30, for a brief account of Adamski and other contactees. See also David Jacobs, *The UFO Controversy in America* (Bloomington: Indiana University Press, 1975), 109, for a detailed look at some of the contactees.

10. Fuller also wrote articles on the Hills that appeared in *Look* magazine, which at the time enjoyed a wide readership.

11. Of course, as astronomer Dr. Jacques Vallee was the first to show, accounts of humans being spirited away by nonhuman entities go back centuries (see *Passport to Magonia* [Chicago: Henry Regnery Co., 1969], and *Dimensions* [New York: Ballantine Books, 1988]). In October 1957, in Brazil, an encounter with extraterrestrials allegedly took place that was in one respect similar to the Hills' experience, in that it involved an abduction of a human being against his will. The case is important, for it represents the first appearance of two essentially new elements in the UFO phenomena, that of forcible abduction and the use of humans for breeding purposes. Antonio Villas-Boas, a farmer, claimed to have been forced aboard a spaceship and subsequently ordered to have sex with an attractive but somewhat unusual looking female alien. In spite of this, the Hill case was brought to the attention of the public *before* that of Villas-Boas. Since it is the purpose of this study to analyze these accounts as part of a continuous nar-

rative evolution, the Hill case must be seen as the true harbinger of the abduction phenomenon as far as North America is concerned.

12. One notable exception is the famous star map that Betty Hill was shown by her alien abductor, purporting to identify the aliens' home planet. But the Hill case is unique in this respect; no similar star maps have been forthcoming.

13. Raymond Fowler, *The Andreasson Affair: Phase Two* (Englewood Cliffs, N.J.: Prentice-Hall, 1982), 12.

14. The view that aliens may not be merely physical beings was originally put forward by Dr. Jacques Vallee, astronomer, computer scientist, ethnologist/folklorist, and former colleague of the late J. Allen Hynek (the highly respected, originally skeptical astronomer who became "converted" to a belief in the reality of UFOs as something other than weather balloons or misidentified natural phenomena). While accepting that there is substance to many UFO reports, he rejects the "nuts-and-bolts" extraterrestrial hypothesis as an inadequate explanation of actual UFO behavior. Concerning abductions, he is scathing in his indictment of the claims of abductees concerning the extraterrestrial origin of the abductors, and argues at length that the behavior of the aliens as described is inconsistent with their supposedly vast technological sophistication. At the same time, Vallee still believes that the events are in some sense really taking place, and may involve transdimensional beings who have coexisted with us for countless centuries, and who may be behind the traditional accounts of encounters with fairies and elves.

15. Kenneth Ring, *The Omega Project* (New York: William Morrow, 1992), 218–19.

16. Baker, "The Aliens among Us," 159.

17. The aliens presented in the two books Budd Hopkins wrote during this period are decidedly unfriendly. Betty Andreasson's abductors are, by and large, kindly, at times communicative, and profess to be deeply interested in her, although their physical treatment of her is often difficult to square with their well-meaning claims.

2

UFO ABDUCTIONS
AND THE NATURE OF NARRATIVE

All books dealing with UFO abductions present their readers with something akin to a historical text, in that they maintain they are describing real events in the past. As is the case with a history book, in any abduction narrative the reader encounters a functional mix of the factual and the interpretive, the alleged facts of the abduction experiences, and, exerting an influence on the entire text, the author's interpretation of and response to those experiences.[1] It is probably safe to say that, as far as the central or core events are concerned, exactly what happened will probably remain a mystery to everyone, including the abductees themselves, forever beyond unequivocal verification or refutation. Because we can never verify these core events, exactly how they are being conveyed in narrative form to the reading public is a crucial factor in determining public response.

As I mentioned in the preface, *all* books are, of course, in some sense "made up," in that the manner each event is presented to the reader is the result of decisions made by the author, and no two authors will express themselves in exactly the same way. Although many readers have trouble accepting this, it must be admitted that no facts are indelibly engraved in stone; rather, they come to the reader through the medium of written language, a medium that, as we shall see, is surprisingly fluid.[2]

It must also be said that authors of abduction narratives employ many of the techniques of fiction, despite claiming that the events presented constitute historically precise records. This does not mean they are consciously fabricating untruths, but the demands of narrative leave them no choice to do otherwise. As the historian Hayden White has observed, the writing of history is not altogether different from the writing of fiction:

> No given set of casually recorded historical events can in itself constitute a story; the most it might offer to the historian are story *elements.* The events are *made* into a story by the suppression or subordination of certain of them and the highlighting of others, by characterization, motific repetition, variation of tone and point of view, alternative descriptive strategies, and the like—in short, all of the techniques that we would normally expect to find in the employment of a novel or a play.[3]

Obviously, if we accept the validity of White's contention (and it is pretty hard not to), it follows that writers of any kind of record of the past play a seminal role in how the story finally appears to the reader. We are at their mercy for those core events, because "we cannot go and look at them in order to see if the historian has adequately reproduced them in his narrative."[4]

Hayden White makes another importantly related point: Historical narratives are "verbal fictions, the contents of which are as much *invented* as *found* and the forms of which have more in common with their counterparts in literature than they have with those in the sciences."[5] Literary critic Wallace Martin likewise observes the power of the narrator: "Between the story and the reader is the narrator, who controls what will be told and how it will be perceived."[6] *All* authors (including myself) have an agenda, a point of view, and a thesis to promote, even though they may not always be consciously aware of that thesis themselves. In the interests of promoting their position, authors will exclude or minimize certain events which we might well consider as valuable to our understanding of the situation in question as is the information which the authors *have* chosen to put before us.

In the case of UFO abduction narratives, then, it is essential to keep in mind that we are *not* encountering objective scientific studies that many such books purport to be. Rather, we are confronted with an account of mysterious happenings that we can read only through the medium of the authors' biases that color their every utterance and are behind virtually every literary technique and strategy they employ. As we will see, even the most seemingly insignificant linguistic and rhetorical decisions made in the act of constructing a narrative are determined by those biases of the writer, and cumulatively contribute to how we will respond. Of course, to say this is not to say in turn that books about history are nothing more than a string of events manufactured through language alone; the vast majority of the events historians write about unquestionably occurred. Nor is it meant to imply that a writer's employment of literary strategies negates the value of the written discourse that ensues. As Wallace Martin again notes, such devices make discourse possible, indeed, they "create the possibility of narration. Without them, and confronted with a sheer mass of facts, the historian would have nowhere to begin."[7]

But in the case of an experience as subjective and unverifiable as a recalled abduction experience, we are dealing with something that leaves absolutely no record of itself other than in the mind of the self-professed abductee. Given this, we are completely at the mercy not only of the abductees' frequently muddled memory, but also of the innumerable decisions that authors of the ensuing narratives have made in deciding how to convey the abductees' stories to the reader. The point here is that the very need for the writer to "form a hypothesis concerning why something happened as it did" can be dangerous, insofar as "this hypothesis determines which facts will be examined and how they will be put together," to say nothing of that which will be discarded as immaterial or irrelevant to the author's purposes.[8]

In the ensuing chapters, I hope to show more particularly how and why abduction authors' various strategies profoundly influence readers' responses to the events in question.[9] In saying this, I do not, of course, mean to accuse the majority of authors of deliberately lying or cynically attempting to perpetrate hoaxes to mislead their readers for nefarious purposes. What I *am* saying is that, because of the nature of the abduction phenomenon and of narrative itself, all abduction narratives can be nothing more than highly speculative documents.

The Author's Role
in Forming a Narrative

Abduction authors commonly reinforce an abductee's account by
making extensive comments about his or her general reliability as
a character. Sometimes the authors will make straightforward editorial declarations that are easy to identify. The credibility of such
comments the reader can simply check against factual evidence
adduced in the book in support of the abductee's stability. Often
such confirmation is not hard to find, but in some cases a lack of
supporting evidence will obviously weaken the author's claim.

On other occasions, the authors will label certain individuals in
a manner that cannot help but create a favorable impression in the
mind of the reader that may not in fact be warranted. In their discussion of the Villas-Boas case, for example (see the section titled
"One Abduction, Many Versions," below), many commentators
cited in support of Villas-Boas's credibility the fact that he refused
to capitalize on his experience by selling his story to the press; presumably, as a man of integrity who had nothing to gain financially
by fabrication, it followed that the story was more likely to be true.
They also stressed the credentials of Villas-Boas's attending physician, Dr. Olavo Fontes, described in one account as "a *distinguished*
local physician."[10] Given this alleged distinction (in support of
which, incidentally, no compelling verification was offered), when
the doctor "concluded that [Villas-Boas] was completely truthful,"
subtle pressure is put on the reader to accept the experience he
allegedly had.[11]

We will encounter both of these techniques, and others more
sophisticated and subtle, throughout abduction literature. Of
course, in the above examples there is no necessary relationship
between the credibility of the claims made and the professed stability of the persons making them. For one thing, we have no
knowledge that Villas-Boas did not benefit in other respects (maybe
he craved fame or notoriety, for instance). But another problem
with such strategies is that they can backfire. For instance, if no corroborating evidence is produced to support the claim, say, of Dr.
Fontes being "distinguished," readers may well dismiss it outright,
and confront other claims made by the author with increased skepticism. Furthermore, if (as frequently happens) people who have

been described as psychologically stable are subsequently perceived behaving inconsistently, the credibility not only of the character but of the author as well is called into question and can affect the reader's reception of this and subsequent information.

Unfortunately, many of us tend to think of written communication as a more or less straightforward process where facts are solid things passed from author to reader, and where the author writes from a vantage point where all is known and thus true. In this spirit, we tend to accept uncritically pretty much everything an author says about these facts, especially when we have been accustomed, or even actively encouraged, to equate the very fact of authorship with the notion of "authority" or "expertise." Consider in this regard the way many people are taught to read and respond to the Bible, for example, as a divinely inspired document every word of which is literally true and beyond challenge. When it comes to abduction literature, John Fuller actually *knew* and interviewed Betty and Barney Hill, and Budd Hopkins himself conducted innumerable hypnotic sessions with his many subjects. With this information constantly in mind, it is hard for many readers not to conclude that any questioning of their conclusions can only be presumptuous, given our distance from the events.

In fact, we have every right to dispute such claims, for despite the closer proximity of the authors to the abductees, they are really no closer to the core events than the reader is. Furthermore, despite their assertion that they were initially skeptical or at least noncommittal on the subject when they were first approached by an abductee (in itself an important strategic device that I will discuss), they are never detached or disinterested observers by the time their books have been published. Also, they frequently establish close relationships with the abductees, and come to play active roles in later proceedings such as the hypnotism sessions, which they often conduct themselves. It is understandable that such friendships between author and abductee would develop, and goes far toward explaining why they are usually so ready to accept more or less at face value an abductee's story. But it also does much to qualify their claims of objectivity.

Since there is no way authors of abduction narratives can count on readers being sufficiently credulous to accept the intrinsic events simply by virtue of being told it *"really* happened," other devices and techniques must be employed in the hope that, to the extent that they carry credibility in themselves, they may exert a favorable influence on our response to the abduction. Because the basic event from which everything flows—the abduction itself—flies in the face of most readers' sense of reality, making such an account convincing presents the writer with a formidable challenge.[12] One way to achieve this is to present the material in a manner that is in many respects indistinguishable from those narratives we conventionally regard as purely true or realistic, such as newspaper accounts of commonplace events.

Wallace Martin observes that in order for a work to be considered realistic and hence believable, it must first contain material that "requires no justification because it seems to derive directly from the structure of the world," i.e., material such as names of cities and streets that we simply know to be true: "A narrative saturated with such details . . . declares its allegiance to the real."[13] Our sense that what we are reading is real is enhanced by our sense of how faithfully a writer has reproduced this surface texture of what we loosely call "everyday life" (what the weather was like the night the abduction took place or what was on TV, for example).

It is, then, no surprise to see how frequently realistic details are inserted in the description of the abduction itself. Indeed, it is arguable that the presence of such details is the most important factor in determining the strength of a narrative's claim to credibility.[14] As we shall see, no matter how fantastic are the experiences being described, we are never allowed to forget that the events are taking place in a context that purports to be as real as the reader's living room. A bond between reader and abductee—or the illusion of one—is subtly formed in this manner.

The likelihood that the reader will not dismiss an abduction account out of hand can also be increased by making sure that the laws of cause and effect are seen to be operating, much as we perceive them to be working in our own lives. To achieve this, authors make sure that their stories conform to our sense of logical sequence, that is, to our knowledge of the "series of events involved in thousands of different activities—going to a restaurant, taking a trip," or visiting the doctor or dentist.[15] Realism demands that the writer adhere to these conventions in order for the narrative to be considered "true-to-life."

Proof that structural coherence in a narrative is a crucial factor in determining how it will be received can be found in Bernard S. Jackson's essay "Narrative and Legal Discourse," a discussion of a revealing experiment conducted by two lawyers, W. L. Bennett and M. S. Feldman.[16] Their experiment was designed to determine which factors were most influential in causing a jury to find a narrative credible. "Their hypothesis was that the construction of truth within the courtroom was primarily a matter of the *overall* narrative plausibility of the story told." What they discovered was "that it is not the weighing of individual elements of the story . . . which renders a case persuasive or not, but rather the plausibility of the story structure taken as a whole."[17] The experiment involved two groups of students, one telling a mock jury true stories, the other false ones. "Their results indicated no statistical association between the actual truth status of stories and their perceived truth status. Moreover, they found that the structure of a story had a considerable impact on its credibility; as structural ambiguities in stories increased, credibility decreased, and vice versa." The authors of the experiment also noted "the importance of the confidence of witnesses as a factor in credibility, and the use of qualifications (e.g., of expert witnesses) in order to validate testimony."[18]

What all this means is simply that if a story appears coherent, seems to have logical sequence to its events, contains certain recognizable consistencies, and is endorsed by authorities, it tends to be believed whether it is true or not. As we will see, the above is most relevant to our investigation, for it not only explains why most abduction narratives are so tightly structured, but also goes far toward explaining why they rely so extensively on the views and endorsements of "experts," even though strictly speaking, the experts are no closer to the material than the reader.

Another time-honored method used by writers to strengthen our sense of a story's credibility lies in involving—or appearing to involve—the reader directly in the primary facts of the case. Writers of abduction narratives often draw considerable attention to the accuracy of individuals' memories even in minor matters, and will present detailed accounts of failed attempts to trick abductees into making inconsistent statements in their testimony while under hypnosis. This may also explain why so many of them (John Fuller, Raymond Fowler, and Budd Hopkins, in particular) tend to reproduce at length actual transcripts of the hypnotized subjects. Letting the abductees articulate their experiences in their own words—as they appear to be doing—supposedly presents the strongest case for their credibility, and it serves as well to draw readers directly into the action, as it were, enhancing the illusion that we are actually on the scene of the hypnosis session as the abductee was reliving the experience.

In order to give the abduction story as much credibility as possible, other literary devices are also employed. Readers must not only believe in the abductee's stability and sincerity; they must also be convinced that the author, who plays a central role as narrator, is a person who can be trusted. Often a reference will be made to the "decency" and "integrity" of the author in an introduction or preface written by a presumably objective third party who often possesses impressive academic credentials. Once this has been accomplished, the author's subsequent comments concerning an abductee's integrity or that of anyone else connected with the story will be made with greater authority. The motive behind the use of this device is the hope that all the characters' authenticity will "rub off" on the abduction account and render it more believable, even though the two categories of events are not really related at all.

Of course, abduction authors also emphasize their own attention to detail, stressing those times when they consulted weather reports or astronomical charts in order to verify that the atmospheric conditions (temperature, clear or cloudy skies, etc.) were as the abductee recalled, or that the stars in the sky did square with the abductee's recollections. But for all their attempts to convince us of their scrupulous fidelity to accuracy, there is really nothing in an abductee's memory of a given evening—no matter how accurate it might be—that increases the likelihood that the recalled abduction took place.

Abduction authors are fond of emphasizing the high degree of consistency that can be found within the abductees' various recollections over lengthy periods of time of their abduction experiences, which they frequently tout as compelling proof of the stories' truth. Interestingly enough, to the degree that this may be true, such consistency can be used as evidence *against* the stories' literal truth. Events experienced in real life rarely repeat themselves with exactitude. Fantasies, however, have a structural completeness peculiar to themselves by virtue of being fiction, and are for this reason more likely to be recalled in exactly the same way any number of times.

Incidentally, on the matter of consistency, the authors also make much of the extensive similarities that they allege can be seen among separate abduction accounts. In fact, abduction stories are riddled with inconsistencies, and contain elements many of which are mutually exclusive. As later chapters will reveal, this tendency to minimize discrepancies and distinctions has resulted in claims being made on behalf of a general "consistency down to the most minute details" among abduction reports that the actual evidence simply does not support.[19] Significantly, on those rare occasions when inconsistencies from account to account are too glaring to be ignored, they are usually dismissed as trifling, minor variations of no consequence.

In cases where multiple or repeated abductions have happened to the same person, authors make every effort to stress the extent to which accounts of the separate experiences are similar, or in some cases form part of a discernible pattern of purposeful behavior on the aliens' part. In fact, as will become apparent, the resemblances one encounters from account to account may say more about the nature of a realistic narrative's inner logic than anything else, and the apparent patterns may be as much the product of hindsight as anything else.

All in all, in spite of the presence of these conventional indicators of truth, the reader should not forget that they are not sufficient in themselves to guarantee that what is being alleged really occurred. After all, some of the most realistically presented fictions have been the purest of fantasies, and readers of abduction narratives would do well to keep this in mind.[20]

One Abduction, Many Versions

At this stage of the discussion some readers may be wondering if the extent of the authors' power over their material is not being overemphasized. That even authors without obvious bias can leave their unique stamps on material will become apparent from the following case study, which provides a striking illustration of how writers, consciously or otherwise, can guide the reader's responses. Indeed, this case typifies in condensed form what I discovered was taking place on a larger scale in the abduction volumes. Although in this instance the variations are relatively minor, it is plain that all of the writers concerned have brought to the subject a distinct approach, and that the finished results—the narratives themselves—are far from identical.

It will be recalled from the introduction that the Antonio Villas-Boas abduction case of 1957 was one of the first to receive publicity on a wide scale. Because the point of this exercise is *not* to rank the authors in relation to how closely their paraphrases approximated the original, but merely to demonstrate variation among the accounts, the Villas-Boas testimony need not concern us particularly here. The case involved the forcible abduction of Villas-Boas, a young Brazilian farm worker who claimed to have been taken aboard a UFO one night by a group of five alien beings. Once inside the craft, he was stripped and washed, following which a female alien entered the room and had sex with him. After this, his clothes were returned to him and he was released. Villas-Boas's testimony was duly transcribed and translated into English by Professor Olavo Fontes, a physician who examined Villas-Boas extensively.[21] I chose at random five summaries of this case: Thomas Bullard's 1982 Ph.D. dissertation "Mysteries in the Eye of the Beholder," Jenny Randles's *Abduction* (1988), Keith Thompson's *Angels and Aliens* (1991), Jacques Vallee's *Dimensions* (1988), and Timothy Good's *Alien Contact* (1991, 1993). All the authors are well-known UFO researchers, and all are writers of considerable experience. In the course of my investigation, I discovered many variations from summary to summary, some of them minor, others less so. All contained their own peculiar omissions and/or insertions, and some statements were made which were outright contradictions of each other. Though the writers remain faithful to the substance of the account, the variations are particularly striking when one considers that all five researchers presumably had access to identical source material: the original testimony of Villas-Boas himself as it appeared in translated form. Another interesting feature of the variations is that of the five, four were published within three years of each other (two in 1988, two in 1991).[22]

Bullard's account appears in table form (where it is set against eleven other abductions), although it is buttressed with occasional comments on the case in the accompanying text of his thesis. He makes no reference to Villas-Boas's age (he was twenty-three), nor does he precisely define his occupation (he was a farmer working for his father). The fact that Villas-Boas claimed to have seen UFOs on previous occasions is not stated, nor is mention made of the aliens' growling or barking language. Since this is very unusual behavior for aliens, if not unique as far as contact cases go, one would think it deserved mention if only for its singularity. In spite of the fact that the seduction of Villas-Boas is obviously the most sensational (and fantastic) aspect of the case, Bullard provides no details of the actual encounter, and his failure to describe the physical features of the female alien, combined with his comment in the thesis's text that "the occupants which captured Villas-Boas were almost human," minimizes those physical differences that Villas-Boas *did* describe (they spoke like dogs, in barks; had light-colored eyes smaller than ours; and their heads were double the size of a human's, judging by the size of their helmets).[23] At the same time, of the five summaries Bullard's is the only one to mention the bad-smelling gas in one of the rooms that made Villas-Boas physically ill, and only Bullard alludes to his having been taken to *three* rooms.

Jenny Randles describes Villas-Boas as a "Brazilian cowhand" and gives the date of the encounter as recorded in the original transcript as "1:00 A.M. on 16 October 1957." Bullard, incidentally, mentioned the evening of the fifteenth, but provided no information as to when the actual abduction took place. Randles, alone of the five, correctly gives the aliens' height at "about five feet tall," but she describes Villas-Boas as being given "a rubdown" where other accounts (Bullard and Thompson) more accurately describe his being coated with a strange thick liquid prior to his sexual encounter. To Randles, the alien sexual partner was not quite as normal-looking, but was a "peculiar-looking woman . . . [who] had fair skin, high cheekbones, Oriental eyes, and red hair."[24] In fact, Villas-Boas described her as "beautiful, though of a different type from the women I had known." Furthermore, she had "fair, almost white" hair, and eyes he associated with those of "Arabian [*not* oriental] princesses."[25] Only her armpit and pubic hair was red.

For his part, Keith Thompson notes that Villas-Boas was not

simply a farmer, but an "uneducated" one, a fact corroborated in Dr. Fontes's covering comments. Thompson also mentions the three legs which "descended from the hovering craft to support it," fixes the time and date at 1:00 A.M. on October 14 (rather than the 16th), and has the aliens suitably "helmeted [and] humanoid" rather than human, unlike the other accounts which, in making no mention of helmets and other unusual distinguishing features, imply that the aliens were not markedly different from ourselves.[26] For the first time we are told that a blood sample was taken before the sexual encounter occurred (in the transcript *two* were taken, oddly enough from his chin), and we have the first reference to the barking sounds emitted by all the aliens, which Thompson correctly informs us that Villas-Boas found "repulsive." In Thompson we learn that the female alien was not a redhead; only her pubic hair was "bright red." We also are given some details of the sexual encounter, but hear nothing of the clocklike device Villas-Boas attempted unsuccessfully to take from the UFO, an event that appears only in Bullard and Vallee. Thompson, however, is alone in making a good deal of the physical after-effects suffered by Villas-Boas which were corroborated by Dr. Fontes. But even here, only Randles informs us that Fontes "examined the farmer in his Rio office in early 1958," a fact of some importance considering that much could have happened to Villas-Boas in the intervening months.[27]

Jacques Vallee's account has the aliens communicating "among themselves in slowly emitted growls" rather than grunts or barks, and omits reference to the three-legged feature of the UFO or to the dress of the aliens.[28] Vallee describes the female alien as simply having "blonde" hair, "with a part in the center," unlike Randles's redhead and Good's "bleached" alien. Only Vallee mentions that "She was much shorter than he was, her head only reaching his shoulder."[29] In the other accounts, no mention whatever was made of her height and none is made of Villas-Boas's (himself only five feet four inches tall). Vallee makes no mention of the details of the sexual episode, but he is the only one to mention her parting smile.

Timothy Good prudently provides us with no precise date of the occurrence, claiming only that "Antonio Villas-Boas was apparently twice seduced by a four-and-a-half-foot tall alien female aboard a spaceship in October 1957."[30] Now the aliens are not simply helmeted, but "space-suited humanoids," and his female companion is revealed to have "very fair, almost bleached hair reaching halfway down her neck"; only her pubic (and armpit) hair are "very red."[31] Quoting Villas-Boas directly on the effect the alien's grunting (*not* barking, as Thompson claimed) had on him while they had sex, we learn he received only "the disagreeable impression that [he] was with an animal," but did not find this behavior "decidedly repulsive" as Thompson claimed.[32] Although Good and others make note of the alien partner's pointing to the sky after the encounter was over, only Vallee describes in any detail subsequent events such as the tour of the UFO. Finally, Vallee's is the only account which bothers to mention the length of time the experience allegedly took (over four hours, from approximately 1:00 A.M. to 5:30 A.M.).

Obviously, the above has only touched on the differences visible among the researchers' paraphrasings of this well-known abduction case. What we have just observed is an isolated, but far from atypical, example of something that takes place in every narrative act. One can never narrate without making decisions to highlight certain elements while minimizing others; what we have observed constitutes a most basic and perhaps unavoidable act of editorial involvement on the authors' parts with the original material. Nor is this simply a petty or pedantic question of "style," or of our being presented with different but equally valid ways of saying the same thing. In each case, the authors have ranked raw material on the basis of its perceived importance and relevance as they conceived it, in a manner that can have a significant effect on the reader. To take only two examples, it is arguable that Thompson's use of the word "uneducated" in his initial description of Villas-Boas might negatively affect a reader's assessment of his credibility, and other readers might be distanced by Villas-Boas's own boastful comment, quoted directly, that the aliens saw in him " 'a good stallion to improve their own stock.' "[33] Timothy Good's detailed description of Villas-Boas's illness following the abduction, together with his observation that Dr. Fontes "concluded that he was completely truthful," may help establish sympathy for him.[34] In short, even though such decisions may be barely visible, their effect is far from negligible. One simply cannot escape the fact that without the original document the reader has no way of knowing which summary is to be trusted, and can only conclude that the validity of all is questionable. As ensuing chapters will demonstrate, despite all the claims the authors make on behalf of the accounts' consistency, variations abound from narrative to narrative, making any response but an undecided one all but impossible for the discerning reader.

Notes

1. Even in those instances when the author of the book is the abductee himself (e.g., Whitley Strieber, in *Communion* and *Transformation*), speaking from personal experience, a case can be made that the author and the abductee are not one and the same person. For one thing, when writing the book Strieber was older than he was when the abductions took place, and arguably had achieved some distance from the events.

2. For an excellent summary of the various ways in which literary theorists have distinguished between "story" and "narrative," see Wallace Martin, *Recent Theories of Narrative* (Ithaca: Cornell University Press, 1986). Martin also provides a good bibliography for further reading on the subject. Readers might also wish to consult Mieke Bal, *Narratology* (Toronto: University of Toronto Press, 1985). Bal's book is highly technical, but she makes an important distinction between the story—that which is told in the actual words of the text—and the *fabula*, or the raw material of the story that exists, so her argument goes, independently of any specific expression in written form.

3. Hayden White, *Tropics of Discourse: Essays in Cultural Criticism* (Baltimore: Johns Hopkins University Press, 1978), 84.

4. Ibid., 88.

5. Ibid., 82.

6. Martin, *Recent Theories*, 9.

7. Ibid., 73.

8. Ibid.

9. A good, if extreme, illustration of how crucial this process of editorial exclusion can be, is seen in the so-called scholarship of revisionist historians, who deny that the Holocaust occurred, but routinely ignore data that would conflict with their thesis.

10. Keith Thompson, *Angels and Aliens: UFOs and the Mythic Imagination* (New York: Fawcett Columbine, 1991), 33.

11. Timothy Good, *Alien Contact: Top Secret UFO Files Revealed* (New York: William Morrow, 1991), 93.

12. Here it should also be mentioned that a so-called debunker of UFO abduction stories such as Philip Klass has fewer initial hurdles to overcome, because he can count on common sense as an ally, the majority of his readers already sharing his suspicions concerning the abductees' stability and veracity. But this does not make *his* approach to the subject any less subjective or biased, only apparently more rational because it is consistent with dominant beliefs.

13. Martin, *Recent Theories*, 67.

14. Readers suspicious of this claim should look at John Barth's famous short story "Lost in the Funhouse" for an example of how an absolutely mundane event—a trip to Coney Island—becomes utterly absurd and incoherent, when written in a manner that deliberately violates all the conventions of realistic fiction, conventions that Barth is violating in order to expose them as the arbitrary literary devices they are.

15. Martin, *Recent Theories*, 67.

16. The full account appears in W. L. Bennett and M. S. Feldman, *Reconstructing Reality in the Courtroom* (New Brunswick, N.J.: Rutgers University Press, 1981).

17. Bernard S. Jackson, in *Narrative in Culture: The Uses of Storytelling in the Sciences, Philosophy, and Literature*, ed. Christopher Nash (London and New York: Routledge, 1990), 28.

18. Ibid., 29–31.

19. John E. Mack, *Abduction* (New York: Charles Scribner's, 1994), 2.

20. One need look no further than the works of Tolkien for verification of this point.

21. The Villas-Boas case was originally published in *Flying Saucer Review* in 1964. A thorough account, complete with Villas-Boas's testimony, appears in *The Humanoids*, ed. Charles Bowen (London: Neville Spearman, 1969), 200–38.

22. It should be noted that the Villas-Boas material in Vallee's *Dimensions* (New York: Ballantine, 1988) is identical to that found in his *Passport to Magonia* (Chicago: Contemporary Books, 1969). However, this work was reissued, with a new preface by the author, in 1993.

23. Thomas E. Bullard, "Mysteries in the Eye of the Beholder: UFOs and their Correlates as a Folkloric Theme Past and Present," Ph.D. diss., Indiana University, 1982, 335.

24. Jenny Randles, *Abduction* (London: Robert Hale, 1988), 17.

25. This is taken from the original testimony given by Antonio Villas-Boas and transcribed in Dr. Fontes's consulting room, February 22, 1958, four months after the alleged incident occurred. From *Alien Abductions: True Cases of UFO Kidnappings*, ed. D. Scott Rogo (New York: New American Library, 1980), 66.

26. Thompson, *Angels and Aliens*, 32.
27. Randles, *Abductions*, 17.
28. Vallee, *Dimensions*, 123.
29. Ibid.
30. Good, *Alien Contact*, 92–93.
31. Ibid., 93.
32. Thompson, *Angels and Aliens*, 33.
33. Ibid.
34. Good, *Alien Contact*, 93.

3

JOHN FULLER AND
THE INTERRUPTED JOURNEY

Although the Villas-Boas case had occurred some years before, the 1961 abduction of Betty and Barney Hill was the first abduction account to be discussed in a book that was devoted exclusively to their experiences, and one that would provide a model for later abduction authors.[1] For this reason alone the significance of the Hills' experience in relation to the developing abduction narrative cannot be overestimated. It was also the first of its kind to be thoroughly investigated by an experienced expert in hypnosis who also had a background in medical science, Boston psychiatrist Dr. Benjamin Simon. His appearance in the scenario gave the claims of the Hills an added credibility, even if that credibility was not necessarily justified.

Readers who are unfamiliar with the details of the Hill case may find the following summary helpful. Betty and Barney Hill, a racially mixed couple from Portsmouth, New Hampshire (Barney was African-American, Betty Caucasian), were returning from a brief vacation to Canada on the night of September 19–20, 1961, when, on a lonely stretch of road, Betty noticed a strange light in the sky, near the waxing gibbous moon. The light appeared to follow them, growing steadily larger. Stopping to look more closely at the object (which by now they had concluded was a UFO), Barney walked some distance away from their parked car, presumably to get a better look, seemingly oblivious to Betty's cries to return. Soon after, Barney ran back to the car in a state of great agitation. The next thing they remembered was continuing on their journey, and arriving home somewhat later in the early morning than they should have, had their drive been uninterrupted or otherwise uneventful. The next day, Betty noticed some unusual circular markings on the trunk of their car, the cause of which could not be determined.

About ten days later, Betty began to have a series of strange nightmares that involved their having been taken aboard a UFO; for his part, Barney was also agitated for no reason he could discern. Their interest in UFOs now stimulated, they began to discuss their sighting of the UFO, and eventually came into contact with researchers in the field who brought to their attention the unaccountable time-lapse and suggested that hypnosis be employed as a means of filling in the seemingly inexplicable gaps in their memories of the night in question. Eventually, they sought out the services of Dr. Simon, a Boston psychiatrist who began hypnosis treatment, in the course of which both appeared to recall being abducted by alien beings, taken aboard the UFO, and subjected to a series of scientific tests. Betty in particular recalled having had a conversation with one of the aliens.

Some time after this, Dr. Simon learned from the Hills that a Boston reporter had written a series of ill-informed articles about their experience. To set the record straight, the Hills requested that Dr. Simon release his recordings of the hypnosis sessions for use in a book that they had decided to write with John Fuller of *Saturday Review*, a request Dr. Simon agreed to honor.

Because of its place in the history of abduction accounts, Fuller's work is seminal. At the time it was published it was certainly unique. Not only was the subject matter original and compelling, but the book was also undeniably well-written. An experienced writer, Fuller penned the opening sections of *The Interrupted Journey* with the skill that one would have expected from a successful writer of mystery or horror novels:

> September in the White Mountains is the *cruelest* month. The *gaunt* hotels, vestiges of Victorian tradition, are shuttered, or getting ready to be; motels and overnight cabins flash their neon

vacancy signs for only a few *fitful* hours before their owners give up and retire early. The New Hampshire ski slopes are *barren* of snow and skiers, the trails appearing as *great, brownish gashes* beside the *silent* tramways and chairlifts. . . . Winter is already here on the *chilled and ominous* slopes of Mount Washington. . . . It was in the *doleful* mid-September period of 1961—September 19 to be exact—that Barney Hill and his wife, Betty, began their drive.[2]

This initial, highly literary description of the area where the events occurred, presented in a Gothic manner reminiscent of Edgar Allan Poe's opening sentence in "The Fall of the House of Usher," is plainly designed to fill the reader with a sense of dread and foreboding.[3] Indeed, the opening pages positively abound with tantalizing references to mysterious events to come: "What they both were about to see was to change their lives forever"; "There was no hint at all of what was about to happen later"; "Beside them, the dachshund was whining and cowering"; Barney "tried not to let Betty know that he was afraid."[4]

Fuller may be forgiven these embellishments and literary license (he couldn't possibly know such things as Barney's inner thoughts with such certainty, for example), for he presented the abduction material itself in a sober and restrained manner. The book contained few if any of those lurid or sensational elements that had long been associated with some of the more outlandish UFO-related studies; indeed, at least one graphic aspect of the experience may have been left out at Barney's request.[5] Perhaps for reasons such as these, *The Interrupted Journey* received extensive and largely favorable publicity throughout North America and the rest of the world.

Indeed, Fuller's book proved a standard against which future books on the subject would be evaluated. Also, its features, design, and structure many authors undoubtedly emulated in their attempts to make their own narratives equally convincing, to the point where it is virtually impossible to find a later book on abductions that is not arguably indebted to this work.

The first strategy the reader encounters—one that would become ever-present in the literature—involves Fuller's employment of an expert figure who writes an introductory preface to validate the credibility of the events to follow. This validation process usually takes the form of comments vouching for the integrity of the characters involved, and even affirming that the persons concerned were neither mendacious nor psychologically disturbed. Plainly, the desired effect of such a device is to win readers over to the book's premise—that the abduction actually occurred as stated. Fuller's third chapter, furthermore, contains an extensive list of UFO sightings, and includes many references to investigations carried out by highly educated and respectable individuals connected with UFO organizations, all of whom presumably accept the extraterrestrial hypothesis. As readers will come to realize, authors of abduction accounts frequently lump the sightings of UFOs together with the abduction experience, hoping to establish the likelihood of the latter by making a strong case for the existence of the former. Of course, the two phenomena are not necessarily related at all. Contrary to what many abduction authors would have their readers believe, the acknowledgement that occurrences of an unidentified nature have been perceived in the sky in no way commits or binds one to a corresponding acceptance that alien beings are abducting human beings.

In *The Interrupted Journey*, Dr. Simon himself is the prominent expert used to lend weight to the Hills' abduction claims. Obviously (so the argument runs), if the presiding psychiatrist could be persuaded to endorse the text, as he appears to be doing from his uniquely privileged position of having personally heard and recorded the Hills' testimony, the reader may conclude that the events described are more likely to have actually happened pretty much as they are alleged to have occurred.

Obviously, this device can be effective, and it is a practice hard to resist. Admittedly, at first glance experts can be presumed to speak with considerable authority, especially when within their field. It is for this reason important that the reader look at Dr. Simon's comments carefully. Clearly aware of the role he was being asked to play, Dr. Simon made a clear distinction between those areas where he could speak authoritatively and those that were beyond his area of expertise, and takes pains to establish exactly what he is authenticating in the narrative and what he is not. For instance, it emerges that he was concerned to guard against creating false impressions and conclusions concerning the use of hypnosis. In fact, he explicitly states that he has "confined [his] active

participation in this book to editorial supervision of medical statements." Because there are relatively few such medical statements,
Dr. Simon's relationship to the bulk of the book's material was in
fact minimal. Even where hypnosis is involved, he delivered what
many would consider an extremely cautious summary of the efficacy of this tool as a means of uncovering truth. Although "it *can* be
the key to the locked room," although "most frequently it is" an
accurate reflection of truth, Dr. Simon is careful to add that it is
truth "as it is felt and understood by the patient."[6] As far as the
"ultimate impersonal truth" which he speaks of is concerned, as we
saw in the chapter on narrative, it is highly debatable whether such
a pure state of knowledge can ever be attained.

Actually, Dr. Simon himself seems quite sensitive to this issue.
Repeatedly he qualifies his references to authenticity and truth,
reminding us, for example, that while fully satisfied concerning
Fuller's respectability as a writer, and ready to accept that the book
could be considered "an authentic version of the true story *as they*
[that is, the Hills] *had experienced it*," readers must never forget that
this truth "*is what* [the patient] *believes to be the truth.*" As far as
hypnosis is concerned, Dr. Simon again reminds us that it is
nothing more than "a pathway to the truth *as it is felt and understood
by the patient.*"[7]

Dr. Simon's carefully chosen words allow the reader many
interpretive options, including the possibility that the abduction
scenario might be the product of factors other than those the book
was clearly favoring. For one thing, early in the introduction he
used words from the field of dramatic literature, subtly hinting
that there may be a good deal of fiction or fantasy in what is to
follow: During the Hills' therapy, he tells us, there was no portent
of the soon-to-unfold "drama"; the book would revive the "whole
drama"; it was a "drama" that culminated in Fuller's book; he
himself had a presence on the "stage" as a member of the
"dramatis personae," etc. Also interesting is Dr. Simon's concluding comment that the existence of UFOs as concrete objects is
less interesting to him than is "the impact of past experiences *and
fantasies* on their present experiences and responses."[8] Here his
vagueness reminds us of how difficult it can be to determine this
distinction in any instance where memory is recalling past events,
especially unusual and traumatic ones.

Dr. Simon's final remarks are particularly telling. He first establishes that his interference with Fuller's early versions of the book must have seemed to the author as if he, Dr. Simon, were taking the life of Fuller's child. He then goes on to say the book is "good reading indeed," which suggests that he believed much of the book's appeal was due to Fuller's creative skills as a writer; one is not apt to call a scientific or technical treatise a "good read."

As to why Dr. Simon would phrase his introduction so guardedly, readers should keep in mind that he was in a difficult position. First, his professional reputation was very much at stake. Any comment on his part even hinting that he believed the Hills' story as literally true would have been most damaging to his standing as a psychiatrist. At the same time, to state publicly that he did *not* believe the Hills would have been tantamount to calling them liars. He therefore circumvented the issue by limiting his responsibility to medical issues, and by distancing himself from the interpretive perspective employed by Fuller. The book, he makes plain, is Fuller's creation, not his. What is important here is that Dr. Simon's presence in the book actually adds nothing that would substantially strengthen the case for the validity of the Hills' claims. Impressive though the presence of any expert in an abduction book may appear, that expert is usually nothing more than window-dressing.

Fuller's foreword acquaints the reader with the history of his involvement with the case. In the course of doing this, some unusual facts emerge that the book makes no attempt to resolve, let alone even confront. For one thing, we learn that Fuller first became aware of the Hills when informed of their UFO experience by Conrad Quinby, editor of the Derry, New Hampshire, newspaper, who spoke to him of the Hills' experience and mentioned their reluctance to discuss what had happened to them with any but a few close friends and family. Interestingly enough, in the introduction Dr. Simon had also made much of the Hills' anxiety over the publicity that would ensue in the wake of a forthcoming series of unauthorized newspaper articles in a Boston paper. Fuller's subsequent contact with the Hills was initiated by the Hills themselves, who had volunteered to help him in his work on the UFO sightings that would be published in *Incident at Exeter*. Only after the articles broke in a Boston newspaper did the Hills ask Fuller if he would document their story. Both Fuller and Dr. Simon concluded that since the Hills had been sitting on the story for five years, they couldn't possibly be seeking publicity now. Fuller makes much of the fact that immediately after the sighting, both Betty and Barney agreed not to tell anyone of their experience other than relatives and a few close friends.

In spite of all this, nagging questions still remain about the Hills' desire for anonymity and their supposed distaste for publicity. For one thing, if they were so reticent to discuss their experience, however did all these newspaper people get wind of it, and in the case of the reporter from Boston, how was he able to acquire enough information about their abduction experience to write a *series* of articles on it without interviewing them? For all their supposed preoccupation with privacy, the Hills must have passed on accounts of their experiences to more than just a small circle of relatives and acquaintances—in short, they must already have spoken in public.

Admittedly, in chapter 3 of *The Interrupted Journey* Fuller does summarize how organizations such as NICAP learned of their UFO sighting (Betty had written Donald Keyhoe September 26, 1961—within a week of their experience), but the question of how the story eventually reached the attention of newspaper reporters is not answered until the final chapter, where we learn that the Hills had been asked in September of the following year to give a talk to a UFO study group during which a reporter made a tape of their lecture. Even so, this answer simply raises other questions concerning their supposed reluctance to be put in the public eye: How did the UFO study group learn of their experience to begin with, and why did the supposedly publicity-shy Hills agree to give a public lecture? Plainly, there is a major inconsistency here. Because Fuller makes no attempt to resolve this, the Hills' credibility is bound to suffer.

Fuller's foreword adopts another strategy that will appear in virtually every UFO abduction narrative: a claim made by the author of an initial personal skepticism concerning the events to be described. Presumably, this device is employed to heighten the credibility of the events themselves; if a skeptic can be convinced, so the reasoning goes, there must be substance in the account. To be fair, Fuller does not make as much of his own skepticism as later abduction authors would, but the fact remains that he was hardly a true skeptic since he was in the process of completing a book on UFOs—*Incident at Exeter* (1966)—when he met the Hills. For that matter, Fuller employs the "conversion-of-skeptics" motif throughout the book. NICAP's Walter Webb, we are told, was "skeptical of this type of sighting" until he met Betty and Barney and heard their tale.[9] Fuller also tries to paint Barney as a skeptic when it came to flying saucers, telling us he was indifferent to the subject, at least prior to his encounter.[10] Presumably, that Barney now is a "believer" gives further weight to the legitimacy both of the experience and his interpretation of it. All any of these conversions demonstrate is that the experience, whatever it was, made a deep impression on the people involved; it can tell us nothing whatever about the *nature* of that experience.

Fuller and the Hills

Fuller's opening description of Betty and Barney Hill, evidently designed to present them in the best possible light, includes comments that, strictly speaking, he could not possibly know with certainty. We learn that theirs was a "successful mixed marriage" that "they were no longer self-conscious about"; that Barney's sons "had made a pleasing adjustment to [Barney's] second marriage"; that the "total adjustment [of everyone] to their mixed marriage had been remarkably smooth"; and that although Barney sometimes showed "concern about rejection in public places," their "problems as an interracial couple are minimal."[11] Presumably, Fuller is receiving this information directly from the Hills and has chosen to record it uncritically. But one cannot be blamed for wondering if, even in relatively sophisticated New England, such a marriage in the America of 1961 would be as tension-free as Fuller would have us believe. Readers may also wonder if *any* divorce and remarriage could be as problem-free as Fuller alleges Barney's to have been. That there is more than an incidental undercurrent of racial tension in Barney is unmistakable, he himself admitting under hypnosis that he cannot enter a restaurant without bracing himself against possible racial hostility.[12]

It is entirely understandable that Barney would be constantly on the lookout for manifestations of racism, be it in the little restaurant where they stopped for an evening snack on the night of their fateful encounter, or wherever. But it becomes evident that he is more than "a worrier at times."[13] In fact, Barney never stops worrying. At times he seems to be a man consumed with anxiety, who worries when encountering unfriendly waitresses, tough-looking teenagers, the possibility of bears on the deserted highway, or even strange lights in the sky. What is relevant here is that we eventually learn that there is more than a theoretical reason for Barney's fears. Both Hills had been bothered by hoodlums at least once in the past, "on a lonely highway in New Hampshire, in which two teenagers had followed their car, harassing them for nearly thirty miles."[14] Here, a number of interesting possibilities emerge, but they are pointedly not investigated by Fuller. For example, the reader may wonder if something *else* could have happened to the Hills, an equally horrifying experience but one dealing with human adversaries such as hoodlums (either on the trip home from Montreal or at some point in the past) that was too terrifying or humiliating to be handled straightforwardly and was suppressed by their conscious minds?

Moving through abduction literature, we will find that the authors make much of what they call the abductees' "screen" memories, which are defined as pseudomemories that abductees claim to have (usually of encountering non-threatening woodland animals such as deer or owls) which, so the argument runs, they have created to shield them from the more frightening actual encounter with aliens. But this cannot help but plant a further question in the reader's mind, and one that is pointedly ignored or bypassed by all authors of abduction narratives: The abduction memory itself might be a screen, created to make somehow more palatable a particularly horrifying social and *human* encounter. Interestingly, both Betty and Barney dimly recalled initially encountering a "roadblock" of some sort with *men* on the road; they also felt unclean as a consequence of their experience, even though their memory of the UFO's interior was that it was spotless. In this context, it is also noteworthy that virtually all of Barney's references to the aliens are in conventional language. They are not described in nonhuman terms, or as anything other than human beings: "There's a man there! Is—is—is—he a Captain? What is he? He—he [not 'it'] looks at me"; "One person looks friendly to me"; "I think of a red-headed Irishman"; another looks evil, "like a German Nazi" who "had a black scarf around his neck." Later in the first session, on the one occasion when Barney does refer to the leader as a "creature," the change in terminology follows Dr. Simon's pointed question "Did they have faces like other people?" Soon after, he reverts to describing them as he had before: "They're—*men!* All with dark jackets. And I don't have any money. I don't have anything."[15]

In the second session, as Barney describes the initial stages of the abduction, the beings are *still* "men," even though he is much closer to them than before and presumably in a better position to describe their features: "I saw a group of men, and they were standing in the highway" and "flagged me down," prior to his being escorted from the car. Here Barney explicitly states "it did not seem that they had different faces from white men," and later, in conversation with Dr. Simon, he recalls explicitly that the "fellow" who looked at him from the window of the UFO "was not frightening in a . . . horrible sense, like a distorted, unhuman type of creature."[16]

For her part, Betty also refers to her initial contact as an encounter with *men*, and continues to employ this word throughout; "I was afraid when I saw the men on the road." Even when not hypnotized, Betty remembers men on the road. Indeed, Fuller's own repeated reminder that the hypnotized subject strives for *"complete accuracy in reporting"* comes back to haunt him, for in the interests of honoring that accuracy, surely an alternative interpretation should at least be entertained (that they encountered real men in rural New Hampshire).[17]

Later, under hypnosis, Barney revealed himself to be extremely sensitive to the possibility of hostility at the hands of hoodlums, as when he became quite agitated over the presence of some tough-looking boys in the restaurant in Canada. But Fuller avoids any discussion of this, presumably because such an investigation might detract from the particular interpretation of data the book favors. Indeed, the reference to the harassment incident on the highway is not divulged until late in the book.

Were the Hills harassed, or even sexually assaulted by hoodlums, and did they create a fantasy abduction experience to shield them from this or some other horror? Although authors of abduction narratives have little patience with this notion, it has recently been given some indirect statistical support by Kenneth Ring whose *The Omega Project* reports that abductees are more apt to have had a history of sexual or other forms of abuse than the general public. While in the Hills' case the answer may never be known, it should not be simply ignored or dismissed out of hand.

When the Hills first saw the strange light in the sky, we are told it appeared directly above a bright star or planet that was to the left of the moon. In fact, there were *two* planets near the moon on the night of September 19, 1961, Saturn and Jupiter, the latter of which is the third brightest object in the night sky after the moon and Venus. Fuller conspicuously makes no mention of two planets being visible, presumably to avoid the likelihood of the reader's dismissing their sighting as a mistaken identification of a planet. As we will see repeatedly, such failure on the part of authors of abduction narratives to address such prosaic possibilities can have a negative effect on the credibility of their interpretation. Any readers who took the trouble to check the position of the stars and planets for that night would be more apt to embrace the conclusion of mistaken identification than they might otherwise have done. That Fuller makes no mention of it at all can only weaken the case for the extraterrestrial hypothesis, because readers will be led by his silence to suspect that he was frankly unable to dismiss the possibility that the initial UFO was simply a bright planet misidentified, especially as Betty admits under hypnosis that she knows nothing about astronomy. By doing nothing to resolve the reader's doubts, Fuller succeeds only in increasing them.

One of the aspects of *The Interrupted Journey* tacitly assumed by Fuller to be the most compelling feature of the case was the concept of "missing time," in the Hills' case a period of up to two hours for which they became convinced they were unable to account. Fuller expounds on this in his third chapter, where we learn the time anomaly was first pointed out to the Hills in a meeting they had on November 25, 1961, with three UFO investigators who had come to discuss the sighting. Observing that once the "missing time" had been pointed out to Betty and Barney, he comments that it "became a major mystery" which no one at the meeting could explain. As the book proceeds, it goes on to become the most compelling single piece of evidence in support of the story's credibility. Yet interestingly enough, at the time neither of the Hills had apparently considered this aspect of the trip as striking or in any way unusual. In conversation with Dr. Simon, Barney stated explicitly that neither he nor Betty was "particularly impressed" by their inability to recall this period of lapsed time.[18] For that matter, his recollection of this part of the trip was far from dramatic. Under hypnosis he recalled remarking casually to Betty, "Well—it looks as if we're getting into Portsmouth *a little later than I expected*," suggesting awareness of only a slight delay, doubtless caused by the many stops they made to look at the UFO.[19] Here, as many readers of *The Interrupted Journey* have noted over the years, the numerous pauses in their trip could well be sufficient to account for some, if not all, of this missing time. For instance, immediately after first sighting the strange light they stopped the car at least three times to get a better look at it; during this period they drove their car as slowly as "five miles an hour."[20]

As far as their inability to recall every moment of the drive home, this may simply be because there was nothing remarkable about it that they *could* remember. Nevertheless, Fuller makes a good deal of the "simultaneous amnesia" experienced by the Hills, for it was one of the factors that led to Major Macdonald's suggestion that they try hypnosis as a means of uncovering possibly buried memories and of recovering this period of time of which they had no conscious recollection. For his part, Barney agreed, even though he did not think anything unusual had happened on the drive. In part he assented to undergo hypnosis because, as he said, "this might clear up Betty and her nonsense about her dreams."[21] It is interesting that throughout, Barney never initiated action when it came to investigating the events of September 19. He initially denied that there was anything particularly unusual about the light that fascinated Betty; he had little interest in discussing the sighting with the Air Force personnel; he had no desire to read Donald Keyhoe's book; and he regarded Betty's dreams of an encounter with aliens to be "nonsense." In fact, he only became involved in response to speculations from other people such as Betty or Major Macdonald that what occurred was in any way odd or unusual, and gives the impression of "going along" with them simply to be agreeable.

As far as Betty's dreams are concerned, early in the book we were told that Betty had "hesitated to mention them to Barney," and had only done so "casually"; that in fact, she had "refrained from discussing the nightmares with him."[22] But evidently Barney, as early as November, had acquired enough knowledge of her nightmares to be able to pronounce them "nonsense." (Barney's agitation, mentioned previously, did not emerge until he recalled it during therapy.) For, even though late in the book Barney states that "no dreams were involved in relation to the experience until well after the therapy sessions began," earlier he admitted that he *had* heard of them before they met Dr. Simon, for the dreams occurred ten days after the abduction, and Betty recalled telling her supervisor about them not long after the visit of Robert Hohman and C. D. Jackson, the two scientists who first interviewed the Hills on behalf of Major Keyhoe and NICAP, both of which events took place long before the visits to Dr. Simon.[23] Indeed, Barney himself admits that "she told me a great many of the [dreams'] details."[24]

These kinds of inconsistencies, as always, can have perfectly plausible explanations; in this case, Betty presumably changed her mind and told Barney of her dreams. But to be told earlier that she had *not* confided in him is bound to give added weight to the possibility that the abduction was a real, objectively experienced event that both had participated in, because when under hypnosis and both speak of being abducted, it sounds as if they are corroborating each other's independent experiences. However, if Betty had previously shared the contents of her dreams with Barney, as seems to be the case, the "events" that both are recalling are not as apt to be objective experiences, and the possibility that they are the product of a shared fantasy becomes more likely.[25] As was mentioned, Fuller minimizes the importance of Betty's dreams in the account because it is in his interests not to make too much of them; in fact, although Betty's record of her dreams *is* included, it appears in an appendix, at the end of the book.[26] In so doing, Fuller actually creates more interest in these dreams as a result of his very obvious relegation of them to the back pages.

Fuller and Hypnosis

At this stage of the discussion it is important to stress that up to the point where the reader encounters the actual transcripts of the hypnosis sessions, *all* information, though skillfully presented in lucid and readable prose, has come to us filtered through the consciousness of John Fuller, who, we must never forget, is anxious to favor one interpretation at the expense of many others. In fact, the only hard evidence is contained in the Hills' sessions with Dr. Simon, recorded when they were under hypnosis or in the course of their direct conversations with him.

It is thus not surprising that Fuller, aware as he is of the conventional force of direct testimony, should devote large sections of *The Interrupted Journey* to verbatim accounts of the Hills' sessions with Dr. Simon (either under hypnosis or in conversation with him), even though hypnosis has little if any intrinsic credibility as an investigative tool, probably because of the public's mistaken belief that it can provide an instant and unfailing method of getting at the truth. Furthermore, it gives a facade of pseudoscientific authenticity to the entire process, while also involving the reader directly in the action.

Even here, the author continues to play a major role, for we are still at the mercy of what he has chosen to pass on to us. In fact, we have no way of knowing to what extent we are receiving a highly, selectively edited version of the transcripts. Many readers will also realize that we are actually reading not only the supposedly "bare bones" account by Betty and Barney, many parts of which (especially in Barney's case) are sporadic and fragmented, but also extensive commentary by Fuller. The reader should never forget, then, that Fuller is far from a merely passive presenter of information, even when that information appears to speak for itself. Throughout the transcriptions of the hypnosis sessions Fuller repeatedly comments—in the form of marginal glosses—on the evidence in an attempt to strengthen the book's central contentions. But there is always the possibility that we may come to regard the author in this self-assumed role of interpreter as intrusive and superfluous, interfering with our ability to interpret the data on our own.

In the majority of abduction cases, the bulk of the detail is recalled by the abductee while in a hypnotic trance. It goes without saying that if authors of abduction narratives employ hypnosis, they must believe in its efficacy, although the reader may think otherwise. In this case, for obvious reasons Fuller spends a good deal of time stressing that "a subject under hypnosis has such accuracy of recall and retention" that he will continue exactly where he last left off, and mentions on several occasions how precise Betty and Barney were when it came to remembering even minor details of their trip.

Although Fuller's observation about a subject's recall is true as far as it goes, it does not mean in turn that everything said under hypnosis will be an accurate record of an experienced event, but only that both memories and pseudomemories can be recalled with equal precision. It has been known for years that subjects under hypnosis can and do lie and confabulate material, and that it is not only difficult to prevent such responses from occurring, but sometimes impossible to separate the fabulous elements of testimony given under hypnosis from the literal truth.[27] Needless to say, this is not an aspect of hypnosis that Fuller discusses himself.

Fuller also makes much of how careful Dr. Simon was as a hypnotist in his attempts to insure the accuracy of what his subjects recalled. Before encountering the actual transcripts, the reader learns of the instructions Dr. Simon routinely gave to the Hills just before the conclusion of the first hypnosis sessions, to the effect that when they returned to normal consciousness they would not remember anything they had revealed while in the hypnotic state. In fact, it was only after a number of sessions that Dr. Simon allowed them to recall any aspects of their experiences, and only those portions that would not be too upsetting for them.[28] Presumably, one of the reasons for issuing this instruction was to prevent the Hills from discussing and comparing what they had recalled, and contaminating further testimony.

While Fuller obviously believes that this provides strong support for his contentions, he avoids the implication that, since the Hills *had* already discussed Betty's dreams long before they first saw Dr. Simon, some degree of contamination had already occurred. For example, he tells us "*neither Barney nor Betty is aware of either his own or the other's story.*"[29] Though this is narrowly true in the light of Dr. Simon's instructions, Barney *was* more than casually aware of Betty's nightmares, as we have seen. Thus, Barney's ability to provide apparent corroboration of Betty's testimony is not as significant as Fuller makes it appear, simply because he could be merely verifying the content of her dreams.

This in itself would not be terribly important, were it not for the fact that these dreams do bear a striking resemblance to the abduction as recalled by both when they were under hypnosis. In one session, Betty remains quite sure that her nightmares and the actual abduction constitute two distinct experiences; however, the evidence she offers is far from strong. Indeed, all she can think of is that in her dreams she walked up steps, whereas in "reality" she ascended a ramp. Although she repeatedly states there is "so much more" in the real experience, she offers no further evidence. As happens so frequently, Fuller does not draw our attention to such omissions and reveals the remarkable similarity of dream and abduction only at the end of the book, after all the evidence in support of the extraterrestrial hypothesis has presumably had its cumulative effect.

One of the most familiar characteristics of a dream is that people in them frequently respond to events unusually. Such uncharacteristic or irrational behavior is likewise encountered frequently in abduction narratives (despite the best efforts of the authors to underplay it), and the Hill case is no exception. In Barney's first hypnosis session, for example, the reader will be struck by the degree to which his reactions are especially unusual. Although a large UFO is allegedly hovering above him, he surprisingly makes no attempt to flee. Instead, he inexplicably concludes that he must "get a weapon" and reaches for, of all things, a tire wrench.[30]

Indeed, the reader does not have to be a psychologist to see that many aspects of the Hills' experience (especially concerning the abduction itself) are highly surrealistic and dreamlike, a far cry from the realistic and graphic account of their sighting of the strange light. Barney himself even hints indirectly of this possibility in the second session with Dr. Simon when, describing his abduction, he says, "I feel like I am dreaming," adds that he seems "disassociated," and makes frequent references to his closed eyes during the abduction and medical examination; all are conditions consistent with being in a dream state.[31] Betty also mentions "I'm thinking I'm asleep" immediately after they meet the "men" on the road.[32]

As far as the fragmented or vague quality to portions of their recall is concerned, Fuller attributes this to a reluctance on the Hills' part to face those particularly frightening aspects of their experience. He does not entertain the possibility that the recollections themselves could be part of a highly symbolic fantasy created to mask another experience too frightening to recall, even though as the sessions proceed it becomes increasingly evident that symbolism is playing an important role in the account. Eye imagery, for one thing, is particularly prominent. Dr. Simon certainly noticed the importance of this image, and at a later session reassured Barney that "The eyes will not trouble you." Barney is particularly upset by the disembodied eyes that obsess him: "the eyes don't have a body. They're just eyes. . . . All I see are these eyes."[33] Barney's own eyes are significantly closed, but if his eyes *are* kept closed throughout most of his ordeal, it would be impossible for him to see as much as he says he did. More surprisingly, though Betty's eyes are presumably open in her first meeting on the road, she cannot describe what their faces looked like or even what they were wearing, though they supposedly came directly up to her and opened the car door for her.

Other dreamlike elements include Barney's recollection of "just floating about" in a kind of limbo where nothing is visible. The aliens hold him but he cannot feel their grip. Back in Portsmouth after the experience he remembers feeling dirty, but he earlier described the operating room as "being so clean." After Barney is returned to his car, he feels inexplicably "happy"; they are both "grinning" and "real hilarious," strange emotions to be felt by people who have just been through such presumably massive trauma. As they get into the car, he sees a "bright moon." In the real world the moon was no longer visible, it having set at approximately 1:30 A.M. (EDT) that day.[34] In response to Betty's question "Do you believe in flying saucers now?" he replies, just as inexplicably for a man who has just emerged from one, "don't be ridiculous. Of course I don't." The next day he wanted nothing to do with the mysterious spots on the car trunk, but simply "shut them out" of his mind.[35] For that matter, not attempting to remove the spots is in itself odd for a man who wanted no reminders of his experience. Importantly, Fuller addresses none of these anomalies, though leaving them unmentioned can only allow them to fester in the reader's mind.

As Betty's first session begins, Fuller insists on the accuracy of the hypnotic subject's memory. It is interesting to learn that Betty sees Barney as being just as receptive to the extraterrestrial hypothesis as he saw her to be. Early in the sighting she concluded, in response to Barney's comment about the light that *"they've* seen us" (an odd remark for a self-professed skeptic to make, incidentally), that "his imagination was being overactive."[36] From Betty's opening wisecrack to Barney that he must have watched the *Twilight Zone,* it is plain that, contrary to Fuller's comment early in the book that Barney was indifferent to the subject, both are far from oblivious to UFOs. In fact, almost immediately after their first sighting of the light, both are prepared to entertain the notion that the object is a UFO on the most slender of evidence. The only difference between their responses is that Barney is hoping the object can be explained as a conventional craft, where Betty hopes it cannot.

Also curious is their emotional reaction to the experience. Barney, as we have seen, was consumed with fright throughout, and much more is made of his fear than Betty's. Indeed, in Betty's letter to Donald Keyhoe, although she refers to both of them having initially seen the strange light, her emphasis is almost exclusively on Barney's later experience with the UFO, and his fear. Her reason for writing him, as she states, is part of a search for any clue "that might be helpful to *my husband,* in recalling whatever it was *he saw* that caused *him* to panic."[37] Betty surprisingly admits herself that at the time of the sighting she "wasn't really afraid," adding that she "was looking forward to it."[38] Yet oddly enough, it is Betty who panicked when they drove past a parked car that was partially blocking the road some days after the events took place (which again recalls the possibility of a close encounter with human thugs instead of aliens), and Betty is the one first to have vivid nightmares of an experience involving a roadblock of some sort and a group of similarly dressed men (a motorcycle gang?). Incidentally, fear of UFOs was relatively uncommon in 1961; Barney's hysterical conclusion that "They were going to capture us" was a most unusual reaction to the sighting of a UFO at that time.[39] Flying saucers were not normally thought of as fearful in those days, outside of the pages of science fiction, at any rate; most sightings were purely visual and, far from threatening, were often considered exciting visual mysteries.

One point conspicuously bypassed by Fuller in his role as narrator is the extent to which the Hills' visual descriptions of the UFO and its occupants is replete with a detail that one would not think possible, given the object's distance from them.[40] Betty describes a double row of windows, but adds that she was unable to estimate its distance because it could not be seen too clearly without binoculars. In his testimony, Barney's description included details of the aliens' dress and their facial features; one even smiled at him! But as far as distance was concerned, Barney was also vague. When asked by Dr. Simon if the object was a thousand yards from him, all he could say was that "It's not that far."[41] Fuller claims it to be not more than a few hundred feet from Barney, but without explanation of this estimate, presumably if it were any farther away, the details in Barney's testimony become extremely suspect. Even if Barney's assessment *were* accurate, it is highly doubtful that one could detect a smile at such a distance, especially at night.

Once the testimony moves into the abduction itself, it understandably puts increasing strain on the reader's credulity. It is no accident that Fuller's involvement with the text now becomes more pronounced, the author playing a more active role on some occasions, while on others maintaining a judicious silence when material would seem to point in a direction away from the extraterrestrial hypothesis. In some cases Fuller's silences can have just as significant an effect on the reader as do those occasions when he decides to editorialize. For example, in Betty's description of the UFO's interior the imagery she employs is very domestic, surprising when one considers that if what she is describing is real, it had its origins in a totally alien environment that would very likely be stranger than anything we could possibly conceive. Yet given her references to doors, rooms, stools, gadgets, a "man who spoke English," and even the presence of a book aboard the UFO, she could be talking about the interior of any hospital or operating room in Portsmouth.[42] Significantly, Fuller makes nothing of this, nor does he observe how amazing a coincidence it would be that alien beings would build craft that would contain so many features similar in design to human constructions.

As Betty's testimony progresses, the medical purpose of the abduction becomes more evident, and a sexual component appears that will come to dominate later abduction literature. Needle imagery is pronounced, as is the act of penetration. The pain Betty feels is magically erased with a gesture of the alien's hand, and her fear is implicitly quelled. Even though she claims no sexual advances were made, it does not take a psychoanalyst to see the relationship between the needle inserted in Betty's navel and an act of sexual assault.[43] Fuller's silence speaks volumes.

Fuller's involvement can be similarly telling. When, at one point, Betty pauses in her monologue, the author chooses to opine that her pause is *"as if to recall the picture more clearly."*[44] A more skeptical commentator could argue just as easily that the pause is to allow her time for further fabulation.

Characteristics of the Hill Abduction

The core section of Betty's testimony contains many elements that are of great importance for our study of the abduction narratives' evolving form. It will be recalled from the introduction that one weakness of the contactee stories was the proliferation of details that could be subjected to verification. As the first abduction narrative in North America to receive significant publicity, the Hill case is the one most like the accounts of the contactees in containing by far the most verifiable detail, and hence the most easily challenged. The most significant element in the Hill case that would *not* be repeated in later narratives is the lengthy and extensive conversation Betty has with this most talkative of alien abductors. Interestingly enough, only in the next major abduction narrative, the case of Betty Andreasson, is there any lengthy dialogue with aliens.

One also notices that in the Hill case the aliens are the least "alien" and display the most human traits and characteristics. For one, they have a sense of humor. Betty's interlocutor laughs frequently, and even teases Betty by not revealing where they are from, even though she has asked him where they are located on the map he has shown her. They also display surprise, upon their discovery of Barney's dentures; irritation, when the Hills dawdle or offer them resistance; remorse, when they realize they have caused her pain with their needle; and caprice, when they change their minds about allowing Betty to keep the book. Furthermore, they are far from all-knowing and confess to an ignorance of time, the aging process, and even color (odd, since they sport colored uniforms). Significantly, virtually *none* of these traits will be seen in future abduction narratives, where subsequent aliens tend to behave indifferently, or as austere godlike beings. Any communication that does take place in future will be distinctly one-sided, and almost invariably the aliens reveal nothing specific of themselves or their purposes.

Because Betty's conversation was so detailed, it contains many inconsistencies and anomalous elements that would not appear in later narratives. First, although the leader-alien claims ignorance of the aging process and the passage of time, earlier he spoke of temporal concerns: "You'll be on your way back home *in no time*"; "The *longer* you fool around out here, the *longer* it's going to take"; "We haven't got *much time*"; "If we took you both in the same room it would take *too long*."[45] This anomaly is so glaring that it is even discussed by the Hills later in the book, but in the discussion the only possibility that is considered seriously is that Betty may have been trying to assign words to what was essentially a telepathic and nonverbal form of communication; that it might reflect an inconsistency within a confabulated scenario is a possibility not entertained.

Another significant detail that would not reappear in later abduction narratives is a reference to the location of the aliens' home planet. Although Betty is not told explicitly where they are from, she is permitted to see a map which she later draws while hypnotized. Incidentally, this map would go on to inspire an extended controversy which eventually made it to the pages of *Astronomy* magazine, a controversy many consider as yet unresolved.[46]

The Hill abduction stands out equally for the number of elements it does not contain. For one thing, there is no evidence that a device or "implant" was inserted into Betty or Barney to aid the aliens in their inscrutable designs, although this feature will become commonplace. Nor do the aliens the Hills encounter appear to be participating in a well-planned, systematic, large-scale series of ongoing experiments performed repeatedly on a select number of human beings, as later aliens would be; there is even a haphazard quality to what they are doing. The leader tells Betty they can find her "*if* we decide to come back."[47] It is also interesting to note that they do not seem to have given the matter of leaving Betty with a memento any thought, for when she asked for one, they first acceded to her request, only to change their minds. Aliens in subsequent abduction narratives will appear far more organized.

Nevertheless, elements also appear that do resurface in other narratives. The aliens' ability to track down those they want to, with or without an implant, will become a common feature of abduction accounts, as is the hint that such experimenting may have been going on for some time, for the leader tells Betty "We always find those we want to."[48] Alien employment of a hypnotic suggestion that the Hills will forget their experience is also frequently (but, oddly enough, not always) encountered, as is a commonly experienced byproduct of that suggestion: its failure to take hold in the abductees.

This last point may be one of the most perplexing aspects of every abduction narrative where such suggestion appears. Alien-induced amnesia is frequently unsuccessful, despite the aliens' oft-stated conviction that the abductees will not remember any aspect of their experience. This failure raises some interesting questions that Fuller's text should confront. First, if the aliens truly desired anonymity, surely they would create total forgetfulness (something they must presumably be able to do, since we would have no trouble inducing it ourselves, and they must surely be at least as medically knowledgeable as we are). If on the other hand they wish their presence to be known, why would they block *any* part of an abductee's memory? It is truly ironic that Dr. Simon is far more successful at inducing blockages of memory in the Hills than are the aliens. Betty and Barney invariably recall only what Dr. Simon allowed them to and no more, but in time remember everything about their abduction. Fuller makes no mention of this anomaly anywhere in the book. Nor, for that matter, does any other abduction author examine this, other than to dismiss it as beyond resolution.

The presence of technological gadgetry is prominent in the Hills' experience (as in many later accounts) and the Hills' aliens are clearly identified as beings dominated by a technological agenda, although the leader appears to have retained some individuality in spite of this. Later aliens will become virtually indistinguishable from the technology that surrounds them, on occasion even reminding abductees of robots or automata. Betty's failure to secure an artifact (in her case the alien book) is encountered in those abduction narratives that were among the first to appear, but this feature only occasionally crops up in more recent ones. Villas-Boas, it will be recalled, tried unsuccessfully to steal what looked like a clock, and as the next chapter will reveal, Betty Andreasson *was* given a book, only to have it mysteriously disappear from her home. In later abduction narratives, the abductee is not given such privileges or opportunities for retrieval of hard evidence, thus cutting off yet another avenue of potential verification; the so-called probes and implants allegedly recovered have not to date proved to be convincing.

In the aftermath of Betty's sessions, even she was surprised by a number of unusual aspects to the experience, to say nothing of her own and Barney's reactions. First, Betty's suggestion that she wanted to forget it does not make sense, given her interest in the UFO sighting. Also odd is Betty's failure to remember precisely if they stopped to sleep at some point during the trip, something one would think she would surely recall. Fuller mentions such aspects, but does not give them the emphasis they deserve.

Just as important are the discrepancies between the two accounts which Fuller ignores. For one, Barney described walking "just a few steps" to his examination room, but Betty clearly recalled that "They [led] Barney right past the door where I'm standing." Although Betty remembers Barney's presence, he has no recollection of her. To Betty, the alien leader spoke English with "sort of a foreign accent"—although, to be fair, in a later session she began to question their method of communication—but to Barney they communicated in a manner the nature of which he "couldn't understand."[49] Finally, there are inconsistencies even within individual parts of the Hills' testimony. Barney initially said he had chosen to close his eyes out of fear: "My eyes were tightly closed, and I was afraid to open them. . . . I didn't want to open them. It was comfortable to keep them closed"; but later, we are told he "had been told not to open" them.[50] Fuller does not acknowledge that there is anything of significance in such inconsistencies.

In spite of this, Fuller makes a great deal of the extent to which their recollections appeared similar, and asks rhetorically, "How could they [the Hills] recount remarkably similar details of an abduction by humanoid intelligent beings which defied any encounter documented in history, when neither was aware of what the other had seen or reported under hypnosis to the doctor?" He then goes on to state that "here were two people, neither aware of what he [Barney] was saying, who were telling identical stories" as convincing proof that Betty was not "borrowing" material from her husband.[51] But of course, Barney *had* previously been privy to the contents of Betty's nightmares, which were very similar to the experiences both recalled when hypnotized. Indeed, it is just as easy to discredit abduction accounts by emphasizing the many ways they do not coincide. Obviously, the fallibility of witnesses concerning recalled details is notorious; some degree of variability is to be expected. Still, one would not expect to find mutually exclusive aspects within a single encounter. While, for example, the aliens are firm and brusque, at times even threatening to Barney (when they order him to tell no one about the experience), they are chatty, colloquial, and even chummy with Betty. Likewise, after being shown the drawing he made of the alien, Barney drew another one and was struck by the fact that they were "fairly similar"; in fact, there are major differences, with the second, more detailed version having a definite mouth, fairly thick lips, and smaller eyes that do not "wrap around."

In one of the later sessions, evidence from the transcript suggests that for his part, even as Dr. Simon allowed more information from the hypnosis sessions to be released, Barney's doubts about the reality of the abduction experience remained. Referring to the "incredibility of the whole thing," he began to note the dreamlike quality to much of his recollection.[52] The aliens' lack of mouths, coupled with their ability to smile; their being able to communicate without talking; and their ability to listen to him speak even though they lacked ears, all of these aspects understandably affected his ability to believe that this had really occurred. To his credit, Barney asked Dr. Simon a number of shrewd questions. First, he wondered if it is possible to have a dream of a UFO and later recall it under hypnosis. Dr. Simon's precise reply is not recorded, although at a later stage he does enable Barney to see that there was a high degree of similarity between Betty's dreams and her experience in the alien operating room. Later, Barney wondered why the period of amnesia should have taken place when it did (*after* the abduction), when common sense would favor amnesia occurring *during* the abduction process and terminating when it had been completed. Even years after the event, the closest Barney could come to acknowledging the experience was to say he "felt" that it had happened. Pushed by Dr. Simon to be more precise, Barney only replied that it was more "comfortable" to express himself vaguely.

Fuller makes few comments on the issue of Barney's continuing doubts, but spends a good deal of time discussing instead the import of the warts on Barney's groin which flared up after the visits to Dr. Simon began. Mentioning that neither Simon nor the dermatologist was concerned about the warts, he adds that "to Barney, the gnawing thought remained that this could be evidence."[53] The appearance of a physical gouge, "scoop," or scar on an abductee's body, presumably the result of an excision performed by the aliens, is a feature that will appear throughout subsequent abduction literature.

However much Barney's drawings of the aliens may be distinguished from later pictures of abducting extraterrestrials, their basic verbal description of the aliens contained many features that would be seen in later abduction narratives. Small in stature, large-headed, gray-skinned, and hairless, the aliens' most prominent feature is their eyes, which extend to the side of the head and seem to possess a mind-reading and hypnotic power. As they have only slits where a mouth and nose should be, it makes them totally expressionless and hence unfathomable by human standards.[54] Yet other features cited by the Hills are not commonly found in later narratives. For one, Barney's "humming" aliens do not reappear; in future abductions, the form of communication is almost always telepathic. Also, the Hills' aliens eyes "moved, and they had pupils," reminding Betty of a cat's eyes.[55] This feature will disappear in most of the later literature, although we do encounter it in Travis Walton's experience. In the conclusion we will examine the description of these beings as a symbolically appropriate depiction of what it means to be "alien." For now, it is important to stress that the Hills' aliens are physically the most humanlike of all the gray-skinned abductors described. Barney even likens them in appearance to a group of Indians living around the Magellan Straits, pictures of whom he had seen when attending a lecture. Furthermore, they are as much at the mercy of the restrictions of the physical world as we are. Later aliens would be depicted as far more sophisticated, having acquired a greater power over physical barriers and limitations.

Fuller ends *The Interrupted Journey* as he began it, with another appeal to authority. This time, the authority figure is none other than Dr. J. Allen Hynek, at the time chairman of the astronomy department at Northwestern University and the most famous scientist to acknowledge UFOs as occurrences worthy of serious study. As one might expect, Hynek, like Fuller, uses the assumption that there is "something" to UFOs as a means of endorsing the abduction phenomenon, even though there is no necessary link between them.

The book then wraps up with a list of "nearly irrefutable points" that Fuller believes emerge from the Hill case. The reader would probably have no difficulty with several of Fuller's contentions: a sighting of *something* in the sky probably did occur; the sighting undeniably caused the Hills emotional stress; Barney's racial tensions contributed to this stress; and the case was checked by investigators who supported the possibility of the reality of the experience.

Other items in his list might be harder to accept: the object sighted appears to have been a craft; there was physical evidence to support their story; and under hypnosis they told nearly identical stories. Notably, these more bizarre details are strategically interspersed within the more or less self-evident ones. As to the final item—that the Hills had no ulterior motive for their disclosure—the reader can never know this without knowing what could motivate the Hills. We do know they were far from the publicity-shy couple Fuller depicts them as being, and may well have, on some level, come to enjoy the favorable response their lectures and talks were receiving.

Exactly what happened to the Hills cannot, of course, ever be known. Even Barney admitted he only began to consider seriously the possibility that the encounter with aliens might have actually taken place *after* he and Betty had been permitted to listen to the tapes of their sessions: "I knew, I felt, I was *almost* sure as I listened to the tapes that this was no fantasy or dream. It was a matter of *little* doubt to me." Fuller himself remarks that they were both "vacillating constantly, at one moment feeling that perhaps this could be a dream—at others becoming convinced of the reality of it."[56] Significantly, he does not seriously entertain this equally valid alternative possibility.

What Fuller's book does do for the abduction myth is set the pattern for future works of this type for good *and* ill. In the next major abduction narrative to be discussed, for example, virtually all the elements found in *The Interrupted Journey* appear again, but in a manner that is not necessarily accompanied by a corresponding increase in credibility, as the ensuing examination of Raymond Fowler's *The Andreasson Affair* will attempt to prove.

Notes

1. In a letter to her mother written shortly after the country learned of their experience, Betty Hill spoke with relief at the favorable response with which publication of the account was greeted. Notably, in her list of the number of individuals who responded, she makes *no* reference to anyone having claimed a similar experience. It is for this reason, perhaps more than any other, that the Hills' interrupted journey deserves to be called the first true abduction narrative.

2. John G. Fuller, *The Interrupted Journey* (New York: Dell, 1966, 1987), 17, my emphases.

3. "During the whole of a *dull, dark,* and *soundless* day in the autumn of the year, when the clouds hung *oppressively* low in the heavens, I had been passing *alone,* on horseback, through a *singularly dreary* tract of country; and at length found myself, as the *shades* of evening drew on, within view of the *melancholy* House of Usher." Edgar Allan Poe's "The Fall of the House of Usher," rpt. in *The Norton Anthology of Short Fiction,* shorter 5th ed., ed. R. V. Cassill (New York: W. W. Norton, 1995), 717–18.

4. Fuller, *Interrupted Journey,* 21–28.

5. According to David Jacobs, Barney had claimed that the aliens took a sperm sample from him. Embarrassed by this detail, he asked that this not be included, a request which Fuller honored. See Jacobs, *Secret Life* (New York: Simon and Schuster, 1992), 40. Unfortunately, Jacobs does not cite a source (such as a direct quotation from Barney Hill himself) which would verify this information. Although this feature of the Hill abduction is commonly accepted today as undisputed fact, I personally have not seen it verified in print.

6. Fuller, *Interrupted Journey,* 9.

7. Ibid., my emphasis.

8. Ibid., 10.

9. Ibid., 51.

10 Barney may not have been quite as skeptical as Fuller maintains. If he were a true skeptic, his fear when he first saw the strange light is hard to fathom. Surely such fear is more apt to be the reaction of a man who *has* some knowledge of the possibility that UFOs might be extraterrestrial craft, rather than that of a person truly indifferent to the subject.

11. Fuller, *Interrupted Journey*, 18–22.

12. Barney tells Dr. Simon about entering a restaurant with Betty: "I can't park close to this restaurant, so I park on the street and we must walk to the restaurant. And everybody on the street passing us is looking. And we go in to this restaurant, and all eyes are upon us. And I see what I call the stereotype of the 'hoodlum.' The ducktail haircut. And I immediately go on guard against any hostility" (Ibid., 98).

13. Ibid., 21.

14. Ibid., 322.

15. Ibid., 111–23.

16. Ibid., 147–53, 247.

17. Ibid., 185–86.

18. Ibid., 231. Robert Baker quotes Graham Reed's study of the phenomenon of so-called missing time. In Reed's opinion, "our experience of time and its passage is determined by *events*, either external or internal." Because of this, "What the time-gapper is reporting is not that a slice of time has vanished, but that he has failed to register a series of events which would normally have functioned as his time-markers." See Robert A. Baker, "The Aliens among Us: Hypnotic Regression Revisited," *Skeptical Inquirer* 12, no. 2 (Winter 1987–88): 147–62.

19. Fuller, *Interrupted Journey*, 128.

20. Ibid., 28.

21. Ibid., 67.

22. Ibid., 48–49.

23. Ibid., 335, 79.

24. Ibid., 232.

25. This appears to be the view that Dr. Simon favored (see Philip J. Klass, *UFO Abductions: A Dangerous Game* [Amherst, N.Y.: Prometheus Books, 1989], 39), but it is one of which, for obvious reasons, Fuller makes very little.

26. If readers do not see the relegation of Betty's dreams to the back pages of an appendix as evidence of a strategy on Fuller's part, or as even particularly important, they have only to read Philip Klass's *UFO Abductions: A Dangerous Game* to see how prominent a position they can occupy when the bias of the author is diametrically opposite to Fuller's.

27. Confabulation, a psychological term, refers to the process whereby we compensate for loss or impairment of memory by fabricating or otherwise inventing connecting details. Readily available summaries of these findings may be found in Philip J. Klass, "Hypnosis and UFO Abductions," *Skeptical Inquirer* 5, no. 3 (Spring 1981): 16–24, who quotes Martin T. Orne, past president of the International Society of Hypnosis; see also Baker, "The Aliens among Us."

28. Incredibly, this very sensible practice has not been emulated by later hypnotists (see in particular the works of Budd Hopkins and Raymond Fowler), who allow the abductees to emerge from the hypnotic trance with full recall of what they have disclosed, no matter how upsetting those recollections might be.

29. Fuller, *Interrupted Journey*, 219.

30. The reader may also be thinking at this point that, while such a weapon might provide him with some protection against obviously hostile human adversaries, Barney has been given no reason to conclude that alien beings pose him any threat or mean them any harm, or that they could be challenged by such means.

31. Fuller, *Interrupted Journey*, 148.

32. Ibid., 188.

33. Ibid., 165, 124–26.

34. Ibid., 156–58. Interestingly enough, the sun rose that morning in their area roughly at 6:30 A.M. We are told their kitchen clock registered 5:00 A.M. when they returned. But even if they took three hours to make the trip from the abduction site to their home (a mere eighty-odd miles or so), they would have had to leave some time after the moon set, suggesting again an anomaly that Fuller owes it both to the Hills and his readers to have investigated.

35. Ibid., 158, 165.

36. Ibid., 174.

37. Ibid., 47.

38. Ibid., 178, 253.

39. Ibid., 181.

40. Those readers familiar with Henry James's *The Turn of the Screw* will find these discrepancies reminiscent of a section of that novel. The principal character, a probably deranged governess, describes in minute detail the physical appearance of one of the ghosts she claims to have seen, immediately after telling us that she and the ghost were too far apart to speak to each other!

41. Fuller, *Interrupted Journey*, 112.

42. Ibid., 193.

43. Ibid., 222. Barney also recalled a similar sensation of feeling pres-

sure, as if he too were about to be penetrated by some object: "And I felt something touch right at the base of my spine, like a finger pushing. A single finger."

44. Ibid., 193.

45. Ibid., 190–92.

46. Intrigued by Betty Hill's map, amateur astronomer Marjorie Fish discussed with Betty Hill exactly what she had seen, and learned it was a three-dimensional star map, something like a hologram. After many attempts to duplicate the map by hanging beads from strings, Fish eventually produced an accurate configuration of the immediate stellar neighborhood, after removing all but the beads that represented "sun-like" stars, that is, those stars capable of supporting planetary systems with earthlike planets. When examined from a certain angle, it appeared as if the aliens' home star was Zeta Reticuli, a binary-star system consisting of two basically sunlike stars revolving around a common center of gravity, both of which could have planetary systems. Naturally, many astronomers were quick to object to the Fish conclusions, arguing that one can always find evidence of a pattern in random data. For further information see Terence Dickinson, *The Zeta Reticuli Incident* (Milwaukee, Wisc.: Astromedia, 1976).

47. Fuller, *Interrupted Journey*, 211.

48. Ibid.

49. Ibid., 190–221.

50. Ibid., 154, 222.

51. Ibid., 226–27.

52. Ibid., 270.

53. Ibid., 284.

54. Interestingly, in Betty's dream the aliens had noses "like Jimmy Durante" (344).

55. Ibid., 309.

56. Ibid., 302–304, my emphasis.

4

RAYMOND FOWLER
AND THE INTERSTELLAR SAGA
OF BETTY ANDREASSON

Raymond Fowler's *The Andreasson Affair* is in a number of ways strikingly similar to *The Interrupted Journey*. The book chronicles the abduction experiences of an individual who also sat on her story for some time (over eight years) before consulting an expert for badly needed advice. This expert (Prof. J. Allen Hynek) eventually fills a role similar to the one occupied by Dr. Simon, for he, too, pens an introduction. In the opening chapter the author establishes his own relevant credentials, outlines how he learned of the case, and much as Fuller had done, announces himself as a converted skeptic who now accepts the literal reality of the experiences as told to him. Hypnosis is also relied upon extensively and is defended as being a valid way of uncovering the truth. Large sections of the book also contain purportedly verbatim transcripts of sessions conducted while the abductee was hypnotized. Finally, much of the information is acknowledged by Fowler, at least initially, as putting a strain on the reader's credulity, which gives the impression of objectivity to the author's tone.

It is easy to see why Raymond Fowler should have structured his book like Fuller's: *The Interrupted Journey* had, on the whole, been well-received and had enjoyed considerable popular success. At the same time, such imitation can be risky to the extent that it invites comparison. Many of Fowler's readers had likely read Fuller's book, and any comparisons of two such similar works will usually be at the expense of the more recent one, which, as it is apt to be perceived as a mere imitative sequel, will be scrutinized more closely and perhaps evaluated less charitably. Here, readers familiar with both books will immediately see that Fowler's presence is far more intrusive than was Fuller's in *The Interrupted Journey*. For one thing, unlike Fuller he played an active part in many of the hypnosis sessions. Also, most of Fowler's comments identify him specifically from the outset as a sympathetic and biased participant in the events.

Fowler's weaknesses are reinforced by comparison with Fuller, as the two introductions will serve to illustrate. Although both Simon and Hynek could claim to possess a certain expertise concerning the subjects at hand, Hynek had no direct involvement with Betty Andreasson and her case. The role he played, such as it was, was both passive and peripheral, and consisted only in his having received a letter from her where she informed him of her experiences, a copy of which he later passed on to a UFO research group that had requested such information. Although Hynek knew Raymond Fowler, he acknowledges no other relationship with the abductee.

Perhaps because he was not very close to the material, Hynek's attempts to align readers on his side are far from successful. Observing that in the past he would not have considered alien abduction seriously, he admits he has learned to "broaden" his view of the entire UFO phenomenon, having come to appreciate it in its full complexity. Although such a comment seems innocuous enough, actually this is little more than rhetorical bullying, for Hynek is condemning anyone disinclined to accept the fact of abductions as narrow-minded. Since few of us like to think of ourselves in this way, the ploy may be counterproductive.

Hynek then goes on to stress the complexity of the UFO phenomenon and warn readers that reducing the problem to a simple question of the physical existence of UFOs does not do justice to the issue. His point is fair enough. Oddly enough, though, for a man who has just disclaimed as simplistic any attempt to reduce the UFO problem to the single "either/or" issue of their physical reality, Hynek proceeds to force an equally simple dichotomy on the reader when he comments in Betty's defense that there is not "the slightest evidence of hoax or contrivance" in the Andreasson case.[1] Here the implication is that her experiences must either be real or the product of a hoax. In saying this, Hynek is again attempting to pressure the reader into accepting the credibility of Betty Andreasson's experiences. While Hynek does allude in passing to a third possibility—that Betty Andreasson's experiences are "the result of some complex psychological drama"—throughout the book readers are relentlessly discouraged from giving this option serious consideration, even though it is just as easy to see much of Betty's story as emanating from the recesses of her psyche as it is to see it originating in interstellar space.

Hynek takes another leaf out of Fuller's book by discussing the general UFO phenomenon as if it were one and the same with the very specific and idiosyncratic abduction experiences. First, he states that readers who have the "courage" to take "an honest look" at Fowler's book will be "sorely challenged" to maintain that "the entire subject" of UFOs is nonsense. This, of course, is an opinion with which few could disagree, since it does not take much of a leap of faith to concede only that there *might* be aspects of the UFO phenomenon that need to be taken seriously. Hynek then goes on to insert Betty Andreasson's abduction experiences under the umbrella of "the entire subject," knowing as he does, of course, that readers may be pushed by his reasoning into extending a similar tolerance to the abduction narrative to come.

But readers do not become less than honest or courageous if they choose to dismiss the Andreasson story. One's response to *The Andreasson Affair* must be based solely on the credibility of the evidence and the manner of its presentation; intellectual acceptance or endorsement of an issue is not so much a matter of character as of mind. All in all, when Hynek's introduction is stripped of its rhetoric, the strength of its endorsement has relatively little value.

Preparing the Reader

Like Hynek, Fowler draws a distinction between the "majority of adult Americans" who believe in UFOs and the "still-skeptical minority" who do not. This is nothing more than a transparent attempt both to categorize belief in UFOs as *de rigueur* and label any skepticism eccentric or stubborn. All will agree, Fowler confidently claims, that the evidence is "too substantial and compelling to be easily dismissed."[2] While this may be true in the most general sense, Fowler pointedly ignores that dismissal can assume many forms. For example, readers might be loath to dismiss the significance of what happened to Betty, seeing what happened to her as an important psychological phenomenon, while having no trouble dismissing from consideration the possibility that what she was saying had actually happened.

Fowler also attempts to establish himself as a man to be trusted when it comes to UFOs, but his very closeness to the UFO "movement" can backfire to the degree that it decreases our readiness to see him as an objective or open-minded chronicler of the events. Further, he has received no formal training in those disciplines that would make him a sophisticated interpreter of Betty Andreasson's experience; he is not a psychologist, nor has he any medical, psychiatric, or literary background. Dr. Simon's relative objectivity concerning the Hills was established by his professional background as a psychiatrist, together with his personal indifference to the subject of UFOs. His very distance from the scene actually added to the intrinsic credibility of the Hills' recollections. Knowing as we did that Dr. Simon himself was unfamiliar with the subject of UFOs, it was highly unlikely that their testimony could have been contaminated by any involvement in the form of factual insertions or leading questions on his part.

As Fuller did with the Hills, Fowler paints a picture of Betty Andreasson's childhood background and present family environment as normal and happy, presumably to guard against the likelihood that the reader will see the traumatic events to come as being related to psychological stress, family dysfunction, or mental instability. As we will see time and again, this is a typical device employed by virtually all authors of abduction narratives.

However, just as often these claims are unsubstantiated. Here, no corroboration is provided that Betty's childhood was idyllically happy and trouble-free. As far as her adult life is concerned, there must have been considerable stress in the family for some time, for well into the book Fowler states somewhat obliquely that a mysterious marital problem had developed, one "that Betty patiently bore for years."[3] Although unidentified at this point, it must have been quite significant, for we eventually learn that just before the hypnosis sessions began she had separated from her husband. Importantly, one cause of their problems, and possibly the main one—her first husband's alcoholism—is not mentioned until the third book in Fowler's Andreasson trilogy, *The Watchers* (1990). Obviously, to have been presented initially with more thorough information regarding their domestic unrest might well have affected our response to Betty's abduction narrative in any number of ways, including steering us away from accepting the contention that it was literally true. And, of course, any conspicuous omission of potentially relevant information is bound to call attention to itself.

From the outset Fowler himself is perfectly aware that Betty's story is an extremely bizarre one. To refresh readers' memories, Betty Andreasson was a New England housewife. On the evening of January 25, 1967, she and her family allegedly saw a UFO outside their house. Shortly after, she noticed that the other members of the household appeared to have been put in a state of suspended animation. At this time, four aliens entered the house, amazingly enough by passing directly through the door. Betty spoke to the leader, who told her his name was Quazgaa. When Betty presented Quazgaa with a Bible, he gave her a small blue book which was written in a language she could not read. She kept the book in her house, but some days later the alien volume mysteriously disappeared.

Betty was then taken aboard the aliens' UFO and subjected to tests similar to those Betty Hill had experienced. The aliens also appeared to remove a small pelletlike ball from her nose. They then proceeded to take her on a trip to another planet (presumably the aliens' home base), different areas of which were characterized by different colors; one part of her journey (which amounted to a kind of sightseeing tour) was enveloped in red, another in green. Strange little headless animals with huge eyes were also seen climbing around walls, which Betty observed as she was escorted to a type of shrine. There she encountered a huge phoenixlike bird and claimed to have a near-mystical experience (which she has been forbidden by her alien hosts to relate) behind what she called the Great Door. The aliens themselves were of a decidedly religious nature, and were favorably impressed by Betty's faith in Christ.

Betty was told by the aliens that, much like an Old Testament prophet, she had been chosen to serve a presumably communicative purpose and that they would inform her when the time was ripe for her to pass on their messages for humankind. In the series of hypnosis sessions that ensued, a number of bizarre and novel facts surfaced, among them that Betty had been encountering the aliens since childhood; that Betty's second husband, Bob Luca, whom she met in Florida under circumstances she considered highly unusual, had also been abducted; that after their marriage, mysterious phone calls were made to their home, where an unintelligible voice spoke to them in angry tones; and that strange unmarked helicopters "buzzed" their house after publication of Fowler's first book, as if to intimidate them.

Fowler's second and third books on Betty Andreasson contain material that is equally bizarre, but both are thematically similar to the initial volume. In *The Watchers*, his third, it emerges that Fowler himself discovered that he, too, had a history of alien encounters, and may well have been abducted as a child.

In an attempt to prevent the reader from a wholesale dismissal of the account, he acknowledges in his opening remarks that parts of her narrative seem to deal with a reality so alien that it can only be described metaphorically, "and perhaps only understood in terms of an altered state of consciousness."[4] But to mount such a defense before the reader has been presented with any of the facts is a dangerous strategy. First, it is difficult to know exactly what he means by the extremely vague "altered state of consciousness." Second, apparently without realizing it, Fowler has acknowledged the legitimacy of interpreting parts of Andreasson's story metaphorically—and hence, as nothing more than a richly symbolic but fantasized experience.

Other problems that surface in the first chapter may also be occasioned by Fowler's fears about readers rejecting the story outright. When he establishes immediately that "our" disbelief gave way "under the sheer weight of the supporting evidence," Fowler's use of the plural form of the possessive pronoun clearly implies that he was neither eccentric nor unique in being bowled over by Betty Andreasson's story. But Fowler offers *no* documented support on behalf of his contention that anyone but he was similarly convinced. Surely on such an important issue, brief testimonials by these people could have been included in an appendix. As we will see, Fowler's numerous claims regarding the presence of corroborating evidence are also largely unsubstantiated; the case still rests almost entirely on Betty Andreasson's personal credibility.

All in all, Fowler's introduction raises more questions than it answers. Why, for example, did Betty wait so many years before communicating her experience to anyone? There were several nationally based UFO organizations in existence at the time from which she could have received information; one would think that at least one would have given her a sympathetic hearing.[5] The time gap, one of many facets of the case significantly not discussed, is important because as many readers will know, a period of ten years provides more than adequate time for a family to create a coherent but greatly expanded and embellished narrative out of quite fragmented and sketchy material, which they will then appear to corroborate separately.[6] What was originally rumor or mere speculation can become hardened into historical "facts" that are rarely challenged, because it is to everyone's interest to believe that the events in question really occurred. While few readers would expect Fowler to be an expert on such matters, surely the possibility that a degree of interactive creativity had taken place should be examined at some point in the Andreasson trilogy, since he makes so much of the family members' corroboration of Betty's original sighting of the UFO and the presence of the humanoids.

After reminding us that the witnesses believed the events happened, Fowler adds self-consciously "And so, for that matter, do I," resting on the assumption that with his credibility established he can weather any criticism that might proceed from his having staked out his position on the matter.[7] But such a commitment at this stage of the book is risky, because readers have been given no hard evidence. It also makes a mockery of the paragraph's opening sentence—"Is the story of the Andreasson Affair true?"

In defending his position Fowler emphasizes the Andreassons' sincerity, stressing that "it soon became apparent to me that both witnesses were wholly sincere" (only Betty and her daughter Becky recalled the encounter in any detail), but the reader must wonder if the question of sincerity is in fact as relevant a factor as Fowler (like other abduction authors) believes when it comes to determining the truth of the experience. Betty's sincerity, as readers will see, has nothing to do with questions concerning the actual nature of the experiences; after all, many people believe themselves to be Napoleon or Joan of Arc with perfect sincerity.

New Elements and Inconsistencies

In the opening chapter Fowler alludes to the "subtle similarities" the Andreasson case had with other similar cases, by way of strengthening the case for its authenticity. It is true that there are some resemblances between the Hill and Andreasson abductions. For one, the physical examination performed on Betty Andreasson by her aliens, as reported, is quite like the one that was conducted on Betty Hill. In both cases the examining rooms appear similarly antiseptic; a large lens-shaped object figures in both procedures; the aliens conduct "pregnancy" tests on the women; and needles are inserted into their navels for this purpose. Oddly enough, these dramatic and painful tests prove to be a meaningless waste of time; neither woman is able to have children because of a previous operation.[8] Betty Andreasson's aliens also debate issues and argue over whether to conduct more tests on her. Finally, though both are told to forget their experiences, this does not happen in either case.

But there are also many unique features that distinguish the Andreasson abduction, features that would put even greater strain on the reader's credulity. The first new element encountered is the ability of the aliens to defy the molecular structure of matter and penetrate doors and walls as if they were not there: "They passed through its solid wood as if it were nonexistent."[9] In this instance, it is not impossible to imagine, for example, that an advanced civilization could manufacture three-dimensional, animate holographic extensions of themselves that could appear to materialize at will, pass through solid matter, and even have the ability to manipulate their immediate surroundings. It is also conceivable that alien technology could be applied to us as well, thus accounting for the "trips" abductees frequently claim to have made through windows and walls.

The problem emerges not when we consider that such technological abilities are theoretically possible, but when we perceive the lack of consistency within or between abduction narratives concerning the aliens' possession of these abilities.* Even within Betty

---

*A few abduction researchers have tried to resolve such differences by postulating the presence in our skies of many different types of alien beings who hail from different planets and accordingly possess distinct characteristics and abilities. While anything is possible, most abduction

Andreasson's own story her aliens possess these skills only sporadically. Though in the alien realm Betty and her guides passed through a wall of some silvery material "without encountering any resistance," and even though they all passed through the front door of her house and floated to the waiting UFO, Betty later makes much of doors and stairs both outside and also within the UFO, the presence of which makes no sense given their ability to float about at will, together with their frequent indifference to material obstacles.[10]

While the Andreasson aliens' ability to pass through solid objects is the most significant distinction, there are others just as important in their implications. Their clothing, for one thing, is differently colored from that which the Hills observed, at least as Betty Andreasson describes it. The Andreasson aliens are definitely alien-looking; they have three-digited hands, and at times look a bit like bees, while Betty Hill's aliens were far more human in appearance. Both alien abductors had big eyes, but the eyes of Betty Andreasson's principal alien are of two different colors (one white, one black), which is probably unique in the literature. The Hills' aliens had no insignia on their light blue uniforms, but one wore a scarf, where Andreasson's have an eaglelike bird with outstretched wings on dark blue uniforms. Betty Hill spoke to a fairly chatty alien, but they were otherwise reserved, businesslike, and anonymous; Betty Andreasson's aliens exude an "aura of friendliness." They also provide her with (usually cryptic) packages of scientific and religious information, and, in a feature that may be unique in the literature, tell her their names: the leader was called "Quazgaa," one of his subordinates was named "Joohop," and a third who functions almost as a spirit guide in a seance is known as "Andantio." Of course, readers are apt to question why there should be *any* such differences—especially when it comes to moving through walls—for, if the aliens do possess the powers Betty Andreasson ascribes to them, there should have been no need to erect a roadblock or open the Hills' car doors.[11]

Anticipating a decidedly fantastic turn to Betty's testimony, Fowler tries to prevent his readers from summarily repudiating what they will encounter by reminding us that he, too, initially

authors refrain from making much (if anything) of this, perhaps recognizing that the very notion of such a plethora of aliens in our skies would be beyond the ability of all but the most credulous readers to accept.

found it all hard to swallow, and acknowledging that "The events that followed in rapid succession are utterly alien to the logical *model* of reality *that we have been taught since early childhood.*" Likening the human mind to "a computer that is automatically programmed to reject extraneous data," he adds that we have lamentably been trained to reject "such claims [as Betty's] with the comfortable labels of hoax, dream, or hallucination."[12]

Many readers may be inclined to raise a number of objections to these quite arbitrary and manipulative statements. First, it is far from self-evident that our sense of the universe is a mere "model" as Fowler states, that is, a totally artificial and arbitrary construct, only one of many, all of which are equally valid and just as capable of sustaining us through life. Fowler's assumption that such a rejection of the bizarre is bound to be "automatic," that is, a mindless knee-jerk reaction to anything unusual, the consequence of "training" rather than education, is only warranted if it has occurred exactly as he says. His implicit hint that *any* rejection of the peculiar or the atypical is the sign of a narrow and unreflecting mind is simply false; it could easily be the result of careful and extensive deliberation. In particular, he has no right to make such statements, especially when we consider that the corollary—blanket *acceptance* of the bizarre—is hardly a guarantee of a successful journey through life.

Questionable Methods in Hypnosis

Fowler's need to defend hypnosis is understandable, and such defenses surface at various times throughout *The Andreasson Affair.* Although he appears at one point to agree with Dr. Simon that the truth recalled by a subject under hypnosis is the truth "as he or she believes it to be," in the very next sentence he shows where he truly stands when he remarks on "the mind's remarkable facilities for storing *memory*," and goes on to comment that deep-trance hypnosis "can produce near-total recall of everything a subject has ever experienced."[13] The author's mind is made up, despite the many dreamlike and literally fantastic aspects of this abductee's story.

In a very strange development, Fowler admits that Betty's hypnotist, Harold Edelstein, at that time director of the New England Institute of Hypnosis, "allowed [Betty] total recall of what had occurred under hypnosis," an extremely questionable, even irresponsible, decision from the standpoint of her psychological well-being.[14] Oddly enough, Fowler gives no reason to explain this singular decision, one that becomes even harder to fathom when we remember that Fowler had read Fuller's book and knew Dr. Simon's opinion.[15] Fowler can even agonize over Betty Andreasson's anxiety and feels like "shouting out in protest at what we were allowing this poor woman to relive," but the decision is nevertheless made to allow her to retain these painful memories in her conscious mind.[16] Whatever the psychological effect on her, the reader may well suspect that one result of allowing her to retain such memories would be to enable her to build on her narrative from session to session, while enabling her also to render each separate story more elaborate than its predecessors. It is undeniable that her experiences grow steadily more bizarre with the passage of time.

Another new development that will become a common feature of abduction narratives involves the insertion of some kind of implant by the aliens for purposes unknown at this stage of the narrative's development. In Betty's case, we learn it was inserted into her body years before her first recalled abduction, and may have been eventually extracted from her nose. Later she also mentions a grisly scene when the aliens removed her eye from its socket—which amazingly neither caused bleeding nor other aftereffects—in order to insert or remove something. This extensive tampering with an abductee's body represents an important new element in the history of the narrative. Although by the 1980s the insertion of implants—itself a most appropriate symbol of technological intrusion—will have become as commonplace an aspect of alien procedure in the literature as the pregnancy test and the needle in the navel, in 1979 it was only one of two such incidents of which Fowler was aware. Since he had many years of experience working for the Mutual UFO Network investigating UFO sightings—he is the author of *Casebook of a UFO Investigator* (1981)—the reader can reasonably conclude that such incidents were rare indeed at that time.

Other new elements involve the aliens' ability to put the members of the Andreasson family in a state of suspended animation for some hours while Betty was being abducted. This fact will become a staple of future abductions, but it was not commonly encountered at this time. Also novel is Betty's disclosure late in the book that she has had a history of abduction experiences going back to her childhood. This element will figure prominently in the majority of future abduction narratives. Finally, a psychic component can be observed. As we will see, the presence of such features in the abductee's past as the experiencing of poltergeist phenomena* or the sighting of ghostly apparitions clearly moves the abduction narrative away from the more scientific scenarios chronicled by the Hills and others. These elements will become increasingly common, and appear frequently in many of the cases discussed by John Mack in his 1994 book *Abduction*.

Other elements are peculiar to Betty Andreasson's story and do not become permanent fixtures of the overall narrative. Her ability to understand the aliens when they spoke together is one such claim that does not appear often again. Conversely, it will be recalled that Betty Hill claimed when the aliens "talked among themselves, they were entirely impossible to understand."[17] Most significantly, Betty Andreasson describes being taken on a trip probably to the aliens' planet of origin; elaborate procedures are employed, presumably to make the journey safe for her. She is encased in a plastic chair, immersed in protective liquid, and is given strange syrup to drink.

At that time, no American, including George Adamski, had ever claimed to have been treated to such a trip or tour.[18] When Betty begins to describe her trip in detail, the narrative becomes even more dreamlike and less bound by the conventions of realistic continuity. Much of her story is conspicuously fragmented and inconsistent, as the following will illustrate: Although still presumably in the small UFO that landed in her back yard, Betty's description of her movements suggests that she is within the body of a very large craft, yet this is incompatible with its size when she first saw it from her window. At another point, the aliens inexplicably don black hoods over their heads. Her clothes, made wet by her immersion in a shower of presumably protective liquid, suddenly (and just as inexplicably) become dry again. As they travel around the aliens' planet they again pass through solid material, in this case a mirror much as Alice did in *Through the Looking Glass*.

---

*As readers will know, a poltergeist is a mischievous spirit which manifests itself in a house, usually by throwing objects about noisily.

Another peculiarity one sees in Betty's exchanges with the aliens is the decidedly religious tone to their conversation. More than any other abductee, Betty's journeys to exotic lands, heavily populated as they are with strange beings in surreal settings, are similar in many ways to a biblical visionary experience. Indeed, the reader soon sees that it is precisely the sort of alien abduction experience that one would expect a religious fundamentalist to envisage. The aliens she converses with employ a kind of quasireligious diction, referring to her as "child" and saying things like "Fear not—Be of comfort." They frequently talk in a formal, dignified manner befitting gods, or at least angels: one employs the first person plural when referring to himself (*"we* know"). For that matter, the Andreasson aliens resemble biblical angels more closely than those of any other abductees, that is, messengers who tell her they "have come to help" and also perhaps test her. At one point, when she asks if she is ready to serve them as their emissary, they reply in the negative, telling her "You are not completely filled with the light"—arguably another religious echo. Finally, specifically Christian beliefs are evoked when the aliens tell Betty that she "must release [her]self of . . . fear *through my son.*"[19] In her initial talk with the alien named Quazgaa, his claim that they can only eat burned food is suggestive of Old Testament burnt offerings; his exchange of books with Betty is ritualistic; and his otherwise inexplicable ability to multiply the number of the Bibles Betty gave him may make some sense when we recall Christ's multiplication of the loaves and fishes. In fact, the entire encounter contains echoes of biblical stories and themes too numerous to mention. As for the phoenixlike bird that she encountered on the aliens' planet, its rising from ashes makes it a most appropriate Christian symbol (as indeed it *is*), entirely consistent with the pervasive religious element.

Also significant is Betty's claim that she has been "chosen" for some great task which we later learn is "to show the world." Precisely what she is to reveal, Betty never gets around to saying, and Fowler notably does not press the point. In this she sees her function very much in the tradition of Old Testament prophets. For his part, Fowler becomes positively maudlin here, describing what Betty is allegedly reliving to be "the most moving religious experience that I have ever witnessed."[20] Readers may be somewhat less moved for several reasons: first, just because *he* was affected does not make it necessarily meaningful; second, without knowledge of how many religious experiences Fowler has witnessed, the reader can take no meaning from his reference to its being the "most moving"; and finally, meaningful though it might be, the intensity of her emotional state tells us nothing whatever about the true nature of the experiences in themselves.

What is of importance in the development of the abduction narrative is that this represents the first instance where the abductee considers herself to be serving an important missionary function, ministering to the rest of humankind on the aliens' behalf. Betty is soon led to believe that the day will come when she will be allowed to share her received wisdom with the rest of humanity, but only when "the time is ready."[21] Here an uncharitable reader might see hints of megalomania. Betty's sense of her status emerges elsewhere, when she said she was told the blue book they gave her "must not be seen by any that were not worthy." Incidentally, this is a strange qualification, since the book "contains strange writing in it" and would mean nothing to any human being, worthy or not. Indeed, why she received the book to begin with is a mystery, since by her own admission she cannot read it; it is untranslatable, and its meaning "cannot be written by our words."[22] Given this, it may come as no surprise when we learn it has vanished from her home.

Finally, many elements in her narrative seem borrowed not simply from Betty's religion, but from science fiction and fantasy films as well, and *The Wizard of Oz* in particular: Betty and her hosts glide by on a tracklike road reminiscent of the Yellow Brick Road; on their trip to what appears to be the alien city, they pass through a "red place," finally arriving at a "green place" that reminds her of "some legendary underground kingdom."[23] The reader will be struck by its kinship with L. Frank Baum's Emerald City, and her encounter with the "Great Bird" not unlike Dorothy's final meeting with the Wizard himself, following which she, like Dorothy, returns home.

One unavoidable fact emerges in the course of Betty Andreasson's revelations that were not as obvious in the Hill case. The prominence of the very earth-bound religious allusions give Fowler considerable trouble, for they suggest that at least a portion of what the reader is encountering is a fantasized, visionary experience, the product of a woman's imagination working in conjunction with her religious and cultural background, rather than a recollected "real" event. Of course, as a symbol in a fantasy, there is no reason for the phoenixlike bird to be regarded as "unsettling" by Fowler, or for it to remain "a puzzle"; indeed, its presence on the symbolic level is easily explained. But the appearance of such a recognizably terrestrial creature as described in a supposedly alien world casts grave doubt on the likelihood of the story being literally true, and its presence *would* be decidedly unsettling to anyone fervently hoping, as Fowler is, that he is really investigating a woman's actual encounter with alien lifeforms.[24] Accordingly, whenever possible he avoids all but a cursory discussion of the implications of the religious themes, remarking awkwardly, "It *somehow* [*sic*] seemed completely out of place."[25] Although it may be "out of place" as an event in a typical UFO sighting, the religious theme has been an ongoing part of Betty's entire testimony and is entirely in keeping with what she has been saying all along, *if* we are prepared to see her account as fantasy. On those occasions when it is simply impossible to ignore this testimony, Fowler suggests it may have been Betty's strong faith that provided her with Christian images whereby she could explain otherwise ineffable, but nonetheless real, events. The more mundane alternative—that the images came from within Betty's mind—is impossible for him to entertain, for obvious reasons.

The Investigators' Intrusive Presence

Unwittingly or not, Fowler played an active role in the creation of Betty's story, which in its original form was far from the more coherent narrative it eventually became. Indeed, as one moves through *The Andreasson Affair* his intrusions and those of the other interrogators become ever more obvious. For example, the investigators frequently introduce notions and volunteer information that fill in gaps that appear in Betty's original testimony. At one point, in a particularly unusual portion of Betty's narrative that is rich in color imagery but otherwise unintelligible, she speaks vaguely of being in a strange realm which Fowler and the others immediately determine to be the aliens' planet. During her travels there, she speaks of moving from a milieu that she saw as uniformly green in color to one that appeared to be solidly red. Throughout this section, rather than simply let the narrative speak for itself, the questioners repeatedly put notions forward, ostensibly in an attempt to help Betty find the "right" words to describe her experiences.

Fowler, for example, at times appears irrepressible in his desire to be helpful and fill in the blanks. He provides an explanation for the separation between the two colored realms by suggesting the presence of an "invisible force field," which Betty immediately embraces, lost as she was for appropriate words to explain the scene. Elsewhere, he helps Betty account for the dominance of bird imagery by saying it might be an emblem, the alien equivalent of the American eagle, to which Betty, again groping for answers herself, quickly assents. But in fleshing her narrative out, he not only gives it continuity and a new form, but changes significantly its effect on the reader. In fact, the narrative has become a joint creative effort.

At the same time, Fowler makes no attempt to draw any implications from Betty's material that would lead in a direction other than the extraterrestrial explanation. That an alien civilization would sport emblems on uniforms virtually identical to our own; that this civilization would employ terms remarkably similar to those of the Christian church; that they would choose an uneducated fundamentalist Christian to be their spokesperson for the entire world;[26] none of this is at any point even touched on by Fowler, who seems as uncritical as he is enthralled by what he regards as the sheer richness of Betty's account.

Fowler's belief in this richness the reader may not share. Indeed, the aliens rarely say anything that is not meaningless or even silly. Some are mere fragments of verbiage: "Within fire are many answers, within ashes," or, "It is through the spirit, but man will not search out that portion."[27] Most of the others fall into the category of pseudoaphorisms, and are nothing but vapid, self-evident cliches that have a superficial sound of profundity. To wit: "Man must understand many of the natural things on earth"; "within the highest of the high and the lowest of the low are many answers"; "Man is not made of just flesh and blood." Significantly, the Andreasson aliens will be the last ones to offer an abductee such precise tidbits of wisdom. With a few exceptions, information conveyed to humans in later visitations relates almost exclusively to topical concerns (such as the environment) rather than moral precepts, and tends to be conveyed in the form of vivid images or pictorial displays of destruction or chaos that we are supposedly bringing about by our wanton ways.

Evidence also emerges that Betty did not find many of her original experiences particularly unnerving or as upsetting as one would expect had they been real. For instance, when Fowler asks her about the presence of possibly confirming marks or scars inflicted on her in the course of the tests she underwent, Betty's reply is most revealing: it turns out that she "never checked. I couldn't. With seven kids, I had to keep well."[28] An odd response, all things considered. Given Barney Hill's burning desire to inspect his groin immediately after he arrived home, Betty's indifference to such matters is singular. Does her reply even make sense, given her frequently painful alleged experiences aboard a UFO?

But even more surprises are to follow. We learn that other than "vague memories of the creatures entering the house, the rest of the experience had somehow been blocked out of her conscious mind."[29] In fact, even this is not strictly correct. Betty herself says that all she ever remembered from the outset was "the pulsating light" (which could have been something as mundane as a passing police car). As far as the aliens' magical entry into her home is concerned, she incredibly cannot remember precisely when the memory of this event came back to her. Surely the recall of an event as dramatic and momentous as any in her life would strike her suddenly, just as the date of such a recollection would remain forever in her mind.

Fowler's readers, forced as they are to rely on their much-maligned powers of logic, may well conclude that one is apt either to remember vivid encounters of extraterrestrial aliens in one's home, or not have any memory of them at all. But Betty remains vague throughout the book when the issue of her memory is ever brought up. When her daughter came to tell her about her "dream" just two or three days after the experience occurred in January 1967, Betty claims she replied that "it was no dream, honey. It really happened, but don't tell anybody," at which point she showed her daughter the blue book "from Jesus" that the aliens had given her.[30] Here Betty has clearly contradicted herself, for earlier we learned that "it was about 1969" before she recalled

anything other than the pulsating light, but it is a contradiction
Fowler overlooks.[31] We also learn that Betty's father, who was not
told by Quazgaa to forget anything, said nothing of his sighting of
the aliens for some years. The excuse he offers for this silence will
strike some readers as lame, but typical of so many in today's
society: He did not want to get involved!

In another new element, while under hypnosis, Betty begins to
speak what appears to be the aliens' language, followed by a few
unintelligible phrases. Significantly, this feature is unique and
appears nowhere else in the major abduction narratives under consideration. Many readers must have noted that Betty's abilities in
this regard are identical with those of certain members of the Pentecostal Church, who also speak in tongues. That Betty is indeed a
member of this faith one would think was a point of considerable
relevance to the case, surely deserving of mention. However,
Fowler only alludes to Betty's faith much later in an appendix, and
as evidence only of Betty's deeply religious and sincere nature. Virtually the same event is discussed in Fowler's second look at Betty,
The Andreasson Affair: Phase Two. At one point Betty speaks in a
"strange" language, to which Fowler can only report that "The phenomenon is similar to the 'speaking in tongues' practiced by some
denominations of the Christian church," carefully failing to mention that Betty was raised in one of these very denominations.[32]

In one session the aliens allegedly speak in English directly to
Fowler and his colleagues, using Betty as a medium in a manner
similar to New Age channeling. Many readers may emerge from
this exchange entirely baffled, if they were not already. Frankly,
nothing the aliens tell Betty—nothing that comes out of her mouth,
that is—is anything but the same gibberish we heard before, and
those bits which make a kind of linguistic sense have no discernible
intellectual content. For example, Betty repeats the phrase "Star
Seeso" several times. When asked if this is a location, Betty replies
in the affirmative; when asked if it is where the aliens come from, we
are simply told that it is not. We are also given a unit of distance
called a "sunburst" which would presumably help us determine
where they hail from; however, it proves to be of no help because the
aliens refuse to tell us how long a measuring stick it is. When asked
directly what the term "sunburst" means, Betty replies with the less-
than-edifying information that "It is something about the darkness

that is left there after the sun has been exploded, I guess, or something or other."[33] The aliens have something to tell us, Betty affirms, but in response to her interrogators' questions, she proves as hard to pin down as the Oracle at Delphi: We learn that scientists "must bury the past"; that old walls "need to be broken down"; that the aliens caused a recent New York City power blackout "to reveal to man his true nature"; that we seek in the wrong directions; that we must "understand man's hatred—to deal with it righteously."[34]

As far as their science is concerned, we learn that the aliens can reverse time; that they "have metals that they cannot penetrate"; and that some stars are in a "heavier space" than we are.[35] To be sure, there is meaning here, although not the sort Fowler intended to reveal. For one thing, we can discern an underlying exhortation throughout to get back to basics and the simple life; the aliens, it appears, are Luddites as far as their advice to human beings is concerned. Much of the information conveyed has an antiscience and antitechnological bias, quite in keeping with the suspicion of science traditionally exhibited by many fundamentalist Christian sects. When asked if the aliens have a "message" for humankind, for example, the aliens, speaking through Betty, chastise us for our greed and exhort us to seek "Simplicity."

The bulk of Betty's testimony is incredible enough in itself. But the total absence of any form of critical commentary by Fowler of these aspects of her tale has a disastrous effect on the book's credibility. As so frequently happens in abduction narratives, the author's silence winds up bringing even greater discredit on the favored hypothesis.

The book concludes with Fowler's apparent corroboration of certain incidental details in Betty's testimony: On the night of the first sighting, "Bozo the Clown" was on television; the weather had been balmy for that time of year; and a power failure had occurred, all as Betty recalled. This, of course, does little to advance the extraterrestrial hypothesis. All it does is reveal that Betty had some contextual memory of the evening the power failed and a strange light was seen, both relatively uncommon and dramatic events that a family might well continue to recall for years. In one last attempt to strengthen his thesis, Fowler demonstrates the number of ways Betty's story tallies with other close encounters, but in doing so he succeeds only in weakening it again, for it turns out that Betty could have heard or read in other UFO encounters about virtually every feature Fowler cites: the stillness at the outset of the UFO's appearance; the power failure; the interference on the television; and the physiological effects she suffered. Betty "admitted having read books and articles on UFOs following her 1967 experience."[36] For example, the medical experiments and physical examination, the telepathic communication, the eyelike lens she observed in the "operating" room, even the overall appearance of the UFO in the yard, each of these features can be found in the Hill abduction.

Wrapping up, Fowler then rhetorically asks a number of questions based on the assumption that the events concerned did occur: Where was Betty taken? Was the alien base an underground colony on earth, the moon, or an asteroid? Did Betty visit a vast mother ship? Did she leave our solar system entirely? Of course, the one question Fowler does not direct to the reader is the one the reader has been asking all along: Is the Andreasson affair true, or a highly charged and symbolically rich fantasy, the product of an imaginative mind undergoing an intensely vivid visionary/religious experience, sparked in part by the domestic turmoil in her life?

Fowler's epilogue to *The Andreasson Affair* reads like a prologue to a sequel, suggesting that one was already being contemplated; it is also here that he indulges in the wildest of speculations. We learn of Betty's meeting and eventual marriage to a man who, it appears, brought with him similar experiences—UFO sightings and missing time. Fowler considers their meeting nothing short of remarkable and quite possibly alien-inspired![37]

Not surprisingly, Betty interprets all of these events as part of an unfolding "supernatural battle between good and evil."[38] Indeed, at one point Betty states that the aliens "definitely" have something to do with the second coming of Christ. Again, Fowler allows her response to stand without comment, presumably because, as we will learn in the sequel, he evidently shares many of Betty's religious beliefs himself.

The book ends quite conventionally, with scientific testimonials such as the results of polygraph tests to bolster the case for the abductee's credibility; poor Dr. Simon is even unconvincingly cited yet again in support of hypnosis's efficacy.

Betty's Adventures Continue

The Andreasson Affair: Phase Two (1982) picks up at the point where the original volume had concluded, with Fowler's hint that Betty's abduction experiences could have begun in her childhood. Much of the sequel elaborates on the contention that she was indeed "chosen" at an early age to make a key contribution to the aliens' still-unfathomable plans. For all that, in most respects this second book is virtually identical to its predecessor as it continues the chronicle of Betty's adventures, most of which will strike readers as even more bizarre and pointless than were those we encountered in the first volume. Fowler again calls upon experts, but his efforts in this regard are similarly unsuccessful. Just prior to discussing an extremely fanciful out-of-body experience Betty claimed to have had, Fowler introduces a female hypnotherapist (whose credentials consist of an M.A. in sociology) who was invited to provide a psychological evaluation of Betty. Needless to say, the profile is uniformly glowing, describing as it does a woman "so pure of heart, so innocent and incorruptible that it was difficult to understand how this [the possibility that the tale might not be true] was possible."[39] Elsewhere, the therapist also likens Betty to Dorothy from the *Wizard of Oz*, evidently unaware of the ironic significance in the comment.

One element in *Phase Two* given more emphasis is the suggestion that psychic phenomena are often associated with the abductees; Betty and her second husband, Bob Luca, are cited in support of this contention. Fowler, as before, claims to be won over in part by his knowledge "that they were both normal, healthy, individuals"; as he "watched them relive some of these [psychic] experiences, [he] found it very hard to be skeptical."[40] By now, many readers will probably see how transparent and manipulative are Fowler's avowals of skepticism. Yet he maintains the pretense of objectivity to support the case he is making on Betty's behalf, claiming that he is "applying cold logic" or affirming his "unusually objective, logical mind."[41] Only once does he question the literal truth of one of Betty's more extreme statements. Late in the book he wonders timidly, "Is this actually what the being said [the being in question made an explicitly Christian allusion to 'the Son'] or was Betty integrating her religious beliefs into the experience?"[42] It is here that we learn that Fowler is also a committed Christian, which goes far toward explaining his uncritical acceptance of the explicitly Christian elements in Betty's story, while further undermining his credibility as an unbiased observer.

As before, *Phase Two* is liberally sprinkled with Fowler's intrusions. In his introductory chapter, he retells Betty's story to acquaint readers who might be unfamiliar with her background. Readers of *The Andreasson Affair* will be struck by the smoothness and lucidity of the summary, which reads as if Betty's experiences had been originally recalled with complete clarity. Fowler also tries to shore up his thesis by quoting his principal investigator, who had observed that Betty's story "is so unbelievable that it *is* believable!"[43] To assent to this logic is to throw all critical caution to the winds and accept the literal truth of virtually any narrative on the basis of its richness and detail alone.

Fowler's attempts to manipulate the reader's responses are also in evidence when he asks if stories like Betty's may "have been filtered out of history by a society that has artificially constructed its own comfortable version of what reality should or should not be," and goes on to wonder if myths and tales of elves and the like "may have a forgotten basis in reality."[44] Readers may well have some sympathy with this position; ours *is* an age—officially at any rate—committed to denying the reality of anything not verifiable by science. But Fowler's tacit assumption that our "comfortable" version of reality has been "artificially" constructed (many readers might ask here, just what *is* so comfortable about it, and for whom?) is itself based on the unsupportable view that there is somewhere a less artificial construct that we have willfully ignored or disregarded.

In the course of *Phase Two* Fowler resorts to other devices to strengthen Betty's credibility. For one, he begins to make a great deal of the similarities between an experience Betty recalled which she claimed occurred in 1950, and the one she first remembered that took place in 1967. But so committed is Fowler already to the literal truth of Betty's stories that he appears completely oblivious to the equally likely possibility that she is simply restating the same basic fantasy. Finally, in the concluding chapter, Fowler quotes extensively from skeptics and UFO experts alike in an attempt to demonstrate his objectivity, and even summarizes an unsympathetic review of *The*

Andreasson Affair that appeared in the *Skeptical Inquirer*, probably hoping that the reviewer's intemperance will backfire. Many will emerge more convinced by the review than they were by the book, for the author of the review, a psychiatrist, makes a convincing case that Betty's abductions were fantasies. Fowler then refers to a number of friendly sources, among them Dr. Leo Sprinkle, who has himself worked with alleged abductees and determined that his subjects failed to support any claims that they were abnormal or psychotic in any way; D. Scott Rogo, the "noted parapsychologist"; UFO researcher Willard Nelson; and others. Actually, Nelson draws some interesting parallels between Betty's experiences moving through colored realms and that of Sufi mysticism,* where "the color of the space one finds in meditation is indicative of the realm (or sphere) of consciousness one has entered."[45] Of course, this does not make those experiences literally real.

What one is struck by in Fowler's conclusion is the extent to which he himself seems to have learned nothing from his own reading of his detractors' opinions. As far as hypnosis is concerned, Fowler seems momentarily aware of how dubious a tool it can be in recovering memories, and even quotes the extremely wary Dr. Martin Orne. But as far as practicing what he preaches is concerned, Fowler seems thoroughly convinced of its infallibility. Furthermore, he and his colleagues put dozens of leading questions before Betty and her husband, despite his own avowal that "the last thing we wanted to do was to influence a witness."[46] But the most glaring evidence of questionable practice concerns the hypnotist's request to Betty to recall specific experiences as if she were watching herself at "a movie." At one point Betty is encouraged to "imagine that you are six feet away from your own body. . . . This isn't happening to you."[47] Here it is almost impossible not to see in this a veritable invitation to Betty to fantasize, for in asking her to project a scenario onto an imagined screen, she is being encouraged to use her imagination to flesh out a "picture."

Interestingly enough, it is roughly at this point that one notices

---

*Sufism is the name given to certain mystical groups within Islam, first developed in Persia and Iraq in the ninth century. It advocated asceticism and meditation as a means of attaining a rapturous union with the Divine. Certain forms of dancing were frequently used to induce an ecstatic state.

a marked change in the nature of Betty's drawings of her experiences. In *The Andreasson Affair*, Fowler made a lot of how fortunate the investigators were to have a subject who had some artistic ability, and could buttress her oral recall with visual depictions. In the first book, it became apparent that every picture Betty drew was consistent in one respect: Each one presented the alien realm around her from her perspective of the actual position she occupied. That is to say, the drawings never portrayed Betty herself, but rather what *she* was observing, or imagining herself observing, at any given time. Significantly, at the point in *Phase Two* when the hypnotist asks Betty to imagine that she is watching herself, Betty predictably begins to include herself visually in many of the scenes. In a later chapter, we will see that while Betty's artistic abilities continue to grow from book to book, by the appearance of Fowler's third volume, *The Watchers*, virtually all the drawings feature Betty herself in them, often from a perspective that would be impossible for her to have attained.

The presence of the questioners throughout the sessions and their influence on the hypnotized subjects' emerging narratives simply cannot be overlooked. During one session where Betty's husband Bob was reliving a childhood UFO experience, he had referred to "people in the light" talking to him "inside" his head. Beyond that, he said nothing about their physical appearance; indeed, the entire encounter had been quite vaguely described. He was then asked if he could physically see them, which he had just explicitly denied (they were inside his head, after all). Naturally, once this suggestion had been planted in his mind, Bob answered in the affirmative. Even though the questioners were initially told by the subject that this was a mental experience, they persisted in asking questions of a "nuts-and-bolts" nature, such as "How far away are they?"; "Do you leave the ground and go somewhere with them?"; and most pointedly, "Did you scream when you saw them?"

Bob, of course, did not originally say he saw them at all and had made no reference to screaming, at least not in any of the transcripts within Fowler's book. The only evidence that he saw anything outside of his own mind came when he replied to the question "can you see the little people?" with the cryptic "Yes, well, a little bit," an oddly vague answer. Soon after, the hypnotist says, "Suppose we progress in time to your next UFO sighting," making an implicit suggestion that such a sighting had occurred; Bob, of course, picks up on this as well.[48]

But the most potentially contaminating involvement of investigator with subject takes place when hypnotist Fred Max says he wants to speak to the beings and ask them questions, a request that again is little more than an overt invitation to Betty to concoct answers to those questions, which of course she does. Of course, the effect of such tampering is to invalidate *all* the information contained in a given scene.

The Andreasson Case and the Abduction Narrative

The matter of objective validation aside, we must still ask what can be made of the Andreasson case in relation to the development of the abduction narrative as a whole. In some ways it is similar to the Hill account, with one major difference: It is far richer in detail and more detailed and dramatic in every respect. The experiments performed on Betty Hill pale when set against the eye-removals and other probes and implants Betty Andreasson endured. Furthermore, where the Hills were human guinea pigs who seemed to have been picked up randomly, Betty Andreasson enjoys great status with the aliens, having been "chosen" for some significant purpose, the exact nature of which is not revealed (even Fowler's third Andreasson book, *The Watchers*, fails to answer the question satisfactorily). This aspect of the unfolding narrative—are abductees "special," acting as agents for an extraterrestrial messiah, or are they being used indifferently, as we would laboratory animals?—has yet to be resolved within the myth. Instances of both motifs continue to appear, with neither dominating.

Other elements in Betty Andreasson's narrative are entirely novel. The suggestion that encounters with aliens heighten one's psychic power is not present in *The Interrupted Journey*, but will appear with increasing frequency in later narratives. The sense that abductees have had a history of abductions going back to their childhoods is also a most important innovation, and becomes a staple of subsequent narratives, with the majority of abductees after Betty Andreasson claiming similar histories.

For the above reasons, the Andreasson abductions can be seen as an important step in the building of a communally created abduction narrative. Many aspects of the Hill case—the initial sighting of a UFO, the loss of will, the performing of experiments on the abductees, the telepathic communication, the aliens' reassurances not to be afraid, the enforced amnesia, the partial recovery of memory—are reinforced by the appearance of similar elements in the Andreasson narrative. Others, such as the basically human-looking Hill aliens, are discarded, and a few new elements are introduced for public inspection. Some of these new features—the explicitly Christian element in Andreasson's story, for example, or the journey in the UFO to the aliens' planet—do not survive, probably because it is simply too difficult to accept that alien beings could also be Christians, or that they would take the trouble to give guided tours of their home base. Just as evolutionary mutations in the physical world that encounter hostile environments do not survive, such unacceptable narrative innovations also die off quickly.

Other aspects of Betty Andreasson's story, such as the notion that the abductee is an emissary of sorts, reappear in a number of future accounts. The almost supernatural power and control the aliens have over their physical surroundings is another feature that will become commonplace in the literature. Aliens also seem to have learned about the passage of time since their encounter with the Hills, for it appears they now have a chronologically unfolding plan that involves the abductees. Still not present in the narrative as yet is the aliens' preoccupation with egg and sperm retrieval, or the widespread use of women as breeders and incubators; that feature would have to await the arrival of Budd Hopkins on the literary scene. It is possible that Betty's upbringing—which occurred at a time when open discussion of sexual matters was less common that it would become—could explain the absence of an explicit sexual dimension to her abduction. However, as we will see in chapter 8, by the time of *The Watchers*, Betty's reticence has all but disappeared, for the use of women as breeders comes to play a part in her developing abduction narrative.

The extensive dialogue Betty enjoyed with her abductors is not an element that finds expression in later narratives, and it is easy to see why. Whenever Betty's aliens speak, they reveal themselves to be incredibly vapid and vague, for all their sententiousness; at no point do they speak clearly or answer questions in simple, straightforward language. Much of what they say to Betty is unintelligible. At one stage in her tour Betty is shown glass or icelike butterflies that magically come to life with the touch of her hand (the resemblance of this and other scenes to the Disney studios will be discussed in a later chapter). When she asks what this demonstration is in aid of, she receives the less-than-satisfying reply, " 'This is for you to remember so mankind shall understand.' " Elsewhere we are told "The Great Door shall guide" us, even though the aliens explicitly forbade Betty from revealing what she experienced there.[49]

At times Betty's aliens are irritatingly evasive, sidestepping questions put to them with irrelevant questions of their own or by simply changing the subject, but always refusing to be pinned down. When asked what the great truth was that Betty discovered behind the Door, they reply, "You have had the truths before you. Why did you not partake of it?" (at times, the aliens' grammar fails them). When asked when it was that we had these truths, they answer "That is for you to find."[50] In one of the sessions where Betty serves as a channeler through whom the aliens speak, Fred Max sensibly observes that "many others would believe your message if you could convince them that you had something superior to offer," something that the reader will also feel has been noticeably missing up to now.[51] In answer to this, the aliens answer testily, "We do not make deals."

But more importantly, none of the questions that readers would be apt to ask is addressed in either book. Fowler sees much in the mysterious helicopters that allegedly harass Betty and Bob, seeing them as proof that "something" is really happening to them. But what possible purpose or advantage could there be to anyone in monitoring them in such an obvious and clumsy manner? What could ever be gained from such activity, anyway? Finally, why would such a presumably secret government agency use unmarked helicopters conspicuously painted black, when normally marked and painted ones would serve as well and create no suspicion? Of course, the biggest question of all—why extraterrestrial beings would take Betty when she was a thirteen-year-old girl, show her a being that appears to be God, implant mysterious probes in her body and fill her mind with wisdom that even she is not privy to, and then induce amnesia for a period of years—is never answered.

If there is an overriding flaw in Betty Andreasson's narrative it lies in the large number of these unanswered questions, to say nothing of the staggering amount of purposeless and irrelevant detail that clogs her story. Many of the events that occur in the course of her various abductions lead nowhere and occur for no discernible reason, while others are distinctly reminiscent of the world of science fiction or children's fantasy, as our discussion of *The Watchers* in chapter 8 will examine in detail.

Notes

1. Raymond Fowler, *The Andreasson Affair* (Englewood Cliffs, N.J.: Prentice-Hall, 1979), 9.

2. Ibid., 21.

3. Ibid., 160.

4. Ibid., 17.

5. Jim and Coral Lorenzen's Aerial Phenomena Research Organization (APRO), for example, had always been receptive to the more dramatic and bizarre UFO cases.

6. This creation of "family myths" is quite a common practice as some readers will know, and is often effected as a means of binding separate members of a family together, especially in times of crisis. One common form involves scapegoating, where stories based on the obnoxious behavior of a particular family member will frequently be forged out of very tenuous or sketchy original material. As belief in these stories takes hold, it permits other members of the family to be united by the bonds of a common dislike of the scapegoated party.

7. Ibid., 21.

8. See John G. Fuller, *The Interrupted Journey* (New York: Dell, 1966, 1987), 318; *The Andreasson Affair*, 53. In Betty Andreasson's case this examination makes absolutely no sense, for we later learn that the aliens have supposedly been monitoring her since she was a child, and would presumably have knowledge of her medical history and present condition.

9. Ibid., 23.

10. Ibid., 75.

11. Later abductees will speak of being physically removed from moving automobiles; in one case the entire car was transported to a UFO. But if this could happen once, why would it not happen all the time?

12. Ibid., 27.

13. Ibid., 42, my emphasis. In fact, Fowler's comment is surprising since at the end of *The Andreasson Affair: Phase Two* (Englewood Cliffs, N.J.: Prentice-Hall, 1982), he quotes Dr. Martin Orne, who wrote extensively about the fallibility of hypnosis in this regard. Of course it is possible that he was not familiar with Orne's work at the time *The Andreasson Affair* was being written.

14. Ibid., 55.

15. Many subsequent abduction authors also allow their hypnotized abductees to retain memories. Other highly questionable techniques appear quite frequently as well. In Budd Hopkins's *Missing Time* (New York: Berkeley Books, 1983), which is discussed in chapter 6, abductee Steven Kilburn is also asked to imagine himself while hypnotized as being in a movie theater viewing a film of his experience, just as Betty Andreasson and the Tujunga abductees (discussed in chapter 5) were. Although Ann Druffel and Scott Rogo (see chapter 5) are suspicious of this method, Hopkins is as uncritical concerning its use as Raymond Fowler is.

16. Fowler, *The Andreasson Affair*, 60.

17. Fuller, *The Interrupted Journey*, 310.

18. Betty's fantastic claims surfaced at approximately the same time as those of Swiss contactee Eduard "Billy" Meier. Betty first contacted J. Allen Hynek in August 1975, informing him of her experience, which she stated occurred in January 1967. Although Billy Meier first announced to a "metaphysical study group" his January 1975 contact with aliens, his more bizarre stories would not be made public (to a North American readership, at any rate) until November 1979. (See Kal K. Korff, *Spaceships of the Pleiades: The Billy Meier Story* [Amherst, N.Y.: Prometheus Books, 1995], 25, 32.)

19. Fowler, *The Andreasson Affair*, 32, 54, 100.

20. Ibid., 100.

21. Ibid., 130.

22. Ibid., 152–54.

23. Ibid., 79.

24. Ibid., 182.

25. Ibid., 99.

26. See Fowler, *The Andreasson Affair*, p. 208: Neither Betty nor her daughter Becky "had fully completed high school, nor did they obtain special training of any kind"; or p. 209: "Both Betty and Becky could be classed as fundamentalist Christians who accept a very literal interpretation of the Bible and believe it to be the Word of God."

27. Ibid., 121.

28. Ibid., 131.

29. Ibid., 132.
30. Ibid., 149.
31. Ibid., 133.
32. Ibid., 196.
33. Ibid., 143.
34. Ibid., 139–41.
35. Ibid., 144.
36. Ibid., 181.
37. In *The Andreasson Affair, Phase Two*, he actually wonders if their meeting "might very well have been programmed by an outside [i.e., extraterrestrial] source" (14).
38. Fowler, *The Andreasson Affair*, 199.
39. Fowler, *Phase Two*, 134.
40. Ibid., 5–6.
41. Ibid., 131–32.
42. Ibid., 194.
43. Ibid., 12.
44. Ibid., 90.
45. Ibid., 229.
46. Ibid., 23.
47. Ibid., 45.
48. Ibid., 30, 80.
49. Ibid., 124, 130.
50. Ibid., 142.
51. Ibid., 196.

5

TRAVIS WALTON, ANN DRUFFEL, AND D. SCOTT ROGO: ABDUCTIONS IN ARIZONA AND TUJUNGA CANYON

Two books that appeared within two years of each other—*The Walton Experience* (1978) and *The Tujunga Canyon Contacts* (1980)—are of considerable importance for our purposes, both historically and in terms of the approach they take to their respective subjects.[1] First, they provide us with excellent examples of what happens when respect for the facts is either present (as it is for the most part in Ann Druffel and D. Scott Rogo) or when it is not (in the case of Travis Walton). Second, they present two markedly different abduction scenarios, each of which is traceable to one or the other of the two abduction cases we previously examined. On the one hand, in Travis Walton's personal account of his abduction readers can see distinct echoes of the Hills' experience. There, the aliens' agenda is presumably scientific, although in the Walton abduction even more emphasis is placed on the abductors' uncommunicative and technocratic demeanor. The abductions dealt with by Druffel and Rogo, on the other hand, are similar in many respects to Betty Andreasson's account and represent the "spiritual" strain of the developing abduction myth. Here, the experience of the abductees in certain respects is almost mystical. Communication between the abductees and basically benevolent aliens occurs, in the course of which information presumably of benefit to the entire human race is given to one of the women involved.

The two books are also important for the strategies they employ, and for what they reveal of the power of narrative conventions. Many readers will find *The Walton Experience*, written by Walton himself, significant as an example of how *not* to go about composing a convincing abduction narrative, for the author evidently has little idea of the conventions of his autobiographical format or of the restrictions and responsibilities that attend the use of a first-person narrator, if that voice is to convince the reader; indeed, he makes virtually every narrative mistake possible.

Travis Walton was a member of a tree-cutting crew working in Arizona. Late one afternoon at the close of a working day, the men saw a light that they soon concluded was a UFO. Travis inexplicably walked toward the object, whereupon a beam shot out of the UFO and immobilized him. In a panic, the other crew members raced to their truck and drove off. Soon after, feeling guilt over having abandoned their friend, they returned to find he had disappeared. An extensive search for Travis was mounted by police, but turned up nothing.

Five days later, Travis returned with a tale of having been taken aboard the UFO. Regaining consciousness, he found himself being stared at by a number of large-eyed, humanoid beings. Jumping up, he confronted them in anger, at which point the creatures ran off. After attempting escape, he encountered a being of human appearance wearing a helmet. This being did not speak, but escorted Travis to another area where he was met by three other aliens of similar appearance. These beings lifted him on another table and put a mask on his face, at which point he lost consciousness.

The Walton abduction narrative is arguably the only one of its kind that is, frankly, boring. The first several chapters are rambling and disjointed, full of irrelevant information about the life of a tree-cutter and sprinkled with wishy-washy sociological platitudes about the dangers of overlogging the wilderness. Unlike later abductees, Walton's environmental sensitivity (such as it is) does not claim to be alien-inspired. It is hard for the reader not to conclude that such padding was prompted by a desire to make his account long enough to be published as a book rather than out of any concern for ecological issues.

Interestingly, Walton is the only abductee who does not have much to say about the time he spent with the aliens; most of the account details events that occurred back on earth, during and immediately after the time of the alleged abduction. And his attempt to convince us that the abduction is true is seriously undercut by his approach. For though he proclaims self-righteously that he "tried very hard to stick strictly to describing the events as [he] *experienced* them, not as [he] interpreted them," the reader will see almost immediately that large sections of the book are nothing more than highly speculative, purely imaginative recreations on his part.[2] Walton seems utterly unaware of the need for authors of autobiographies to confine themselves to stating as fact only that which they experienced personally. Any conversation or event they only heard about cannot be reproduced in the form of direct speech, but must be presented indirectly as the hearsay it is. For example, early in chapter 3 Walton tells us of being rendered unconscious and taken aboard the flying saucer (he reappears on earth only at the beginning of chapter 7). Yet virtually four chapters contain what purport to be exact transcripts of conversations to which he could never have been privy. To wit:

> "It got him!" Steve yelled.
> Dwayne screamed, "Let's get out of here!!"
> "Get this son of a bitch moving!" Allen shrieked hysterically.
> Mike did not need to be asked. He fumbled as he groped for the ignition switch. His shaking fingers finally seized on the key and the engine roared to life. . . .
> "Is it following us?" he yelled over his shoulder.
> Nobody answered.
> "Is it after us?" he shouted again.
> When no reply came again, he turned to see the emotionless looks of stupefied shock on the faces of his crew. Their pale faces stared straight ahead blankly. He knew then that it was entirely up to him to get them all to safety.[3]

Nor is it even remotely likely that these sections were the result of any kind of retrospective interviews with the people involved, for a large group of individuals under conditions of stress is unlikely to agree on such detailed recollections. Had Walton been content to paraphrase the conversations and only speculate on what his friends may have been thinking, his account could at least have been accepted as such. As it stands, it is not only utterly worthless as information and irrelevant to the abduction, but suggests as well a lack of concern for literal accuracy that the reader cannot help but suspect is characteristic of the entire work. Despite the brief, approving introduction by the obligatory expert—L. J. Lorenzen, the head of the Aerial Phenomena Research Organization (APRO), a well-known UFO organization at the time—who states that he would be "pleased to have [Travis] as a neighbor, as a friend, or as a son," Walton's own literary blunders nullify any credibility such an endorsement might otherwise have given him.[4]

The detail is flimsiest precisely in those sections where it is most needed; that is, those that deal with the actual abduction. Indeed, only 24 of the book's 181 pages are devoted to the abduction itself. Even here, Walton apparently remembers only those events that occurred immediately after he regained consciousness in the UFO, events that could not have taken more than an hour to complete. Initially, he recalls waking in a disoriented state, in what he first thought was a "very hot and humid" medical operating room in a terrestrial hospital. When his blurred vision cleared, he discovered three "horrible creature[s]" with eyes "the size of quarters" who were staring at him. In fright he jumped up and lashed out at the "horrid entities," knocking one of them down. Despite his "weakened" condition, "aching body," and "splitting pain in his skull," maladies for which no cause is suggested, he has no trouble jumping up from his operating table, seizing a conveniently placed glasslike rod, and, assuming a karate "fighting stance," frightening them with this display of macho aggressiveness, enough at least to cause them to run away.[5]

Walton's physical description of the aliens tallies for the most part with that of the Hills. They are about five feet tall, have five-digit hands (but no fingernails), and, like the Hill aliens (but in sharp contrast to most later accounts), heads that are *not* disproportionately large for their bodies. Also like the alien who spoke to Betty Hill, they do not appear entirely fearsome. For all their ugliness, Walton "felt there was also something gentle and familiar about them," which makes his own aggression toward them somewhat surprising. One major difference concerns their silence; Walton's aliens do not speak. The most significant parallel concerns their "incredible eyes" that have a capacity to mesmerize him, much in the way Barney had been captivated. Staring intently at him, they make him feel "naked and exposed under their intense scrutiny." All in all, the beings remind him "disturbingly" of a human fetus, a description that will crop up in the future. The intense, almost hypnotic quality of their gaze also anticipates some future abduction accounts, and is a feature that David Jacobs will make a great deal of in his 1992 study of the phenomenon, *Secret Life* (see chapter 9). Interestingly, though they were "the creepiest, most frightening things" he had seen in his "entire life," the Walton aliens' eyes are not biologically different from our own, and are complete with irises, pupils, and lids, giving them "a certain catlike appearance." They also blink conspicuously.[6]

Attempting to escape, Walton leaves the room and enters what seems to be some sort of control room. Inexplicably deciding to play with the controls, what appears to be a huge star map appears on the wall. As he experiments, he finds he can manipulate its appearance by moving a lever that is similar to a switch found on children's video games; when moved, the stars shift their positions. Only after some minutes of this does it dawn on him that the star map *may* be a window, and that " 'If this thing is flying, I could crash it or throw it off course and get lost or something!' "[7] Readers may find Walton's explanation—that he knew what he "was doing was *risky*, but I was desperate"—something of an understatement.[8] At any rate, at this point a silent, human-looking, and helmeted alien enters (Walton initially thinks he *is* human) and takes him to another area where he is met by three other entities of similar appearance (two men and a woman) who, oddly enough, are not wearing helmets. Put on a table, Walton is anesthetized, at which point the part of the abduction he could recall comes to an end.

Upon completion of this section of *The Walton Experience*, the reader will be struck by the number of distinct features this particular abduction contains. True, other abductees will continue to be "beamed aboard" UFOs, and many will encounter similar-looking, equally uncommunicative creatures complete with human-looking accomplices; but beyond that, the similarities end. In some ways, Walton's experience stands out by virtue of its *not* being particularly bizarre as far as abduction accounts go. For one thing, he is shown nothing particularly strange or fantastic; for another, he has complete freedom of movement in the UFO, at least initially. Though weakened, he is able to sit up on the operating table with such force that it knocks to the floor the device that was on his chest. Only David Jacobs's abductees manifest on occasion a similar ability to resist. The vast majority are powerless in the face of the aliens' advances. Although no explanation is ever given as to how the aliens induce this powerlessness, as we will see it makes a good deal of sense when regarded thematically, as a part of the overall myth.

Walton's aliens do not display any unusual abilities such as the capacity to move through walls; nor do they behave in otherwise mind-boggling ways. Travis Walton is the only major abductee who finds himself alone in a spaceship experimenting with the controls. Finally, he stands out in having been anesthetized prior to whatever operations were performed on him; as a consequence, he has *no* recollection of what went on during this period.[9]

Here it should be noted that anesthetizing the victim is obviously a sensible way for the aliens to proceed, for a comatose patient is obviously easier to handle. But it raises the question as to why alien scientists would not treat all their human subjects in a similarly prudent manner. One reason for this is that the administering of anesthetic by the abductors creates a kind of dead-end in the narrative, preventing further development of the story line from occurring. Given this, the failure or refusal of the aliens to render their victims unconscious is essential if there is to be any ongoing narrative at all.[10] But there is another possible reason. The very indifference of the aliens to our pain and discomfort is an important attribute of their "alienness," and quite basic to the thematic role they are playing in the unfolding drama, as the later section on the mythic significance of the abduction narrative will illustrate. If Walton's aliens and those of the Hills do not prevail, it is partly because they are simply not alien enough.

Walton spends a good deal of time—the whole of his tenth chapter—defending himself against charges of hoax and fraud, in fact more time than any other abductee or author spends on such self-defense. This seems a risky strategy, for readers may conclude that the abductee is protesting his innocence too much. For example, he embarks on an extensive criticism of William Spaulding of the organization Ground Saucer Watch, which seems suspiciously motivated by Spaulding's own eventual repudiation of Walton and his story. Walton himself claims that Spaulding "suddenly switched to making negative comments to the press" because he "found he had blown it so badly that he could not re-enter the case."[11] Precisely how Spaulding "blew it" is not specified, although it may be related to Spaulding's having recommended that Walton see a "Doctor" Steward for a medical checkup (following his reemergence on earth); this person turned out not to be a physician but a hypnotherapist. For a man who claims he tried hard to avoid the sins of interpretation, Walton has no trouble reading a great deal into something that could easily have been an honest error on Spaulding's part.[12]

Walton is on somewhat stronger ground when it comes to his speculations on the meaning of it all, although again, it is interesting how significantly his sense of the aliens' motives differs from those speculations found elsewhere in the literature. For instance, he dismisses the likelihood that some sort of biological or scientific purpose is behind his abduction, arguing that the aliens probably already have all the information they need. Of course, extensive experimentation as an element in the narrative had not gained the prominence that it would in the ensuing decades. But Walton also anticipates astronomer and UFO researcher Jacques Vallee's later observation that such clumsy and repetitive experimentation on the part of the aliens is simply too absurd to be believed of technologically sophisticated beings.[13]

Interestingly, many of the questions Walton asks in this section come to be answered in later narratives. Having no idea why he was picked as opposed to anyone else, he concludes (as did the Hills) that it is most likely he simply happened to be on the scene when the UFO appeared. Perhaps inadvertently, he raises a valid point about "the more ego-inflating of the two possibilities," hinting as he does of the extent to which the desire for status, combined with other factors, could be behind the creation of at least some abductees' abduction accounts.[14]

Finally, attempting to account for the "family resemblances" he observed among the human-looking aliens, Walton alludes to the possibility that they could have been cloned, a feat that he argues they could easily have perfected, since even we are familiar with it in principle. In doing this, he again inadvertently provides the reader with an excellent argument against the need for all that sperm and ova gathering that will later become a staple part of the narrative, for cloning makes such practices unnecessary. Continuing in this vein, Walton prefers to suspect that humanity as a whole may be in the process of being conditioned to an awareness of the existence of the aliens by randomly exposing certain men and women to them, with the hope that the publicity these encounters generate will make us less fearful when large-scale contact occurs. In an interesting addendum, he mentions that while his sighting of the UFO may have been planned, his abduction may have been an accidental byproduct of his foolhardy curiosity.

The Walton abduction is the least far-fetched narrative and the one with the fewest inconsistencies concerning alien behavior. Perhaps for this very reason it is not exactly the most convincing of abduction accounts; Walton's aliens are far too much like ourselves to be credible. His narrative style, then, more than any other single factor, has had a damaging effect on the overall credibility of his story.

The Tujunga Canyon Abductions

In sharp contrast with *The Walton Experience* is *The Tujunga Canyon Contacts*, jointly written by UFO researcher Ann Druffel and parapsychologist D. Scott Rogo, an abduction narrative that does make an effort to treat the evidence with some degree of respect and critical detachment. First published in 1980, it investigates the alleged abductions of a number of women who lived in the Tujunga Canyon area north of Los Angeles. The story involves five women who experienced a number of separate but related encounters with strange, presumably alien, beings over the years. The events first surfaced in 1975 when "Sara Shaw" contacted UFO researcher Ann Druffel with a claim that she and a friend, "Jan Whitley" (all names are pseudonyms), had experienced a missing time period in 1953, when as young women in their early twenties they were living together in a cabin in the Tujunga Canyon area of California. Under hypnosis, Sara revealed that alien creatures entered their cabin in the middle of the night and took them both to a UFO, where she was placed on a table and examined with light beams, and mysteriously branded with an invisible tattoo on her back, the latter presumably to enable the aliens to locate her for future encounters. After her examination, the aliens chatted with her and gave her what they led her to believe was a cure for cancer.

Her friend Jan's corroboration of this abduction was far from satisfactory or complete, although she and a mutual friend named "Emily" had an experience some years later where they allegedly encountered aliens while sleeping in their car one night at a highway roadside stop. Two other women named "Lori" and "Jo," friends of Emily's, turned up in the course of the investigation, and were also found to have had similar memories of more recent encounters in downtown Los Angeles. There, both women saw a bright light outside their apartment; Lori seemed mesmerized by a strange sound the aliens made. Although taken aboard the nearby UFO and subjected to a physical examination, Lori was able to resist the aliens' request that she join them aboard their mother ship by making a mantralike sound of her own, whereupon she found herself suddenly back in her apartment.

While the authors' attitude to the subject is far from unbiased and while their readiness to favor extraterrestrial or other paranormal hypotheses blinds them to more prosaic interpretive possibilities, the book reveals a refreshing willingness to examine critically at least some of the evidence and the manner in which it was obtained. Druffel and Rogo are also to be commended for entertaining alternative theories in trying to account for the highly unusual experiences of the Tujunga abductees.

The first indication of this greater frankness is the authors' readiness to criticize the hypnotist's behavior. While generally supporting the methods employed by hypnotist Dr. Bill McCall, they freely admit that his habit of questioning his subjects aggressively "had its advantages and disadvantages," one of which may result in his client "concocting some of her memories" when he begins "asking leading questions."[15] Likewise, they observe that a particular response of Sara "could easily have been architectured [*sic*] by her unconscious mind to satisfy Bill's line of inquiry."[16]

The authors also seem more than passingly suspicious of the "remote viewing" procedure, whereby the hypnotist asks the subject to picture a scene from an imagined, "out-of-body" perspective. Although eventually giving it their approval, they only do so after considering the method at some length, and even there they do not appear totally convinced that it is a sure way to arrive at the truth. Importantly, the reader's own suspicions have been tacitly acknowledged and possibly mollified as well. Again, when observing of one session that "quite a bit" of the abductee's testimony was "polluted by strong fantasy elements," they succeed in strengthening the credibility of those sections of testimony that do *not* appear as obviously the product of fantasy.[17] On one occasion they ask if a question put to Sara by McCall was really leading—"It may seem as though Bill was asking leading questions"—in order to demonstrate that it was not—"Sara had no reason to confabulate such an answer"—and in doing so produce a positive response from the reader concerning *their* methods and approach to the material in the process.[18]

The authors also guard against readers concluding that, if some of the account is admittedly the product of confabulation, it could *all* be, by frequently couching statements in nonthreatening language that does not back us into a corner: "It is our *guess*" that they underwent "*some sort of abduction* during which Sara *believed herself* aboard a UFO—*either physically or mentally*—before being returned to the cabin."[19] As far as the relationship between fantasy and real memory is concerned, Druffel and Rogo openly concede that the stories could be at least partly the products of the women's imaginations. In Sara's case, they speculate that "many of her life experiences during those years were intricately related to her abduction experience."[20]

In the second alien encounter dealt with, Jan and Emily were apparently accosted by aliens while sleeping in their car one night when they were returning from a vacation. The aliens asked Emily to go with them, but she refused. In the course of recalling this incident under hypnosis, Emily alluded to finding herself outside the car and being able to look in and see herself still sleeping within it. Druffel and Rogo suggest that Emily may have had an out-of-body experience as part of her alien encounter, but they are careful to note that some researchers consider these experiences illusions or hallucinations, and add that it is difficult to determine how much of Emily's "rather confused" testimony may have been confabulated. Much later, discussing Lori's experience, they dismiss part of her testimony as a likely "prebirth or 'womb' fantasy."[21]

Druffel and Rogo also draw attention to some of the inconsistencies in a witness's statement. Once, when describing the initial abduction that involved her friend Jan and herself, Sara says aliens gave her a tranquilizing injection just after mentioning that Jan put up considerable resistance. Here, Druffel is quick to point out the inconsistency: why was Jan not given one, while Sara was? The possibility that Sara's abduction story "might be a symbolic fantasy" generated by "hostility toward her friend" is also entertained, and the "conference" Sara describes having with the aliens after her examination, as it was "an entirely new incident" not previously reported, is considered "immediately suspect" for that reason.[22]

One element prevalent in the earlier contactee stories was the imparting by the aliens of some message for humanity. Only rarely does the new generation of aliens provide precise information in abduction accounts, and what *does* surface tends to be concentrated in earlier (pre-1980s) narratives such as those of the Hills and Betty Andreasson. In Sara's case (published just after *The Andreasson Affair*), the aliens gave her a cure for cancer which involved the application of vinegar on the cancerous tissue. Sara was amazed to learn subsequently that vinegar as a cancer cure had long been used as a folk remedy.[23]

To the authors' credit, after learning from experts that there is no evidence to support the efficacy of this claim, they openly admit that this is the "least credible" part of Sara's account, and in doing so, they allow us to dismiss the "miracle vinegar cure" without necessarily having to discard the entire package, because we have not been forced into an "all-or-nothing" situation.

Reading all this, some readers may conclude that this display of objectivity is disingenuous, itself a strategy, part of a shrewd attempt to appear fairminded in order to win the reader over to the thesis the authors have favored all along. If so, initially it would appear to be effective as a device; it certainly makes the authors seem scrupulous and fair. But on balance it is quite a risky strategy as well, for the very mention of the possibility that the hypnotist may be leading the witness or that the abductee may be confabulating cannot help but alert the reader to the possibility that all the evidence is pretty suspect.

The following example will serve to show how scrupulousness can get abduction authors in trouble as well. At one point, stating

that noncorroborated, one-witness abduction accounts have a relatively low priority, Druffel and Rogo make a good deal of the importance of Sara's friend Jan's testimony, which if it were to corroborate
the details Sara presented, could "resolve the entire case."[24]

Unfortunately for Druffel and Rogo, Jan fails for the most part
to deliver that reinforcement to Sara's account that the authors earlier admitted was so crucial. Jan, apparently not easy to hypnotize,
gives far from precise responses to the questions put to her. Even
when asked the extremely leading question "have you ever been
frightened by some shapes or beings that came into your bedroom? Who perhaps kept you from moving, who might have taken
you aboard a flying saucer, who might have examined you?" her
answer is an unequivocal no.[25] All she recalls with any certainty is
the initial feeling of being immobilized and a subsequent fear of
the dark that persisted for some months; she does not even recall
being told by Sara about the missing period of time.[26] Those details
she does volunteer tend to be impressions and feelings, or are the
direct result of the hypnotist's invitation to "make" up a story "any
way you want," a directive the authors acknowledge "might seem
a little suspicious."[27] It is perhaps understandable that much later
in the book, they would argue bravely that "Despite the fact that
Jan has never been successfully regressed, we don't feel that this
lack of corroborative evidence mars the importance of the Sara
Shaw case," but this remark represents quite an about-face.[28]

Flaws in the Authors' Approach

To say that The Tujunga Canyon Contacts has narrative merit is not
to say that it is flawless. One immediately notices the presence of
characteristics that have become standard practice in the narratives. It goes without saying that the abductees are all given
glowing character references: Jan and Sara are both "objective,
intelligent, and honest"; Jan herself is also "practical and courageous"; Emily is "honest, level-headed"; and Lori is "remarkably
intelligent."[29] The gap in time between the event as it occurred and
Sara's recollection is also typical. Sara Shaw only contacted Ann
Druffel twenty-two years after her abduction experience.
Although the authors attach no importance to this fact, the reader

must find this time gap odd to say the least, especially when no satisfactory explanation is offered. Missing time is also a prominent feature, and as one would expect, the authors make numerous references to the similarities between Sara's and Jan's experiences and the Hill case, the most conspicuous of which is their inability to account for over two hours in the cabin immediately after seeing a mysterious glow that filled the yard and woke them up. But the Hill case itself is incorrectly summarized, Druffel and Rogo claiming that both Hills' stories of their abduction were the same. Incidental oddities are also ignored. Jan's unusual lack of curiosity concerning this presumably singular event in her life is made nothing of, nor is the significance of her refusal to relate the event to UFO activity.

Also important is what is *not* said. For one thing, the introductory section called "The Beginning" summarizes the events of the Sara Shaw–Jan Whitley abduction with a chronological precision that it never had when recalled in fragments by the women two decades later under hypnosis. Given this, it is actually a bit misleading for Druffel and Rogo to summarize the initial encounter, together with the abductees' awareness of missing time, as if it had been recalled with crystal clarity immediately after it allegedly occurred. Although Sara's recollections are reasonably clear, Jan's are markedly vague, as the following extract will illustrate:

McCall: Go back to 1953 in your mind and tell me what it was you were afraid of.
　Jan: . . . Can't find anything.
　McCall: But you told me you were afraid.
　Jan: Yeah. I remembered being afraid.
　McCall: But you can't remember what you're afraid of?
　Jan: No.
　McCall: O.K. (*Pause.*) If you were going to describe what an alien looked like, what a being from a flying saucer would look like, what would you describe? Just tell me what you think one might look like.
　Jan: Probably something I couldn't see.[30]

Nothing in this testimony corroborates anything Sara said. Sara's aliens were definitely physical—she even shook hands when saying goodbye to them!—and were described in considerable detail. Possessing gray but cold skin with bodies "very much" like ours, they wore suits and communicated telepathically. Though Jan was described by Sara as "pretty panicky" during the abduction, Jan herself "can't find anything" to be afraid of.

Despite these discrepancies, the events surrounding the 1953 abduction—involving the aliens' initial entry into the cabin and the women's loss of time—are described at the beginning of the book as if they were indisputable, corroborated facts, even though Jan is able only to verify the initial sighting of the light. (Jo similarly corroborated Lori only on this one point.) Like many other abduction authors, Druffel and Rogo make the mistake of concluding that Jan's inability to support her friend may be because "something" was blocking her memories, and do not entertain the possibility that there may have been no memories to block in the first place.

In support of the women's stories, the authors also make much of the abductees' professed ignorance of UFOs, telling us Sara "had shied from reading anything about UFOs"; Jan had read "practically nothing on UFOs"; Emily "had hardly any interest in UFOs"; Lori "knew very little about UFOs."[31] Of course, it is impossible for the authors to be as sure of this as they purport to be. No one could make such a claim with certainty, especially when over two decades had passed since the alleged abductions occurred. Even if these facts were verifiable, they would raise more questions than they answer, when we recall the authors' own comment that the Tujunga area was full of UFO activity. Frankly, it is hard to imagine anyone in North America as oblivious to UFOs as Sara and the other women purportedly were.

Many of the inconsistencies commonly encountered in the literature can also be seen here. In an attempt to preclude the likelihood that the first encounter could be otherwise explained, the authors speak of the "strange light that had invaded the *secure* confines" of the rural cabin.[32] Yet only pages before a reference was made to a "cycle gang" they had seen that very day in the area, suggesting that they were not as safe as might appear. In a manner reminiscent of *The Interrupted Journey*, some other form of invasion and abduction—by humans, rather than aliens, that is—is at least a possibility, but it is never investigated, since it is obviously incompatible with the authors' preferred thesis.

Frequently, bias causes Druffel and Rogo to overlook obvious and ordinary explanations, even when such solutions are staring them in the face. On one occasion they refer to a Brazilian named Caetano who claimed to see and be abducted by a UFO while his traveling companion Elvio, looking in the same direction, could only see a bus. The authors explain this anomaly by arguing that the aliens must have caused Elvio to perceive the UFO as a bus, ignoring the more likely possibility that Caetano was the one probably hallucinating. Surely, if aliens could cause such hallucinations they would presumably cause *every* abductee to see a nonthreatening object such as a bus instead of a UFO. Later, the authors allude to an extremely dubious-sounding story of photographs having been taken of aliens, as if the authenticity of the pictures were beyond dispute; conclude that Jan and Emily both saw the "entities" that approached their car, despite Jan's denial that she saw anything physical; and make the usual case for consistency, ignoring the numerous instances where stories do not concur.

It is certainly true that Sara's story bears some similarities to other abduction narratives. For instance, like Betty Hill, Sara was also shown a map, although Druffel and Rogo suspect (to their credit) that this memory is probably the result of confabulation on Sara's part, in response to McCall's asking her if she saw one. Sara's case *is* similar to Betty Andreasson's: Both are "floated" to the UFO; tested by the aliens; have brief discussions with them; are given information; and are returned with virtually no conscious memory of the incident, although Sara does not recall being told to forget the encounter. Also, her description of the aliens' appearance tallies in certain respects with that of Betty Andreasson; both groups of aliens, for instance, had three-digited hands.

That Sara would describe the UFO as "Saturn-shaped" will not strike many readers as particularly surprising, considering that both the planet Saturn (with its rings) and the flying saucer as traditionally seen on edge are both elliptical objects well-known to the public. For that matter, readers may wonder if these similarities suggest only that an abductee unconsciously assimilated information from another abduction (say, the "map scene" from Betty Hill's abduction) or from having watched Betty Andreasson promoting her book on television, and reproduced it as a feature of her own.[33]

As is so frequently encountered in abduction narratives, the authors not only fail to mention this possibility but also minimize the significance of the differences between the Tujunga accounts and others. Sara's aliens are uniquely dressed in one-piece, black body-stockings "which enclosed their entire bodies, including their hands and feet."[34] Indeed, on the matter of their appearance, no mouth can be seen (given the all-covering body-stocking), and the reference to smooth but otherwise featureless heads is reminiscent of burglars who wear nylon stockings to disguise their features; it is also unique in abduction narratives and does not reappear in any of the other books we will consider. Emily's aliens are markedly different from Sara's; they are light-toned, wear no body-stockings, and they shimmer. Notably, in the days before implantation by the aliens of so-called tracking devices in their victims was a common feature in abduction accounts (*The Andreasson Affair* had just been published), Sara claims that the aliens inscribe an invisible tattoo on her back (by a remarkable coincidence, a mark identical with the astronomical symbol for the planet Jupiter), presumably for purposes of tracking or future identification. Perhaps because the insertion of an implant is more consistent with the dominant technological motif so prevalent throughout abduction literature, the inscribing of such a tattoo does not appear in later narratives, even though it may seem more functional than the relatively clumsy implant.

The Tujunga women's descriptions of the aliens' height and general appearance, though strikingly distinct, are simply mentioned without comment, as if such differences were of inconsequential importance. Descriptions of height vary dramatically and range from three or four feet (Emily's later encounter, and Lori's); five feet three inches through five feet seven (Sara); to as much as seven or eight feet tall (Emily's first encounter). Concerning the tests performed, these are conspicuously nonsexual in nature. No probes are inserted, and the experiments seem to be relatively innocuous and painless. It is thus surprising to read the authors' reassuring observation that "All these details about the examination are totally in keeping with what has been reported by other UFO abductees." Neither Barney nor even Betty Hill would ever have characterized their abductors as "really nice" or described their experience as "sort of fun," as the Tujunga abductees do.[35]

In Lori's account of her abduction, the aliens possess a strange mixture of traits, some of them appearing in the literature for the first time. Essentially formless, they can apparently change their shapes at will, and are also distinguished by their use of a painful, high-pitched sound to gain control over their subject. As is also typical of earlier alien abductors, they are not particularly fearsome, despite the pressure they put on Lori to come with them to their mothership. Indeed, she claimed not to be afraid during her experience and said they seemed friendly and concerned for her welfare. Incidentally, Lori's lack of fear—reminiscent of Sara, but otherwise extremely unusual in abduction accounts—is neither registered as strange, nor is it even remarked upon. This may simply be because at the time, truly menacing alien abductors had not as yet made their way into the literature and for this reason had not become an accepted feature of many narratives.

Inconsistencies within a specific abductee's narrative are frequently ignored. At one point Lori speaks of the aliens "urging her to come with them," which she refuses to do. Despite this resistance, she finds herself "floating" out to their UFO. Readers will immediately wonder why the aliens bothered to coax her to do their bidding when they were already prepared to take her against her will. One alien, Lori notices, "did not seem to have clothes on, but neither was it naked," an anomaly that merely "puzzled" her; again, this unusual comment, clearly reminiscent of a dream, fails to draw comment from the authors.[36] Lori's unusual tendency to fall asleep suddenly while visiting friends, then wake just as suddenly, only to fall asleep again—possibly pointing to the condition known as narcolepsy—is relegated to a footnote, and the obvious implication that her abduction could have been a dream while in such a state is not examined, just as the significance of the very atypical command by the aliens to Lori *not* to forget her abduction is not discussed.

Like most abductions, the Tujunga cases seem in many respects to be similar to dreams or fantasies. Sara admits feeling as if she is "conjuring the whole thing up." Emily and Jan "were very tired" when they pulled off the road to sleep just prior to their encounter. Seeing the UFO, Emily observed that it shone, but "didn't reflect any light on the ground beneath it," a property of light quite impossible anywhere but in a dream. Lori had been convinced by friends that her experience was "some sort of bizarre dream." Yet the authors reproduce such remarks without comment.[37]

Because the hard evidence for all of these abductions is quite weak, it may have caused some disagreement between the book's authors, as the epilogue suggests. There the authors acknowledge that they came to distinct opinions and decided to write two separate conclusions. It is obvious that Ann Druffel is far more accepting of the women's face-value testimony, to say nothing of UFOs generally, than is her colleague Scott Rogo. For one thing, Druffel's rather rambling, disjointed, and often-irrelevant concluding comment assumes the existence of UFOs as indisputable truth. But more important, although virtually nothing in the Tujunga women's experiences supports such claims, Druffel nevertheless argues that these abductions are serving some cosmic or divine purpose by seeding our species and teaching us spiritual truths such as monotheism; and that UFO entities are "pure energy beings who could fashion their material, temporary bodies as they wished."[38]

Although Druffel attempts to distance herself from the "ancient astronaut" school of UFO studies, she only partly succeeds, and winds up leaving readers with the same criticisms that such theories invariably produce. They assume a need for such extraterrestrial intervention in human affairs that history tells us is both unnecessary and superfluous as a means of accounting for our evolution and intellectual development.

Druffel is not content to stop here. Instead, she goes on to speculate à la Fowler that the demons and angels of folklore and religion may be UFO entities taking "physical form." Alluding to the sometimes paranormal aftereffects that have purportedly occurred in the wake of more recent UFO encounters, she offers the theory that UFOs and their occupants may be deliberately expanding human consciousness by stimulating such extrasensory powers in the people they encounter, bent as they are on "teaching us something, forcing us to change our study methods from purely material to parapsychological."[39]

While anything is possible, one cannot help but feel that this is properly the stuff of another volume. It goes without saying that all these manifestations can just as easily be seen as psychosocial constructions the origins of which are in the human imagination;

that they are symbolic projections of our own beliefs, ideals, and fears, the psychological importance of which is beyond dispute, but which need not be physically tangible in order to be important. One also feels that in trying to formulate a unified theory to account for all aspects of the UFO phenomenon, Druffel has lost sight of the abduction motif, for she has gone far beyond the limits defined by the book's contents in her attempts to be all-encompassing in her conclusion. Finally, it cannot be denied that her theory raises more questions than it answers. If the UFO entities are pure forms of energy capable of fashioning their appearance "as they think the witness would expect them to look," there is no reason for them not to appear human in every respect.[40]

D. Scott Rogo's concluding comments are far less religious in tone than Druffel's. Many of his remarks virtually invite the reader to consider psychological explanations for the events dealt with in the book. Pointing out that poltergeist manifestations are often associated with families undergoing considerable strain, Rogo wonders if UFOs and their occupants may be "quasi-physical" manifestations, similarly created "in times of psychological stress." Very much in the tradition of psychologist Carl Jung, he adds that a "UFO is often symbiotically linked to the individual mind that perceived it." While this is an intriguing possibility, it obviously leads in the direction of dismissing their physical reality altogether; this Rogo is reluctant to do. Instead, he suggests that UFOs and abductions may be real events that the abductee "structures a hallucination around."[41]

In support of their physical reality, Rogo offers as evidence the fact that UFOs leave traces of their presence and residue, and that people often suffer deleterious physical and psychological reactions in the aftermath of a UFO encounter. The case of one Calvin Parker is cited; Parker spent time in a mental hospital after his abduction. At this point readers might well wonder if Rogo is confusing cause with effect. Surely it is just as likely that individuals like Parker may experience an illusion of UFO abductions as a *consequence* of some abnormality in their personalities, rather than having their personalities affected as a result of an alien encounter.

Furthermore, the reader cannot help but wonder what reason there could be to retain a belief in the abduction as a real, physical event, when Rogo himself acknowledges the necessity of incorporating a psychological or hallucinatory element into the theory to account for the numerous discrepancies among abduction stories. In short, it does not seem necessary to cling to the claim that "The abduction may actually take place, but the witness does not perceive what is really happening to him." Rogo's reluctance to think in terms other than the physical leads him to formulate a theory virtually as bizarre as Druffel's, where a mysterious force or intelligence he calls The Phenomenon beams "projections of various kinds" into our world.[42] This force, he argues, may provide us with visions that reflect and objectify human concerns.

Rogo makes much of physical evidence presumably left by UFOs, such as "marks on the ground," multiple sightings, and livestock mutilations, which he accepts on faith even though such evidence is a matter of considerable dispute; multiple hallucinations can and do take place frequently; and there may be perfectly prosaic explanations of the so-called mutilated cattle.[43] As before, we see the author going to extreme lengths to avoid having to view the abduction experiences of the Tujunga women as having a psychological or social origin, which is odd since he otherwise appears not to have an extraterrestrial axe to grind. It becomes increasingly obvious that Rogo's "supermind"—the entity he postulates that beams down visions of UFOs and abductions to people in a state of psychological need—is frankly unnecessary and superfluous. A merely human mind in all its complexity is all that is necessary to create such experiences when in a state of distress or extreme agitation. Thus, while Rogo's summary of the psychological element in the Hill case is impressive and his discussion of the symbolic dimension in Sara's experience is equally valid, there is simply no reason to cling to the belief that any of these experiences have an objective component. That both authors refuse to abandon the possibility that the Tujunga aliens are real says more about *their* belief system than it does about what really happened in Tujunga.

The authors are similarly reluctant to see any particular significance in the abductees' sexual orientation, or acknowledge that it might possibly be an influential factor in the kind of abductions the women had. Only in the book's conclusion do we learn that "Of the Tujunga women who witnessed close encounters, most were or are oriented toward the gay life-style"; that Sara spent much of her life attempting "to deny her sexuality"; and that "Jan had been molested repeatedly by her stepfather, starting at the age of seven."[44] Of course, such information may not be crucial or even relevant to the truth or falsity of the abductions, and could well be used in support of the contention that people from all walks of life are equally likely to be abducted. Still, it is hard not to see it as a potentially significant psychological factor. To take only one example, the tests performed on the Tujunga women do not involve any explicit phallic imagery so commonly found in abduction accounts; no needles or probes are inserted into vaginas, ears, or navels. For this reason alone one would think that the question of the abductees' sexual orientation deserves greater attention than it receives because there would appear to be some kind of prima facie relationship between sexual orientation and the type of abduction experience that people describe.

Initially, the authors tell us only that the women are a "special breed" of people who escaped the "suburban nightmare of tract homes and condominiums" for the "solitary surroundings" and "primitive comforts" of rural life, where they were free to live in their "unconventional way," without the bother of "curious neighbors." Here, a discerning reader might sense unstated undercurrents of meaning. But all we receive is the odd reference to Sara's "personal problems" or to her having gone through a "difficult time in her life" when the first abduction occurred. Though we also learn that "Due to an unfortunate and depressing home situation, [Jan] left home at the age of fourteen and lived with foster parents"; it emerges that she was the victim of sexual abuse.[45]

The authors' decision to deny us this information at the outset creates more problems than it avoids. Druffel's defense of her silence in this regard—that "the search for truth cannot justify violation of privacy"—is neither convincing nor even particularly honest, since reference *is* eventually made to the sex issue.[46]

It is undeniable that the authors of *The Tujunga Canyon Contacts* should be complimented to the degree that they do manage to acknowledge even the possible presence of a psychological component in abduction accounts. Still, their refusal to pay more attention to the issue of human personality and social context as they relate to the abduction phenomenon constitutes a serious flaw in their approach, and one that we will see occurring time and again in the narratives.

Notes

1. Travis Walton, *The Walton Experience* (New York: Berkley Books, 1978); Ann Druffel and D. Scott Rogo, *The Tujunga Canyon Contacts* (Englewood Cliffs, N.J.: Prentice-Hall, 1980).
2. Walton, *The Walton Experience*, 148.
3. Ibid., 29.
4. Ibid., ix.
5. Ibid., 105–107.
6. Ibid., 109. Although descriptions of the aliens' eyes vary considerably from case to case, their importance as a feature of alien anatomy is encountered repeatedly. In the majority of instances they seem to be seen as the vehicle through which alien power flows, whether it be to mesmerize and control victims, or more benignly, to impart wisdom or bits of knowledge to the abductee.
7. Ibid., 119.
8. Ibid., 118, my emphasis.
9. In a recent issue of the *MUFON UFO Journal*, Walton admits that the film version of his abduction experience "took serious liberties with some of the facts" and bore little resemblance to the book on which it was allegedly based; incidentally, Walton "revised" his original version of the book "to relate to the film made from it." Although there is a tacit assumption that neither he nor screenwriter Tracy Torme had any option other than to " 'Do what they [i.e., Paramount Studios] want or don't have a film' " (19), some readers will be hard pressed not to question their decision to alter the facts in such a way. See Dwight Connelly, "Ufology Profile: Travis Walton," *MUFON UFO Journal*, No. 364 (August 1998): 18–19.
10. In fact, narrative development could only occur under such circumstances if abductees were to be picked up in groups and anesthetized one at a time while the other victims looked on. Though many abductees speak of observing others in the process of being experimented on, usually all participants are at least partly conscious.
11. Walton, *The Walton Experience*, 93–94.
12. For a critical reading of Walton's veracity see Philip Klass's *UFO Abductions: A Dangerous Game* (Amherst, N.Y.: Prometheus Books, 1989), 25–37.
13. See Jacques Vallee, *Dimensions: A Casebook of Alien Contact* (New York: Ballantine, 1988), 228–41.
14. Walton, *The Walton Experience*, 149.
15. Druffel and Rogo, *The Tujunga Canyon Contacts*, 42, 50.
16. Ibid., 45.
17. Ibid., 58.

18. Ibid., 50.

19. Ibid., 60, my emphasis.

20. Ibid., 250.

21. Ibid., 185.

22. Ibid., 54, 57.

23. This may cause readers to suspect immediately that Sara had probably heard of this folk remedy many years ago and forgot about it, only to have it re-emerge in its present form as alien-inspired.

24. Druffel and Rogo, *The Tujunga Canyon Contacts*, 135.

25. Ibid., 114.

26. Ibid., 140.

27. Ibid, 105–106.

28. Ibid., 148.

29. Ibid., 10, 99, 65, 166. In the updated edition of *The Tujunga Canyon Contacts* (1988), Druffel evaluates the five women as constituting a "group one" class of witnesses, that is, people who "appear rational, honest, and socially productive" (275); in other words, basically normal. Of the four remaining women (Jan is deceased), Sara has been divorced twice, gave up a baby for adoption, suffers from clinical depression, was in a mental hospital for an extended period (six months), and has such poor health that she is no longer able to work. Emily is also in poor health, experiences periods of sleep paralysis, and claims to travel astrally. Jo could not be reached by Druffel and Rogo. Only Lori appears by all accounts to be in stable condition.

30. Druffel and Rogo, *The Tujunga Canyon Contacts*, 110.

31. Ibid., 19, 138, 35, 171.

32. Ibid., 29, my emphasis.

33. This process is known technically as "cryptamnesia," and refers to the process whereby long-forgotten memories, often fictional in origin, are recalled by a person at a later date and remembered as facts. Some— but by no means all—"past-life regressions" have been traced to an individual's having read a work of historical fiction or encountered a person who told them stories that years later emerged as actual memories.

34. Druffel and Rogo, *The Tujunga Canyon Contacts*, 26.

35. Ibid., 55–56, 45.

36. Ibid., 188.

37. Ibid., 31, 67, 83, 172.

38. Ibid., 230.

39. Ibid., 223.

40. Ibid., 232.

41. Ibid., 236–37, 241–43.

42. Ibid., 243–44.

43. Curtis Peebles's *Watch the Skies* (Washington, D.C.: Smithsonian Institution Press, 1994) offers such an explanation.

44. Druffel and Rogo, *The Tujunga Canyon Contacts*, 217, 251, 272.

45. Ibid., 3–10; 134.

46. Ibid., 201.

6

BUDD HOPKINS:
MISSING TIME AND
I N T R U D E R S

While often frightening, the abductions that have been examined up to this point were not continuously negative experiences for all concerned. Some of the Tujunga abductions were almost pleasant, and even Travis Walton in the midst of his fright sensed that there was something "gentle" about his abductors. This mood changes abruptly in the abduction narratives compiled by Budd Hopkins, whose aliens are rarely communicative, never humorous, and frequently take on a decidedly sinister and even malevolent demeanor. Gone is Betty Hill's chatty interlocutor, and the avuncular aliens Betty Andreasson encountered will only appear again occasionally in some of the narratives compiled by John Mack.

Hopkins's first book, *Missing Time* (1981), contains no introduction by an expert (one of the abductees' hypnotists does write an afterword), but it does begin with quotations from two supposedly impeccable observers of the phenomenon, physicist Edward Condon and the renowned psychologist Carl Jung. Summarized are the *Condon Report*'s account of three unexplained UFO sightings by astronauts, and Jung's apparent endorsement of the objective reality of UFOs contained in his remark that "only one thing is certain: it is not just a rumour: *something is seen.*"[1]

Hopkins's use of these sources is a shrewd strategy in itself, knowing as he did the prestige both of these individuals commanded, but it is also somewhat misleading. First, many readers will not have forgotten that Condon's overriding opinion was that there was no compelling reason to continue the scientific study of UFOs. As far as Jung's position on the subject is concerned, while there is no reason to doubt that he used these words (oddly enough, Hopkins does not give a source for the 1954 quotation), they give a misleading summary of where he came to stand on the matter. Indeed, the first chapter of Jung's classic work on the subject is titled "UFOs as Rumours," and he continued to refer to them in this manner throughout that book; that is, as something unverified or unfounded in fact. Although Jung did indeed say at one point that *"something is seen,"* he was careful to add *"but one doesn't know what."* Furthermore, he went on to observe that "It is difficult, if not impossible, to form any correct idea of these objects, because they behave not like bodies but like weightless thoughts," and added emphatically, "As a psychologist, I am not qualified to contribute anything useful to the question of the physical reality of UFOs." That there may have been a physical basis to what Jung was investigating as a psychological issue he acknowledged as possible, but noted that so much about them is uncertain "that it must remain for the time being an unproven conjecture, or rumour, until we know more about it."[2] From Jung's standpoint, the matter was of interest as a symbolic manifestation with its roots in the psyche.

Hopkins, in his introduction, proceeds to divide all people into two groups as far as UFOs are concerned: those who believe the subject to be important and worthy of study, and those who "out of lack of information or mere indifference, simply ignore the phenomenon."[3] He tries here to align the reader on the same side as he is by lumping all members of the opposition into one obviously unattractive camp. The reader will also see a pretty obvious attempt to win readers over (notably, *before* presenting any of the evidence at hand) in Hopkins's frequent use of qualifying words and phrases. On one occasion, he argues that "No one can deny that this [the extraterrestrial hypothesis] is *possibly* the correct explanation of the UFO phenomenon."[4]

Hopkins also provides his readers with a brief history of UFO sightings in America since the Great Airship sightings* of 1896–97,

---

*From early winter of 1896 to the spring of 1897, across the United States and Canada large numbers of people reportedly saw huge objects

and he summarizes the well-known Lonnie Zamora case* at length, in order to establish a background of credible, reliable sightings of UFOs over the years, the better to prepare readers for the far more bizarre events to come. Of course, readers of this book will be as familiar with Hopkins's method here as with its logical flaws, having already seen it employed by John Fuller and Raymond Fowler.

Hopkins follows the example of his predecessors in stressing the extent to which abductees are persons of honesty and integrity, which as we have seen in previous chapters adds little to the credibility of their accounts. He then stresses the similarities among the various abductions with which he was involved, similarities he sees as evidence that some kind of actual event is taking place, probably a systematic research program carried out by alien beings. He supports this contention by presenting a short, composite abduction scenario that he considers typical. Notably, this prototypical description will remind readers of the Hill case, to which it bears considerable similarity. Understandably, Hopkins makes much of the element of missing time and amnesia that so bothered the Hills and their investigators, although he exaggerates somewhat the success of alien-enforced amnesia when stating, "The events immediately before and immediately after the abduction have been *seamlessly* joined, leaving them with little or no sense of missing time."[5] Hopkins and other authors seem to forget, as we have already noted, that the aliens have been far from successful in this regard. And readers do not have to conclude, as Hopkins would have it, that a narrative is literally true simply because similarities can be found throughout its various manifes-

---

in the sky variously described as lights, balls, cigar-shaped objects, or wheels, apparently occupied by human passengers and powered by propellers. Today, the majority of the sightings are generally thought to have been the work of hoaxing telegraph operators or newspaper reporters.

*In April 1964, police officer Lonnie Zamora claimed to observe a UFO land, discharge two occupants for a brief period, and later take off when they observed him. The object left physical traces of its presence in the form of burned brush and tracks on the ground. Although skeptics have suggested the sighting was a hoax, Zamora, who was regarded by J. Allen Hynek as a credible witness, seemed genuinely frightened by his experience. The case was never satisfactorily resolved, and the sighting remains unidentified. See Peter Brookesmith, *UFO: The Complete Sightings* (London: Brown Books, 1995), 22–23, 79–80.

tations. This is because only a finite number of events can ever proceed from a previous event, whether fictional or not, and still remain faithful to principles of consistency and logic.[6] When we consider the alien abduction scenario, once the existence of UFOs is assumed for the sake of argument, the performing of experiments and tests on human beings by their occupants is simply one of a limited number of reasons for their presence here in the first place that makes any sense.

In *Missing Time* several new and important features appear in the narrative. In the introduction, in order to strengthen his contention that the abduction phenomenon is of grave and immediate importance to everyone in society, Hopkins argues that there must be large numbers of abductees everywhere and speculates that there may be tens of thousands of persons—even millions have been suggested—who have experienced such trauma. This notion that many persons could have undergone abductions and retained *no* conscious recall of them is a genuinely new element and one that will open the field up widely. Whether intended or not, mention of these unsupported speculations is a most successful strategy, and many readers have doubtless felt pressure to take the book's contents very seriously, given that there was a chance, no matter how small, of its having happened to *them* without their knowledge. Upon reflection, though, other readers may suspect that Hopkins's logic is not without its flaws. For if the aliens' methods work most of the time, why should they not always succeed?

Another element seen frequently in *Missing Time* is the presence of permanent scars or physical marks left on an abductee, presumably the product of some sort of sample-taking conducted by the aliens in the course of the abduction. This will become an increasingly dominant feature in abduction narratives after this period, and one that most abduction authors point to as incontrovertible evidence that the abduction phenomenon is real. However, as we will see, no attempt is made by the authors either to verify the abductees' claims as to when and how the scars appeared, or to dispel the possibility that the various marks on their bodies did not in fact have perfectly ordinary causes or origins.

His introductory material completed, Hopkins proceeds predictably to present a brief history of his relationship with UFOs. The reader may object to his description of his degree of interest as "casual," given the extent of his actual involvement (as a younger man he claimed to have seen a UFO, and he had read many books on the subject over the years). Again predictably, he confesses to having been initially skeptical on the matter of the Hill abduction, but acknowledges that he became convinced after familiarizing himself with *The Interrupted Journey*.[7] It is interesting to note that by this point in the development of the entire abduction narrative in 1981, the Hill case is simply accepted as a classic and alluded to as if it had been verified as incontrovertible fact. Hopkins even says at one point that "we accepted the Hill case and others like it as a general model," its status as an actual event being presumably beyond dispute.[8]

Reading Hopkins's summary of the Hills' experience, one is struck by how, like Fowler, he gives the Hill narrative a continuity and assigns to the events a degree of precision that in its original form it did not have. As we saw, the Hills did *not* sense immediately after returning home that there was a two-hour period for which they could not account, nor did the time discrepancy strike them as at all unusual until it was pointed out to them later. Hopkins is also incorrect when he says that Barney was the first to have nightmares, he omits completely any reference to Betty's dreams which she shared with her husband, and he alludes only to the similarities in their descriptions of the aliens, saying nothing about the significant differences in the Hills' respective reports.

Presumably to make his readers more susceptible to the initial, highly unusual abduction account of Steven Kilburn that follows, Hopkins first tells us of his investigation of a UFO sighting at night near downtown New York in North Hudson Park. Out of the UFO there allegedly came several little beings who dug holes in the ground and collected soil samples before taking off in their craft. This scene was witnessed by George O'Barski, a liquor store owner who claimed no prior interest in or involvement with UFOs and revealed his story reluctantly to Hopkins, who had known him personally for years as a man of honesty and integrity. By and large, the account of the sighting appears pretty convincing. For one, the presence of a UFO in the area that night *was* corroborated subsequently by a number of witnesses. But even here, many readers will notice that Hopkins has minimized the importance of O'Barski's silence (for six months), which he makes only a half-hearted effort to explain: "the perplexity and fear must have finally have been too strong" to resist.[9] Readers might just as easily conclude that with the passage of this amount of time, memory of the original event would be colored by his imagination.

Moreover, despite Hopkins's suggestions, the O'Barski case has no bearing on the experience of Steven Kilburn. For that matter, the very strengths of O'Barski's alleged close encounter may come back to haunt Hopkins, for such factors are clearly lacking in the case revealed by Kilburn.

Steven Kilburn originally told Hopkins in 1978 that he had a strange feeling about a certain stretch of road on which he used to drive. Under hypnosis, an alleged abduction was revealed that had occurred five years previously, where Kilburn recalled emerging from his car to encounter a number of strange beings with putty-colored skin, who put a painful clamp on his shoulder and walked him up a ramp to their UFO, where they performed various tests on him.

For his part, Kilburn was acquainted with UFOs and had a passing knowledge of the paranormal generally; proof of his more than passing interest is seen in his having once attended a conference devoted to the writings of Charles Fort (1874–1932), one of the first American collectors of UFO sightings. Second, Kilburn's abduction experiences were totally personal; no one was present to corroborate anything he said he saw. Third, where O'Barski waited only several months before telling Hopkins his story, Kilburn (like so many abductees) waited for years before making his experience public.[10] Finally, the fact that he himself initiated the investigative process might lead some cynical readers to entertain the possibility that Kilburn may be using Hopkins and staging the entire scenario. Significantly, Hopkins gives none of these factors any consideration.

Understandably, Hopkins describes Steven Kilburn in glowing terms, but his choice of words reveals as much about Hopkins's methods as it does about his subject. We learn Steven is "shy" (that is, not out for publicity); "intense and haunted" (sincerely troubled); "dedicated to a career in the arts" (presumably sensitive and idealistic); and that his "shyness and seriousness are captivating, accompanied as they are by an understated, natural honesty and directness."[11] Later, we will be told that Hopkins's other abductees are similarly impressive: Howard Rich is "gentle and pacific";

Denis McMahon is a person of "obvious integrity"; Virginia Horton is "interesting and highly intelligent"; and Philip Osborne is "not the kind of man who is easily taken in."[12]

In Kilburn's case, we might well wonder how Hopkins can discern such character traits if they are as understated as he claims. But more importantly, the credibility Hopkins is trying to establish in all his abductee-clients rests entirely on how credible we are prepared to find Hopkins as a judge of character. Since he provides no corroborating evidence to support his favorable assessment of any of them, his evaluations are virtually meaningless. Thus, when he says it cost Kilburn a "great effort" to make the request to be hypnotized, we have no reason to accede to his assessment of the situation. Similarly, while Hopkins speaks of Kilburn's honesty, the reader may be struck by Kilburn's vague, guarded, or qualifying phrases like "I don't remember" (if I saw something in the sky); "I believe I did"; (I felt strange but) "I didn't know why"; "I felt that something maybe had just happened to me, or was going to happen"; "Now I can't say for sure, but I believe I was a little bit confused about the time, a loss of time on that one main experience I had"; "It's possible, of course, that I'm mistaken"; it is a "scenario that *could* have happened" (rather than one that "did").[13] This manner of speaking could be seen as proof of Kilburn's scrupulous honesty, but it also serves as a self-protective device should any of these memories be exposed in hypnosis as faulty or the product of confabulation.

While under hypnosis, many interesting features about the Kilburn abduction surface. Kilburn's experience, like that of so many abductees, is both dreamlike and suggestive of fantasy. At one point, referring to an encounter with an alien, he says, "I don't think I really see him, but I do"; recalling the abduction, he remarks that "It's happening, and I knew it would. . . . I almost knew what to expect."[14] Later in *Missing Time*, Howard Rich, Denis "Mac" McMahon, Virginia Horton, and Philip Osborne all give strong indications even while under hypnosis that their experiences may well be dreams: Rich remarks that "It's really just a dream . . . It's not happening"; McMahon says that "it seemed like a dream sequence"; Horton, "The place is like a dream"; and Osborne, "I think it's my imagination."[15]

To be expected, Hopkins discounts the obvious implication that they all *were* dreams—surmising instead that it only indicates a denial process on the abductees' parts when faced with memories of such unusual, but real, experiences.

Like the other abduction authors we have looked at so far, Hopkins also stresses the apparently corroborative features found in the various abductions. Emphasizing that in any abduction account containing one hundred bits of information, eighty will be similar to other accounts, while twenty or so will be new, he sees this as providing strong corroboration of the events' reality. As far as the similarities are concerned, as we saw in chapter 2, all abduction accounts are bound to draw from a certain finite number of basic narrative elements, given the premises involved.[16]

But more importantly, what Hopkins pointedly fails to discuss are the implications of the 20 percent of any account that is not only new, but also frequently in open conflict with information found in other abduction narratives. In Kilburn's case, his experience contains many such inconsistencies, a fact which may call into question the legitimacy of the entire recollection as a series of actual events. For example, Kilburn's aliens are, if anything, similar to Betty Hill's in appearance, being "almost our size," having putty-colored skin (like Walton's "marshmallowy-looking" skin), wearing turtlenecks, and possessing presumably normal, but nailless, hands ("all the fingers are perfect"). Kilburn's temporary loss of control over his car is also mentioned as a point of similarity, Hopkins making much of the "probably" hundreds of cars being "literally lifted off the ground and moved, with driver and passengers inside" as a validation of Kilburn's experience. But this particular aspect of the abduction narrative—a vehicle being "beamed aboard" a UFO—has an unmistakable ring of science fiction to it, and is quite similar to a scene from the 1957 SF classic *This Island Earth*, where an airplane is mysteriously sucked into a UFO. (The possible influence of science fiction and fantasy films on the stories of abductees will be discussed in chapter 8.)[17]

Other inconsistencies are also present throughout the testimony that do much to weaken the stories' credibility. Where Betty Andreasson's aliens floated, Steven Kilburn's abductors hobble as if they "had two really bad knees"; Betty Hill's aliens had no trouble walking at all.[18] Indeed, Kilburn stresses how weak and "skinny" and lacking in muscles the aliens appear to be, in sharp disagreement with one of Hopkins's other abductees, Denis

McMahon, who described aliens who "were built well. They were built powerfully . . . as a normal person would be." Once inside the UFO, Kilburn feels "perfectly comfortable" and "peaceful" with the "perfect" temperature, but Howard Rich felt "so cold" in the alien environment to which he was exposed.[19]

However, as part of an overall developing narrative the presence of these different, and frequently mutually exclusive elements makes considerable sense when seen as experimental variants. Elements that appear to fulfill criteria of appropriateness and relevance to the core narrative tend to remain; those that seem irrelevant, superfluous, inconsistent, or otherwise inappropriate, drop off. For example, alien control over abductees' automobiles becomes a commonplace, probably because it is perceived as being consistent with the fundamental premise of alien technological power and efficiency. But other new elements such as the strange clamp used to immobilize Steven while the aliens perform tests on him are not repeated in later accounts, probably because it has a clumsy and primitive ring to it.

Readers will soon see that the sexual component has become increasingly prominent in the course of Hopkins's abduction accounts. Steven Kilburn feels a "hard finger" poking him in his "back" that "hurt farther down," as well as a "rod" poking his stomach and "sliding back and forth," and a "metal thing" which moves his "legs apart a little bit." Though Hopkins sees this as a retrieved memory of an "operation," many readers may wonder if we are witnessing a displaced memory of some form of sexual assault. This would go far toward explaining Steven's feelings of having been "embarrassed, somehow violated," as would his memory of a "wand" that was "twice as thick" as a thumb and "seven or eight inches long," reminiscent of Betty Hill's memory of the six-inch needle that was inserted in her, or Betty Andreasson's memory of an alien having shot something needlelike in her spine. Hopkins recognizes that the "short, plain cylindrical device is indeed a ubiquitous tool" but his belief in the literal reality of the device prevents him from seeing its appropriateness as a phallic symbol.[20] It need hardly be said that such prodding and poking by metal rods and needles *do* make considerable sense when seen in relation to the dominant theme of violation and helplessness at the hands of an alien (and alienating) technology, a theme that plays such a fundamental role in the unfolding narrative, and becomes such an important part of this narrative when viewed in mythic terms.

Variations among the Abductees' Narratives

Hopkins's next case details the experiences of Howard Rich, whose abduction is of interest for the number of ways it differs from Kilburn's. Like Betty Andreasson, Howard saw a brilliant bluish light outside while watching television in a room in his mother's house late one night. This was followed by a feeling of fear and apprehension. Under hypnosis he recalled walking outside and seeing the source of the light as a UFO. At that point he was immobilized, and claimed to "feel like there's some people there," but no clamp was put on his shoulder to render him immobile. When the abduction was finally recalled, the familiar experience of being touched repeatedly, of being helpless, of feeling initial fear followed by inexplicable peace and calm, and of amnesia, are all present. Although Howard's aliens are slender, they are also physically cold to the touch—"They're cold. Feel cold"—where neither Steven Kilburn nor Virginia Horton would notice any difference in alien body temperature.[21] While Hopkins's fascination with the similarities is to be expected, he fails to examine the import of some of the very points he raises. If, for example, the alleged aliens have "come up with technological feats more staggering to us than color television would have been to Leonardo da Vinci," why, for example, *do* most abductees experience "intermittent pain," when they evidently do not have to?[22] The fortunate Denis McMahon, for instance, claimed to experience no pain whatever, but he represents a small minority of abductees.

As far as alien appearance is concerned, McMahon's abductors have big black eyes, pale skin, and wear what appear to be turtlenecks—all traits we've seen before. But they are also "built powerfully," "looked like miniature people," were "skeletally" similar, and though "compassionless," caused him "no pain." These major differences from other abductions are not examined. Indeed, all Hopkins says about the unique features of this case is that the "description presents a variant on a standard humanoid type."[23]

Also, he tries to account for the many differences by arguing unconvincingly that "these witnesses are trying to describe the same equipment through the use of various homely images, with varying degrees of success."[24]

In what amounts to a final throwing of caution to the wind, Hopkins expresses the opinion that there are no degrees in credibility from story to story: *all* are equally true. As far as differences are concerned, "we are seeing a wide variety of *human response* to the same basic unearthly experience."[25] In other words, if two accounts differ, this only reflects on the linguistic and observational skills of the abductee. The implications of this statement are as wide-ranging as they are damaging to Hopkins's credibility, for it would be virtually impossible to challenge *any* abduction account on the basis of perceived internal inconsistencies or other narrative weaknesses.

Hopkins's presence as a factor in his cases should not be minimized. For example, Virginia Horton's story is distinguished by the presence of a physical scar on her leg which both she and Hopkins came to believe had been inflicted by aliens. Virginia first approached Hopkins with a memory of having sustained a strange, pain-free cut on her leg in 1950, when she was a little girl gathering eggs on her grandparents' farm. Some years after, when she was sixteen, in the course of a picnic in France she disappeared for a period of time, only to emerge from the woods with blood on her blouse. She also described dreams of space travel. Under hypnosis a series of abductions and scientific tests performed by aliens surfaced.

Prepared as he is to agree with Virginia that the scar must have been caused by something unusual, Hopkins strengthens what was in its original form nothing more than a gnawing suspicion on her part that something definitely odd had happened to her as a child, and draws no attention to the time gap between the recalled experiences and the present. No matter how "interesting and highly intelligent" she may be, the reader has every right to suspect the accuracy of a memory this old.[26] Indeed, although there is nothing in Virginia's initial recall of the cut to indicate that she even took it very seriously at the time, Hopkins prefers to erect an elaborate explanation that involves aliens landing near the barn, cutting a sample of skin from Virginia's leg, and controlling the parents' memories of the entire event. Here, even readers unfa-

miliar with the term "Occam's Razor" will suspect that a less elaborate theory could be formulated.[27]

Virginia's aliens are distinguished in several ways. For one
thing, they are kindly, polite, and respectful of her parents (whose
permission to take her they requested!), and in their age, sense of
humor, and patience remind her of her grandfather. In a scene that
recalls part of the alien's exchange with Betty Hill, Virginia's aliens
seem equally ignorant of the aging process, ask her many questions about conditions of life on earth, and show her pictures of
alien lifeforms and color-coded star maps. The seeming purpose-
lessness of aliens telling a six-year-old girl all this information,
only to force her to forget it for thirty years (so reminiscent of Betty
Andreasson that it will strike many as frankly derivative), is not
even acknowledged in passing.

Virginia's aliens may also be able to render themselves invisible at least on occasion, for she comments that they seemed to be
telling her, "You can't see us because you wouldn't understand
how we look. It would scare you." For whatever reason, they do
not "have any direct contact" with her, possibly, she suspects,
because "they breathe different air." Possession of this particular
attribute (invisibility) has not been previously encountered,
although occasional hints of alien invisibility do enter the narrative from this point on. Another distinguishing feature of the
Horton case has to do with the aliens' eyes. Although "different
from ours," Virginia cannot recall in what respect, or even how
many they had, two or three (!); nor can she recall whether they
had hair.[28] Virginia's aliens also possess mutually exclusive attributes such as a mind-boggling technological sophistication combined with an inability to prevent a cut they have inflicted upon
her from bleeding or scarring.

One final point of some interest concerns Virginia's memory of
blood on her blouse that she acquired when on a picnic in France
as a child, together with the remembered sighting of a deer at the
same time. In the course of several sessions it emerges that Virginia
had another encounter with the same aliens who had taken the
skin sample years before. Hopkins speculates that the initial
memory of seeing the deer may have been a pseudoimage
implanted by the aliens to provide Virginia with a euphemized
memory of what happened, although the reader may suspect that

such memories could be explained in many ways (maybe she simply saw a deer and had a bloody nose). At any rate, the implanting of such pseudomemories constitutes a new element in the narrative, and it is one that will reappear, with future abductees such as Whitley Strieber recalling sightings of owls or other animals that they come to suspect may have been such "screen" memories.

As Virginia reveals more information about her woodland encounter, her story becomes increasingly similar to traditional accounts of encounters in the forest with fairies, elves, or witches, though the imagery is technological. For instance, hearing her name called, she obeys the call, enters the forest and eventually joins in a celebration of aliens taking place "in her honor."[29] Avoiding any discussion of these similarities, Hopkins goes on to reason that Virginia's bloody blouse—presumably an established fact, corroborated by members of her family—can stand as proof of the entire experience as recalled. The reader will recall similar offerings of such "proof" in other narratives and recognize the inherent illogic therein.

Abductee Philip Osborne's testimony is conspicuously imprecise, even more than Steven Kilburn's. He uses the phrase "sort of" and "kind of" over forty times in the testimony contained in the book, and acknowledges frequently that he either cannot remember details of his experience or does not know how he behaved. Indeed, many readers must register some surprise that this case is featured at all, considering the lengths Hopkins must go to extract detail from his subject. As Philip's hypnosis sessions proceeded, a number of highly unusual, isolated memories emerged, many of them far from typical of abduction experiences. For one, Philip told of an incident that happened to him when, as a child on vacation with his parents in the Smoky Mountains in Tennessee, he recalled feeling great fear at one point in the trip for no apparent reason. He also remembered experiencing the feeling of hurtling through the air toward a dome-shaped object and being unable to stop. Finally, he recalled an incident in Pittsburgh in 1964 and another in New York, when he became paralyzed for a period of time and sensed a "presence" in his room. Although all of these states could have their origin in a neurological abnormality, Hopkins does not investigate this possibility.

Doubtless because of the account's imprecision, Hopkins's presence as interpreter is more conspicuous here than at any other point in *Missing Time*. For example, when asked to "dream" about how he got his scar, Philip says only, "I sort of saw that hand, that metallic hand that I saw last week only that is not really what it looks like. For a moment, I sort of thought I had a glimpse of it, but I didn't. Couldn't really see it." All he can recall is a "something" that is polished; indeed, he admits having only a "feeling" of some "sort of mechanical apparatus." Incredibly, Hopkins considers these vague recollections evidence of Philip's "scrupulous manner" and observes remarkably that "there were two *distinct* images—a jointed metal hand, and a less-articulated robotlike arm which seems to have done the actual cutting."[30]

Similar interpretive intrusion occurs with the supposed eye that Philip saw when in the strange hospital-like room. Hopkins presses him for more information about this fixture, asking if it was "like a normal eye, or what," to which Philip replies, "I don't know." In answer to the question "was it moving?"—a singular question to ask of an image Philip described initially as a painting on which he observed "kind of ah, um, an eye motif on that"—he replies inexplicably, "neither in a sense." But out of this, Hopkins fills in the presence of an "eyelike apparatus," a technological device far different from anything Philip described, similar to that encountered by Betty Andreasson and others. He then justifies the prominence of his interpretive role on the grounds that "It is more important at this point to see if these observations form a coherent and specific whole which is consistent from session to session than it is to worry over his frequent uncertainties."[31]

Earlier, Hopkins jumped to the conclusion that Virginia Horton was "inside an examining room of the UFO" where the account never mentioned a UFO explicitly, but only a "room."[32] In Philip's case, any testimony that sounds dreamlike, sequentially chaotic, or inconsistent with other accounts is smoothed over in a manner that does not challenge the premise that a real abduction occurred. Hopkins simply shrugs off the oddities in Philip's aliens as described—metallic eyes, semitransparent skin which reveal blood vessels underneath—as a "funny mix, and one that I had never precisely heard of before." From there, he goes on to recreate from vague fragments a coherent narrative, arguing, "If, ten months later, a hypnotically recalled narrative confirms in both outline and specific detail what was recalled ten months previously, then we are probably dealing with an actual, historical event."[33] To say this is to argue that a person's ability to recall twice in ten months the plot of *Hamlet* provided proof that the characters actually existed. With this reasoning, Hopkins has no trouble turning a statement made by Philip such as "I hesitate to say it, but (*I have*) almost a sense of a flying saucer there and I'm just trying to imagine what might have happened next" into "nearby there was a flying saucer."[34]

Missing Time concludes with a series of speculations, both "grim and hopeful." First, Hopkins cautions us not to try to understand or evaluate the aliens in our terms, and adds that to set ourselves and our behavior up as the sole standard constitutes rank arrogance, a sentiment with which few could disagree. But for all that, this does not seem to be the central point he could be making. The issue is not that the alien behavior is inexplicable because it contradicts our notions of how aliens ought to behave, but because it contradicts *itself* on so many occasions. Given all this, it is hard for the reader to believe that Hopkins has indeed followed his own advice: "Simple logic requires us to search for the clearest, most specific patterns we can find within the sometimes misleading mass of UFO reports."[35]

In his attempt to find order in all the data he has amassed, Hopkins himself falls into the trap he warned of earlier in the chapter—of evaluating alien behavior in human terms—by his very human attempts to give it intelligible motive and purpose as we understand such concepts. Accordingly, to him the importance of the physical operations is central, a point that he will elaborate in his next book. But his sense of a logical development in the history of the UFO presence—which he sees as beginning with an initial general interest in human topography, followed by the taking of soil and other samples, and culminating in a specific scientific interest in human beings—is somewhat presumptuous and actually amounts to the same kind of arrogance he earlier deplored, and belies his concluding claim that he has "tried to relate these encounters, these events, as directly, and with as little adornment as possible."[36]

Though an obviously intelligent human being, Hopkins does not appreciate how complex and varied can be the ways we receive information within modern society. Human beings do not live separately in vacuums, but in a communal state where information is continually being exchanged in innumerable ways, many of them subtle. It is impossible to say of any abductee's account that it was "pure," because such accounts are simply too prevalent a part of popular culture. There is no doubt that something highly unusual is happening to these individuals, but their own hypnotically recalled memories of involvement with alien beings may themselves be the results of a creative process, the product of an attempt to come to terms with events in their lives that could have innumerable other causes.

Psychologist and hypnotist Dr. Aphrodite Clamar echoes the above position in her afterword. Indeed, she takes a balanced approach to the subject that readers may wish had rubbed off on Hopkins. Throughout, she is well-reasoned and cautious, and concerns herself mainly with defining the limits of her role as a hypnotist. She clearly avoids committing herself on the question of the reality of the recalled memories. The buried experiences may be "real or imagined," she admits, even after spending considerable time with abductees. This may be because she also realizes that hypnosis, while a useful tool, is "not necessarily a precise one." Indeed, she suggests at one point that the amnesia may be self-induced, observing that "the mind has a way of protecting itself by repressing painful or frightening experiences."[37] Ironically, her very caution actually makes it easier for readers to entertain *all* possibilities, even (dare I say it?) the extraterrestrial one.

Kathie Davis and Her Intruders

Where *Missing Time* focused on a number of abductees, Hopkins's second book, *Intruders* (1987), concentrates on the extensive and traumatic experiences of one female abductee, Kathie Davis, and uses other abductees in a supporting capacity on those occasions when events that take place during their abductions appear similar to Kathie's. Because Hopkins employs basically the same approach to his subject that he used in *Missing Time*, we will concentrate only on those elements that represent new developments in the overall narrative. By now, for instance, readers will have

come to expect from abduction authors the same array of predictable rhetorical devices, and so will not register much surprise
when confronted with yet another announcement of the author's
skepticism, arguments from consistency, glowing assessments of
the abductees, or the obligatory (if rather brief) allusions to
experts—physicians, psychologists and scientists—whom Hopkins thanks in the acknowledgments.

In fairness it must be acknowledged that, unlike most abduction authors, Hopkins does not rely greatly on experts. For instance,
early in *Intruders* Hopkins summarizes the results of a personality
profile of nine alleged abductees conducted by Dr. Elizabeth Slater,
a psychologist who had not been informed that the subjects were
abductees at the time of the tests. Although she saw "no major
mental disorders" among the nine persons tested—a point of which
Hopkins naturally makes a good deal—she did find that the group
displayed mild paranoia, a degree of distrust and wariness, and a
lack of self-esteem. When, after the tests, Dr. Slater was informed
that the subjects were alleged abductees, she was still not convinced
that such abductions had necessarily occurred, but conceded the
above personality disturbances were consistent with the individuals *possibly* having had an experience of this nature. Still, readers
may wonder if the mild personality disturbances were not the
product of real abductions, but along with other factors, could have
contributed toward these individuals' creation of fantasized ones.

Even if we accept the results of these tests, although Kenneth
Ring's study* established a statistical correlation between instances of sexual or physical abuse and abduction experiences, not
much weight can be given to such a tiny statistical sample, and
Hopkins's obvious relief that none of the nine subjects was found
to be mentally ill means very little. Furthermore, his implicit sense
that there are only two options available here—either the alleged
abductees are "paranoid, schizophrenic or otherwise emotionally

---

*Sociologist Kenneth Ring questioned two relatively small groups of
people: a control group composed of persons who had no history of
abduction experiences, and a group comprised of those who had. He
found a measurable, though slight, difference between the two groups,
with the abductees having a higher incidence of sexual or physical abuse
in their pasts. See Kenneth Ring, *The Omega Project* (New York: William
Morrow, 1992).

crippled" or they are "normal" and thus telling the literal truth—
will strike readers as suspect in its all-too-typical simplicity.[38]
Some may even wonder if there might be as yet unidentified emotional or psychological states of mind that could be responsible for
certain individuals who are otherwise functioning members of
society conceiving abduction experiences.

One rhetorical device Hopkins employs has obviously been
prompted by his awareness that many readers will find the
ensuing story even more difficult to believe than anything they
encountered in *Missing Time*. Implicitly hinting that the contents
will be both horrific and improbable, he draws an analogy
between the Holocaust and the abduction phenomenon. Many
readers may find Hopkins's analogy both tenuous in itself and
manipulative. Although both events may be "beyond belief," there
is a crucial difference between the two events in that we have volu-
minous physical proof that the Holocaust took place, so we *must*
accept it, difficult though such acceptance might be for some.

In the opening sections of *Intruders* Hopkins naturally tries
hard to convince us that such abductions are taking place. Plainly
he is working on the assumption that if he can get us to accept this
fundamental premise, it will be easier to brush aside the many
inconsistencies that we encounter from case to case. In fact he is
working backward, hoping to obscure that *within* the phenomenon
the constituent parts do not cohere. Of abduction authors, only
John Mack has made any extensive effort to deal with these inconsistencies, and the success of his attempt is open to question, as we
will see in chapter 10.

Kathie's Abduction Story

Of course, by the time Hopkins began to write *Intruders*, stories of
abductions by aliens had been receiving publicity for over twenty
years. Hopkins's own *Missing Time* was a bestseller that had been
widely read and discussed on radio and television. Yet Hopkins
expresses a blithe confidence that Kathie's "images and memories
cannot be ascribed either to 'contamination' by reading the UFO literature or by viewing its Hollywood version." In fact, contamination is highly likely in the case of Kathie and her sister, Laura, who

were both familiar with *Missing Time*.[39] Nothing in Kathie's initial letter to Hopkins in September 1983 contains anything that she could not have encountered in Hopkins's own book or have found in earlier abduction narratives. Kathie's story begins with her account to Hopkins of having seen a mysterious bright light near her pool house in her backyard in July 1983. The letter goes on to detail similar experiences of her sister, Laura, who had a history of seeing UFOs, and of Kathie and her mother's discovery that they both had strange scars on their right legs. As Hopkins proceeded to investigate the case through interviews and hypnosis, it emerged that Kathie and other members of her family had been repeatedly abducted by aliens over the years. The aliens presumably took "scoops" of skin from Kathie's leg and that of her mother (causing the scars), and performed extensive experiments both on Kathie and her sons, inserting tiny implants into their noses for undetermined reasons. As well, they removed a fetus from Kathie against her will for purposes of their own, and—during a later abduction—showed her a female child who she sensed was the one they had previously taken. Despite the apparent richness of Kathie's narrative, the initial sighting of the light in the yard, the physical traces on the ground, her sister's sighting of a UFO some years before, a missing time experience, the experiencing of unusual dreams, and the presence of scars on the legs of family members are all aspects of the narrative that had been in circulation for years.

Indeed, Kathie's case provides a good example of how the overall narrative is developing. For example, when Betty Hill and Betty Andreasson were first given the "pregnancy test," it had no obvious purpose in *The Interrupted Journey* or the first Andreasson books. But by the time of Kathie's narrative, we are provided with an extensive explanation of all the alien sexual experiments. It is for this reason, among others, that the Davis case is so important. Narratives thereafter tend to incorporate the Davis explanations into their own storylines; David Jacobs, for example, writes as if experiences such as Kathie's involving impregnation and fetal extraction were commonplace. Of course, these new narratives frequently raise additional questions of their own, as we shall see.

As we proceed through *Intruders*, it becomes evident that factual information about Kathie, her experiences, and her family, and Hopkins's interpretive assessments of them frequently work at cross purposes. Members of Kathie's family, for example, speak with an "earthy, candid directness that conveys the habit of honesty"; Kathie, remarkable for her "intelligence and range of information," is "highly sophisticated in surprising ways," a woman with "a particular kind of insight into others, an ability to read and understand people."[40] Even the normality of the environment is stressed at the outset in order to establish the Davises' credentials as a representative family "pleasantly typical of middle-western, middle-class suburbia."[41]

But much of the factual information in *Intruders* about the family in general and Kathie in particular suggests a different state of affairs. Though characterized simply as "candid," Kathie's father sounds like something of a tyrant when stating that he would "whack [his daughters'] butts" if "they ever made anything up," which readers may well consider both an odd and excessive response to the innocent fantasies which children concoct.[42] One hesitates to speculate on the effect such negative reinforcement might have on a child's imagination, possibly suppressing it or otherwise forcing it underground where it might manifest itself years later in unusual formulations.

Kathie's decision in 1978 to marry when pregnant at the age of nineteen is not particularly unusual, but some might find strange her "elation" at hearing she was pregnant at such a young age. Significantly, readers are encouraged to see a great deal in the fact that this pregnancy was "mysteriously" terminated, but we may not find it as abnormal or singular an event as do Kathie and Hopkins, for pregnancies routinely terminate (i.e., miscarry) for any number of perfectly natural reasons. (It has been estimated that as many as one in five women—20 percent of pregnancies—may miscarry.)[43] Soon after her miscarriage, Kathie gave birth to a son, Robbie, in July 1979, and to a second son, Tommy, in September 1980.

More important, we learn that Kathie is far from healthy. She has colitis, an irregular heartbeat, and has "several chronic, possibly psychosomatic illnesses." She routinely consults a psychologist who suspects "buried trauma" as a possible cause of these maladies. Though Hopkins clearly hints that the abductions are the source of this trauma, the reader could be seeing another mistaken designation where the abduction claims are not the cause of her "years of insomnia and paralyzing anxiety," but the *effect* of years of sleep-lessness and worry brought on by other causes.[44] Concerning Kathie's insomnia, Hopkins obviously sees it, too, as a symptomatic reaction to her abductions and he likens many of her symptoms to the reactions of a victim of sexual assault. Significantly, the possibility that female abductees could actually have been such victims who rendered their trauma manageable through fantasy is *never dealt with* in *any* of the major abduction narratives until the 1990s, with the appearance of David Jacobs's *Secret Life* and John Mack's *Abduction*, but even in those works it is summarily dismissed.

Oddly enough, both sisters are strangely reluctant to undergo hypnosis. For her part, Kathie did not even want to be hypnotized in her own home (where, one would think, she ought to feel the most secure), and Laura at no point consented to undergo hypnosis. While some readers might deduce from this that the women are simply afraid that their stories would be revealed as another example of "making something up" (for which they might once have been "whacked"), it is possible, though of course not provable, that the answer may lie more in misgivings regarding the home environment itself, coupled with fear over what might be revealed about that environment. For his part, Hopkins dismisses these anomalous reactions as merely "interesting."

Similarly, even after citing problematic aspects of Kathie's relationship with her parents, Hopkins proceeds to ignore them. One night, even though she fears yet another abduction, Kathie refuses to waken her father, who is a "sound and determined sleeper."[45] Hopkins betrays no concern about a woman who, though evidently believing that she is about to be carried off by extraterrestrial beings, is afraid to wake her father to seek his help. When she speaks to her mother, she is sleepily told to take some aspirin—singular advice indeed! On another occasion, Kathie has another strange feeling that she is about to be abducted, but, claiming her mother would "kill her" for incurring the expense, refrains from calling a fellow abductee long distance for support. Seeking advice from her mother, she is told this time to take heart medicine and Pepto-Bismol! Yet again, one night Kathie thinks she sees a small, gray alien walk past her bedroom door. Terrified, she asks her mother for money to stay in a hotel for the night, a curious request that is in any case refused. The parents' actions suggest apathy, cruelty, or at best a disbelief that readers may suspect to be justified.

Hopkins appears more personally involved with the Davis case than with those abductions covered in *Missing Time*, and he spends considerable time building up the reader's expectations that this abduction may be "the most important in the history of UFO research."[46] In large part, he bases his assertions regarding the unique importance of the Davis case on the physical evidence associated with Kathie's abductions. However, this is a risky strategy, because if mundane explanations can be found to account for this evidence, the entire case is weakened. In this case, the damage to the ground presumably caused by the UFO is inconclusive. Indeed, virtually all of the rest of the "hard" evidence must be taken on faith, especially the physical symptoms which Kathie, her friend, and the friend's daughter claimed to experience following their swim on the night the UFO appeared. Of course, even if they experienced such symptoms it does not mean they were caused in the manner Hopkins is claiming.

Early in the book Hopkins spends what appears at first glance to be an inordinate amount of time discussing a UFO encounter Kathie's sister, Laura, had experienced, and he also makes a good deal of a remembered dream that both Laura and her mother claimed to have had concerning a fear of intruders in their attic. We also learn that shortly after she was married in 1978, Kathie began to receive a number of strange telephone calls similar to those Betty Andreasson received, consisting of a voice which babbled in an indecipherable language. Hopkins's strategy here, despite his claims about a normal family, is obviously to establish the existence of an atmosphere surrounding the Davis family where unusual and inexplicable events occur routinely. Of course, this strategy runs the risk of distancing readers altogether, most of whom have never seen a UFO or even received such unusual telephone calls.

Hopkins is also impressed by Kathie's recollection of the UFO, which he termed "extremely vivid." But less than five pages later she herself admits she saw it but "dimly," adding that she just "*knew* it was there, but I didn't want to look at it." Though he discerns humanoids in his discussion of her testimony, Kathie's initial statement spoke only of a "presence," of "dark things" that pinched and touched her, and inserted a "pencil-like object into her ear."[47]

At times it is hard for the reader not to see Hopkins as simply gullible, and to see this gullibility as more pronounced in *Intruders* than it was in *Missing Time*. Concerning Kathie's son Robbie's claim that a "man with a big head" entered his bedroom and placed a nasal implant in his little brother Tommy, Hopkins accepts that the child's account could be genuine simply because it contained certain details found in his mother's account. Second, he accepts uncritically the family's claim that the adults "tried never to mention the subject" in front of the children. Yet on one occasion Hopkins himself violated this taboo by discussing the abductions in front of the boy, causing the child to say that "when we talk about this it makes my stomach hurt," a remark that clearly reveals the adults *did* speak regularly of these matters in the children's presence.[48] As far as Tommy's bleeding nose is concerned, alien implants are immediately suspected, and no alternate possibility is investigated.

Speaking of implants, readers will note that their prominence in the abduction scenario has been steadily growing, to the point where by the time of *Intruders* they are playing an important role. Kathie claims to have had pencillike objects inserted into her nose and ear, and attributes her subsequent hearing deficiency to this latter action. Hopkins understandably is moved by these claims to liken alien behavior to the "tagging" process which we employ on wild animals, but though he himself is evidently a bit awkward over the anthropomorphic bias of his analogy, he does not give his hesitation broad enough rein. For that matter, anyone familiar with the more sophisticated tagging method employed by the alleged Tujunga Canyon aliens will wonder why these beings would revert to a more primitive and time-consuming process when a more efficient one was at their disposal.

The Importance of *Intruders*

From a historical perspective, *Intruders* is important in a number of respects. First, it contains several elements that we have encountered before, many of which first appeared in *The Andreasson Affair*. Some items that will become increasingly common include the "switching off," just prior to an abduction, of relatives and friends who have been deemed unnecessary to the aliens' purposes. The presence of scooplike scars or marks (which appear on both Kathie and her mother), presumably the result of skin samples taken from an abductee, also come to be encountered with greater frequency from this point on, as are the multigenerational abductions.

Intruders is also remarkable for the number of new elements that figure prominently in the narrative, the most significant of which is the presentation of a rationale for the ongoing nature of the alien experiments: It emerges that Kathie is being used as part of some sort of breeding program.[49] As it turns out, Kathie has also been allowed to see her hybrid offspring. She first broaches the subject by mentioning to Hopkins that she knows she has a living daughter to whom she never gave birth. After that test which indicated that she was no longer pregnant, she somehow "knew" that "somebody" had taken her baby, a belief that initially appears to be confirmed by her testimony while under hypnosis. But Kathie's actual words are quite equivocal in their meaning, and could be interpreted in a number of ways; all she said was "IT'S NOT FAIR! IT'S *MINE! IT'S MINE! (Sobbing)* I *HATE* YOU. *I HATE YOU!* . . . IT'S NOT FAIR!"[50]

Later, when Kathie describes the appearance of her hybrid child (they have been brought together by the aliens), Hopkins sees nothing psychologically significant in the description of the little girl as "just a doll," "real pretty," looking "like an elf" or "angel" with blue eyes and "so perfect" nose and mouth, the little girl she never had, of whom she "should be proud."[51] In later narratives these offspring are more commonly described as sickly, pathetic, or even revolting, and abductees frequently resist alien attempts to force them to hold and cuddle these half-human children. This negative appearance is arguably truer to the logic of what such hybridization (granting that it were possible, which is highly unlikely) would be apt to produce. Nor does Hopkins ponder why aliens would select such an unpromising candidate (given the state of her health) for their program.

At all events, readers do not have to be psychoanalysts to see the implicit wish-fulfillment in Kathie's description of her hybrid child as a perfect and petite being, remembering Kathie's own large frame, small size, and medical history. Nor would the symbolic import of Kathie's being allowed to name her several hybrid offspring be lost on many readers. A powerless, less than well-edu-cated woman (although Kathie is a high school graduate, Hopkins describes her level of education as "obviously less than Ivy League"),[52] as well as a single mother in chronic ill health, obvi-ously victimized by life, Kathie is given virtually the status of an Adam and Eve combined by her alien abductors. But Hopkins prefers to concentrate on the aliens' purpose, taking as he does their existence virtually as a datum. Similarly, because it conforms to his thesis, a good deal is also made of the apparent similarities between the aliens' gynecological procedures and laparoscopy, and he sees much significance in the fact that, as Kathie had not had laparoscopy performed on her, her knowledge of the procedure was striking. Hopkins ignores that laparoscopy* had been invented a century before, and the existence of the laparoscope and its uses would likely have been known to many women of Kathie's age.[53]

The extent of Hopkins's readiness to embrace such claims is also seen in an ancillary case he cites in support of Kathie's allega-tion concerning alien kidnapping. "Andrea" allegedly became pregnant while still a virgin, a virginity allegedly verified by her unnamed gynecologist, who allegedly confirmed that she "still had [her] hymen."[54] Proof that this pregnancy was the result of alien intervention is limited to a dream she had of having sex with a "funny looking," hairless man with "funny" eyes. Hopkins's acceptance of this bizarre story parallels his refusal to see anything odd in the fact that no supporting documentation was preserved, arguing incredibly that "neither her physician nor her parents would have felt a strong need to preserve much information about this *unhappy* situation."[55] Surely an instance of parthenogenesis—human reproduction from an egg unfertilized by a sperm—would have been regarded by the doctor as the most significant event since the conception of Christ, and dealt with accordingly.

Unquestionably, abduction authors often betray methodolo-gies designed to fit their predispositions. Hopkins, for example, informs us that if an abduction "followed the pattern of symptoms [he] recognized as suggestive of a buried abduction experience,

---

*The laparoscope is an illuminated optical instrument which is inserted into the body, piercing the body wall, and is used by physicians and surgeons to examine internal organs.

[he] often phoned the writer directly."[56] That is, it is his a priori understanding of the form an abduction narrative *should* take that determines which abduction claimants who contact him he will investigate, and presumably affects as well which parts of their testimony he will take seriously.

It is doubtless for this reason that he stubbornly refuses to entertain the possibility that the experiences he catalogues could be fantasies or dreams, even though the abductees themselves label their experiences in such a way. Kathie's initial letter spoke of "vivid dreams" shared by her mother and herself, and when hypnotized she made numerous references to dreams or sleep, saying at one point "I must be imagining."[57] Though on one occasion he appears to corroborate an alleged abductee's tearful expression that what happened "had to be a dream," he admits he only did so out of pity.[58]

Hopkins's deep personal belief in the extraterrestrial hypothesis also explains why he plays such an active role in the hypnosis sessions he conducts. Asking his hypnotized subjects to imagine that they are standing behind a black curtain (one that they can open and subsequently see what is simultaneously happening to them) will seem a familiar invitation to fantasize. Telling Kathie that she "got a good look" when presumably inside a UFO doubtless has the same effect and causes her to create a room or environment that she had previously described in vague language.[59]

Another important new feature in the narrative is the growing sense that the aliens are somehow deficient in emotions and that they are anxious to learn about the emotional realm from us. Kathie feels that her emotions "really touched them" and that one alien "was trying to feel something." Yet there is considerable confusion here if not outright contradiction, for immediately after she adds that the alien in question may have been trying to get *her* to feel something, she then suspects that "he felt guilty about how sad I got when I had to leave her" (the hybrid child). Elsewhere, Kathie says under hypnosis that the aliens want "to feel how I love" this child, in order to learn from her about human emotions; this is the explanation Hopkins favors.[60] While this doesn't make much sense as it stands (a few seconds of cuddling a strange-looking baby can hardly provide it with much emotional sustenance or the aliens with much useful information), when viewed as part of a growing myth it is easy to see the thematic relevance of such a statement concerning the value of the emotional life and the sacrifices that result when a society achieves technological prominence, but is otherwise incomplete and deficient.

Finally, *Intruders* reinforces the point made by Betty Andreasson and Sara Shaw (but disputed by other abductees) that abductees have not been randomly chosen, but that they have been singled out or selected and are somehow "special." This sense of the abductee's status will be enlarged upon in the work of one of the most celebrated of abductees, Whitley Strieber, who sees himself as the recipient of a life-long, alien-inspired learning experience.

Notes

1. Quoted in Budd Hopkins, *Missing Time* (New York: Berkley Books, 1983), xi.

2. C. G. Jung, "Flying Saucers: A Modern Myth of Things Seen in the Skies," from *Civilization in Transition*, vol. 10 (Princeton, N.J.: Bollingen Foundation, Princeton University Press, 1959; 1970), 312–415.

3. Hopkins, *Missing Time*, 1.

4. Ibid., 5, my emphasis.

5. Hopkins, *Missing Time*, 9.

6. This point was established many years ago by Vladimir Propp in his *Morphology of the Folk Tale* (1927; Austin: University of Texas Press, 1968). Incidentally, Propp also found that abduction plays a prominent role in folktales, as one of the many possible acts perpetrated by the villain, who is usually responsible for initiating the situation from which the story develops: "A tale . . . may be termed any development proceeding from villainy" (92).

7. This skepticism extends even to some of his own abductees: Concerning Steven Kilburn, "none of the four of us [investigators] expected anything dramatic to occur" (42); with Howard Rich, "I honestly did not think that there was much to discover" (81); it was "highly possible" there was no UFO involvement with Virginia Horton.

8. Hopkins, *Missing Time*, 40.

9. Ibid., 28.

10. Throughout *Missing Time* Hopkins interviews many abductees whose experiences—some very vaguely recalled—go back to 1969 (Denis McMahon) or 1966 (David Oldham), when both were teenagers, or 1950 (Virginia Horton) when the abductee was a small child.

11. Hopkins, *Missing Time*, 39.

12. Ibid., 80, 103, 123, 146.

13. Ibid., 43–44.

14. Ibid., 48, 115.

15. Ibid., 88, 110, 132, 154.

16. Thomas E. Bullard has extensively schematized abduction narratives in his *On Stolen Time: A Summary of a Comparative Study of the UFO Abduction Mystery* (Mount Rainier, Md.: The Fund for UFO Research, 1987). He compiles a list of eight major events that characterize the "ideal," prototypical abduction account. Bullard's approach to the subject differs from mine in that he does not view abduction narratives as a phenomenon evolving in time, but treats all specific details in the same light, regardless of when they appeared. It should also be kept in mind that Bullard's study appeared before Hopkins's second book, Fowler's third and fourth books, or those of David Jacobs and John Mack. See also Bullard's full-length study, *UFO Abductions: The Measure of a Mystery* (Mount Rainier, Md.: The Fund for UFO Research, 1987).

17. Hopkins, *Missing Time*, 49, 65.

18. Ibid., 59.

19. Ibid., 111, 69.

20. Ibid., 72–76.

21. Ibid., 86, 89.

22. Ibid., 96.

23. Ibid., 110–13.

24. Ibid., 141.

25. Ibid., 174.

26. Ibid., 123.

27. This term, borrowed from philosophy, simply says that, among all possible theories offered as explanations for any phenomena, the simplest and least complex one should be preferred.

28. Hopkins, *Missing Time*, 130–35.

29. Ibid., 204.

30. Ibid., 155–67, my emphasis.

31. Ibid., 154–62.

32. Ibid., 143.

33. Ibid., 166–68.

34. Ibid., 170–73.

35. Ibid., 216.

36. Ibid., 231.

37. Ibid., 233–37.

38. Budd Hopkins, *Intruders* (New York: Ballantine, 1987), 31.

39. Ibid., 19; see Hopkins, *Missing Time*, 8, 28.

40. Hopkins, *Intruders*, 15, 39.

41. Ibid., 1.

42. Ibid., 16.

43. Lynn Friedman, *A Woman Doctor's Guide to Miscarriage* (New York: Hyperion, 1996), xi.

44. Ibid., 26, 40.

45. Ibid., 74.

46. Ibid., 101.

47. Ibid., 60–61. This may remind readers once again of Henry James's governess in *The Turn of the Screw*, another person who on at least one occasion "saw" ghosts without the necessity of having actually to open her eyes!

48. Hopkins, *Intruders*, 105.

49. It is interesting to note that at this point in the development of the overall narrative Hopkins can remark with confidence that no female abductee had ever claimed to have had sexual intercourse with an alien; the relationship was effected entirely through alien technological devices. Importantly, in later narratives such as John Mack's, a few women *will* make this astounding claim.

50. Hopkins, *Intruders*, 174.

51. Ibid., 223–24.

52. Ibid., 39, 293.

53. Abduction authors frequently make much of the fact that the description of alien medical procedures as described by many female abductees "anticipates" the laparoscope's use. In fact, the prototype for the modern laparoscope was invented in 1905, and first used in 1914 (the instrument itself had been invented in the nineteenth century). In America, a full-length article on the subject had appeared in the widely circulated *McCall's* magazine as far back as July 1971.

54. Hopkins, *Intruders*, 180.

55. Ibid., 181, my emphasis.

56. Ibid., 15.

57. Ibid., 99.

58. Ibid., 220.

59. Ibid., 164.

60. Ibid., 231, 261.

7

THE ABDUCTIONS OF WHITLEY STRIEBER: *COMMUNION* AND *TRANSFORMATION*

Whitley Strieber's accounts of his abduction experiences are (like Travis Walton's) autobiographical, but they are also unique in being compiled by a professional writer who had begun his career in advertising and had gone on to write several best-selling fantasy and horror novels. In certain respects his professional background was regarded by some with suspicion, for his abduction experiences contain many thematic similarities to his fiction.[1] Strieber's awareness of this is doubtless behind his own dismissal of his fictional works in the opening page of *Communion* (1987) as mere "imaginative thrillers," a comment obviously designed to guard against too much being made of such comparisons. Despite this disclaimer, it is still plain that his professional background and experience as a writer have contributed to the success *Communion* enjoyed, for it is arguably the most sophisticated treatment of the abduction experience encountered to this point in the history of the overall narrative.

Strieber's first recalled experience occurred on December 26, 1985, when he claims to have been taken from his cabin some distance north of New York City and examined by what appeared to be alien beings. Following this, he suffered a number of disconcerting physical symptoms. Thinking he was losing his mind, he sought the help of Budd Hopkins, who recommended hypnosis.

Incidentally, Strieber acknowledges that hypnosis is far from a sure-fire means of uncovering the truth of a person's past, which lends strength to his credibility, especially when we consider the generally uncritical approaches to hypnosis we have already encountered.[2] In the course of these sessions, an earlier experience was recalled from October 1985, and as time went on many other strange experiences that involved various encounters with the beings (whom he calls "visitors"), going back to his childhood, surfaced. One occurred on a train when he was twelve, returning from a vacation with his sister and father. Gaps of time in his past that he had been unable to account for were also recalled, where unusual losses of consciousness, "missing time" experiences, and other strange events also surfaced, all of which he traced to the visitors.

Strieber's autobiographical approach is responsible both for his book's strengths as well as its weaknesses. Unlike Travis Walton, Strieber is scrupulous in restricting himself to a firsthand rendering of his experiences alone. Words are not put in other people's mouths (except when Strieber hears them), and conjecture is restricted to such areas as the meaning of his experiences, precisely at those points where the reader would expect the author to indulge in speculation.

Though an autobiography can convey the impression of immediacy and establish a direct and intimate relationship between author and reader, it also contains its own peculiar limitations, since, as we have already seen, readers may suspect that *all* such writings are ultimately self-serving. What is said in an autobiography—apart from historically verifiable information, of course—is always a bit suspicious, because we have no way of validating anything the autobiographer tells us, at least not without going directly to sources outside the text itself, and this is frequently impossible. In Strieber's case, where the central abduction experiences happen to him alone, we are completely dependent upon how fair he appears in his capacity as autobiographer to all sides of the issue.

In the frontispiece, Strieber acknowledges the "incredible" nature of his story while advising readers not to be too skeptical. Just as Hopkins had hinted in *Missing Time*, he adds darkly that there may be in the reader's past "some lost hour of strange recollection that means you also have had this experience."[3] Strictly speaking, it is hard to avoid acknowledging the connection Strieber has attempted to forge here between author and reader, even though it is actually quite tenuous. He then proceeds to thank numerous members of the scientific community for their help, and in doing so gives the appearance of having obtained their verification without actually receiving it. That none of the scientists mentioned makes a personal statement in support of his conclusions is a fact the author, to his credit, himself points out.

Strieber employs a number of undeniably shrewd strategies in the opening pages of *Communion*. He begins typically enough, first painting himself as an apparently normal and honest man who when the as-yet unmentioned events began to occur was sane enough to wonder initially if he was losing his mind. We are told he and his wife are uncommonly stable, rarely drinking more than wine and never using drugs. In establishing a picture of his own basic normality, Strieber hopes that it will become difficult not to believe in the sanity of a man rational enough to question that sanity, when faced with what the reader knows on some level must be highly unusual events, given the provocative picture of an extraterrestrial being on the book's cover.

Similarly, to claim as he does that the early sections of the book were taken from journal entries written prior to his undergoing hypnosis is misleading, for it implies we are reading an actual day-by-day account, minimally embellished. Strieber is obviously trying to diminish the extent to which the reader will see his book as a crafted work. In fact, the entire book is the product of careful and extensive planning, revising, and editing—as *all* books are—processes that took place long after the initial encounters occurred. Finally, his refusal to summarize any of the events to follow at the outset of *Communion* is itself a shrewd strategy deliberately designed to fill readers with a sense of mystery and foreboding, and recalls John Fuller's method in the opening chapter of *The Interrupted Journey*.

A none-too-subtle denunciation of his potential critics is also included, where such individuals are defined as "vociferous professional debunkers whose secret fears apparently close their minds." Not only are such critics "professional," that is, doing it for money, and thus insincere, but motivated by "secret fears," burdened with neuroses, afraid to confront the unusual, and as such not to be taken seriously. The task of debunking, incidentally, Strieber likens to "laughing at rape victims," thus compounding his indictment of the debunkers' insensitivity.[4]

Like all authors of abduction narratives, Strieber is anxious to impress upon us that unlike his critics, he was free from personal bias or prejudice regarding the subject of UFOs at the time the experiences occurred. Accordingly, throughout *Communion* reference is made to his personal history of past skepticism and indifference to the subject of UFOs and the paranormal in general. He further claims to have "a great deal of trouble with the notions of spaceships and visitors"; acknowledges that a casual look at the preface to the *Condon Report** on UFOs was all that it took to cause him to dismiss the subject entirely; and remembers only vaguely "somebody named Hill" who claimed to have been abducted by aliens years ago.[5]

Yet the facts elsewhere paint a rather different picture of the author's relationship to paranormal activities. The very subject of his fictional work demonstrates more than a passing interest in the occult world, while his self-admitted admiration for the paranormal-debunking *Skeptical Inquirer* is as significant as his reading even the preface to the *Condon Report.*[6] Indeed, evidence rebutting his claim can even be traced back to his earliest childhood, for he recalls as a boy watching *Alfred Hitchcock Presents* and *The Twilight Zone* on television, and telling friends that "spacemen" taught him "how to build an anti-gravity machine."[7] Later, in *Transformation* (1989), he confesses to being remembered by the parents of a friend as a "strange child" who was "always fascinated with the unusual and 'unreal.' "[8]

Indeed, Strieber is manifestly a most unusual human being who lives in an equally unusual world. For one thing, a raw, primordial fear has plagued him throughout his life and has had a

---

*Physicist Edward U. Condon of the University of Colorado headed the group that produced the massive, 1,485-page *Scientific Study of Unidentified Flying Objects* (New York: Bantam, 1969), commissioned by the U.S. Air Force. Although by its own admission as many as 25 percent of the sightings in the study remained unsolved, in his introduction Condon nevertheless concluded that UFOs could be explained in conventional terms and were not worthy of serious scientific attention. See Keith Thompson, *Angels and Aliens* (New York: Fawcett Columbine, 1991), 83–88.

decided influence on him. We see the first inkling of this fear when Strieber tells us of the extensive burglar alarm system he set up in his cabin and the shotgun he kept by his bed. Though he sees these measures as proof of past involvement with the alien visitors that he suppressed from his conscious mind, readers may well wonder why he would ever choose to live in such a remote location if he were so fearful, and, as subsequent events in *Communion* will suggest, are led to suspect psychological reasons rather than cautionary ones. And Strieber's reference to the "horror" he felt when merely seeing a blue light on the ceiling of his cabin earlier that fall might strike some as excessive, and his explanation—that he was "frightened because it wasn't possible for there to be any light there"—somehow insufficient.[9] Although his having "become extremely fearful about living in the New York area" may not be too difficult for readers to accept, when we learn that he was, "if anything, even more fearful in Texas" than in New York, it is harder to see the external environment as a sufficient cause of his fright. Strieber, like Barney Hill, is afraid of virtually everything, from environmental collapse and global annihilation as a result of war to the abduction of his son by the alien visitors; once he even agonized over the possible explosion of the moon![10]

It is interesting that *everyone* connected closely with Strieber is, by his account, also very fearful. Many are, like Strieber, subject to fits of screaming; even the aliens are bothered by his outbursts, and ask him what they could do "to help [him] stop screaming." An early abduction memory (first identified as taking place when on a train as a young boy) contains a vivid and frightening image of his father, less than four feet from Whitley, "just screaming and screaming."[11]

Much later, Strieber claims his wife Anne woke up one morning "screaming and reported that something had poked her in the stomach." A few nights later their son "suddenly began screaming the house down," and will do so again on another occasion.[12] Sometimes, screaming is even heard throughout his neighborhood. In Cos Cob, Connecticut, and some years later, in Provincetown, Massachusetts, they heard "bloodcurdling shrieks coming, it seemed, from above the house."[13]

But for all that, there is evidence that Whitley is the only Strieber to hear these screams. Anne did "not remember screaming when she was awakened by the prodding"; "nothing was ever said by [the Cos Cob] neighbors about the shrieking"; and only one neighbor—who lived a full mile from the Striebers and who was himself an alleged abductee (though no details are provided)—claimed to hear the screaming in Provincetown. Interestingly enough, Anne recalls that it was Whitley and *not* their son who had been screaming the night she was allegedly "poked," and "was terrified by the idea that something could frighten [him] that much."[14] Readers may find that the above scenes have a distinct ring of the melodramatic about them.

Still, Strieber *is* to be commended for his willingness to entertain many possible explanations of what has happened to him. Anticipating that readers may simply not be able to accept that the beings who visit him are real in the usual sense of the word, he goes out of his way not to be too specific regarding his alleged abductors' nature or activities, and this is less easily challenged by the reader. Instead, he terms them "visitors" (rather than "aliens," "UFOnauts," or the like) and he remains vague about their actual nature and place of origin. At the same time, he never allows us the comfortable option of seeing the visitors as merely mental chimera and dismissing them as the stuff of science fiction. In keeping them vague Strieber also makes them more mysterious than, say, Hopkins's more distinctly physical aliens, and more intriguing to the imagination as a result. In fact, although his attitude will undergo numerous changes over the years, throughout *Communion* Strieber remains ambivalent concerning the physical reality of the visitors and distinguishes himself from all other abduction authors by never committing himself to a fixed opinion.[15]

Thus he can speculate that it could be "an essentially mental phenomenon," or "a totally misunderstood *biological* process" emanating from the brain. The visitors could be "a strange form of hysteria" or even the result of "natural electro-magnetic anomalies that trip a certain hallucinatory wire in the mind."[16] One particular encounter could have been nothing more than "an act of the imagination—the act of a mind calling upon itself to provide another argument in favor of this being an experience with an external component," while another could be an attempt by that mind to "create a new deity," just as "we gave" the old gods "to ourselves."[17]

Yet he can state just as earnestly that the visitors "of course . . .

were real [because he] had perceived them," causing him to be "quite certain that the beings [he] saw were not a dream, and probably not a hallucination." In fact, they may have "really, physically arrived sometime in the future, and then spread out across the whole of our history" in order to study us.[18] Late in the book he makes one final attempt to resolve the question by denying the distinction between objective and subjective reality. Just as the ancients realized that "to know the mind is to know the universe," so his visitors may be real, but emanate from a long-forgotten realm of reality that lies within his soul.[19] According to this theory, the visitors are subjective entities that have assumed quasi-material status in order to teach, improve, and eventually transform humankind in part through the use of symbols. Strieber's fence-straddling is most conspicuous in the epilogue, where he states "I do not have it in me to be a believer. Nor can I be a true skeptic."[20] While some readers may well have sympathy with this position, others may suspect that it is another attempt to avoid alienating readers by trying to keep all of them satisfied.

Strieber's Visionary World

Strieber's seemingly honest and forthright attempts to analyze his experiences critically certainly strengthen his claim to be a scrupulous observer. At the same time, the reader should not forget that since Strieber's world purports to be our own, his responses within that world should still be believable and logically in keeping with what we would expect to encounter. Yet this is frequently not the case. For example, in the course of the first hypnosis session a number of incidents come to the surface that are difficult to account for. In the course of one encounter the visitors presumably fill his mind with an image of the world blowing up. Incredibly, Strieber feels "tremendous relief" over being able to bring such a vision to the surface of his mind as a result of being hypnotized, which is not a reaction we would expect of a normal human being made conscious of an alien-induced vision of the end of the world. To his credit he does add that such pictures may have been nothing more than a symbolic vision of his "worst fears" and "deepest secrets," but he does not pursue the possibility that all his experiences might be similarly amenable to a psychological explanation.

In fact, Strieber's actual encounters with his visitors are about as different from previous abduction narratives as they could possibly be. Even the bizarre adventures of Betty Andreasson had a certain temporal and chronological sequence behind them that made some sense within the scenario. In the course of most abductions the abductees are taken aboard some sort of craft, given a medical examination, and eventually returned. Most importantly, events proceed in a linear manner and the abductions usually have a hint of discernible purpose behind them, at least in the form that eventually reaches the reader.

Virtually all of Strieber's encounters seem to be entirely dream-like or surrealistic because their fragmented, discontinuous, and inconclusive nature is unmodified by the kind of temporal logic or continuity we have seen in other abduction experiences. But not only are the abductions themselves without apparent intention, continuity, or purpose (despite Strieber's repeated attempts to find meaning in them); even those events that take place outside the abduction sequences are similarly fantastic in nature. The alleged abduction that took place on the train while he was twelve, for example, is extremely disjointed, containing many memories—the father, close beside him and screaming, but being heard only faintly—that are more reminiscent of a dream or fantasy than a real experience. Similarly, the failure of his alarm system to respond to the intruders also leads us to conclude that nothing of an objective nature was taking place. But these and many other anomalies are as often as not ignored. Strieber claims to be naked when the visitors took him from the cabin in December, but though he has been outdoors in the cold air for an extended period of time, he suffers no physical aftereffects. During the same abduction, he "felt" that he was being carried (would he not *know* this?), but at the same time could not see his carriers. Taken to a place in the woods where, amazingly, there is no snow, he looks around him and is aware of another being's presence; even though the being is "completely invisible," he claims it wore dark blue coveralls.[21] Elsewhere he professes knowledge about his visitors he could not possibly have acquired. Once he sensed that one of the visitors was a "bored or indifferent" female, but he provides no explanation as to how he could ever have reached this conclusion concerning her sex or her emotional state. When the aliens speak, they do not communicate telepathically but rather aurally, in a "subtly electronic tone," the accents "flat and startlingly Midwestern," and they employ colloquialisms like "OK."[22]

Despite *Communion*'s many strengths as a narrative, Strieber has not been able to convey continually a sensation of realism to the reader. For instance, after one of the first encounters he admits waking the following morning feeling distinctly uneasy with a vague sense that something distressing had happened. Though he soon experiences a number of unpleasant and disturbing physical symptoms—alternating chills and fever, fatigue, odd mental sensations, irritability, mood changes, a finger injury that is slow to heal—we are not told if he sought any medical aid for these unusual maladies, even though he was obviously worried about them.

In the course of trying to come to terms with the December 1985 abduction, he begins to recall that during the previous October a number of other strange occurrences also took place at the cabin, when he and his wife were entertaining two friends, the writers Jacques Sandulescu and Annie Gottlieb. As Strieber describes the events, readers will again sense that there is a distinctly unrealistic quality to the behavior of all the participants. For one, Strieber alleges that he observed in the middle of the night a distinct blue light in the cabin which caused him to suspect that the chimney might be on fire.[23] Fair enough. But amazingly, immediately after drawing this conclusion he then fell fast asleep, just as he had during his December encounter.

Upon waking later that night to the sound of a "loud report" like a firecracker—the exact quality of this sound, incidentally, *none* of the four agrees on—he thinks he heard his wife cry out and his son shout. Just at the point when he finally did jump out of bed to alert his friends to what he thought was a continuation of the chimney fire, the light disappeared. Meeting Jacques in the hall, he reassured him that nothing was wrong (unusual in itself) and told him to go back to bed. Oddly enough, both men do return to bed and go back to sleep.

Once Strieber does manage to dredge his friends' memories of the evening to the surface, they are curiously garbled. Although Jacques did see a bright light, he recalled no startling encounter with Strieber in the hall, does not recall getting out of bed, and only remembers hearing Strieber speaking to him from the hall to reassure him that all was well. For her part, Annie initially was of the opinion that Strieber told her that people from a spaceship had come down to visit them. Though she remembered hearing a banging sound, she recalled only "vaguely" the light that was intense enough to wake Jacques out of a presumably sound sleep.[24] Most unusually, the morning after the October occurrence "little was said about the incident" by any of the four, suggesting nothing had happened in the first place.[25]

On another occasion, Strieber has a nighttime encounter with several of his otherworldly visitors (one of whom is improbably wearing an archaic three-piece suit made of cardboard, of all things), and is overcome with a "terror so fierce and physical" that his skin tingles. Though paralyzed, he tries to communicate with them, but can only muster a smile, whereupon they enigmatically vanish. Just as improbably, the following morning, though drained, he eats a "beautiful breakfast" before telling his wife, who "laughed merrily" at his description of the suit. Some time later, he experiences the sensation of flying about his bedroom. When he tells his wife, she "just laughed and continued to act as if everything were normal," a response Strieber incredibly finds "enormously reassuring."[26] All of this cannot help but detract from the book's pretensions to realism, to say nothing of Strieber's own claims to normality. Wives do not normally "laugh merrily" when told that their quarters have been invaded by alien beings, and happily married men do not normally keep such events from their wives if they indeed believe these experiences are occurring.

Past Encounters with the Visitors

Early in *Communion* Strieber revealed his familiarity with the notion of the screen memory—a pseudoevent created to shield an individual from a particularly traumatic occurrence. When Strieber had a memory of seeing an "owl" one night, it could, he reasons, be a screen memory hiding an encounter with one of his visitors. But like other abduction authors, at no point does Strieber examine the possibility that his encounters with the visitors could themselves be screen memories erected to shield him from even more painful memories of physical or sexual abuse by human beings. That he does not do so is strange since there is an unmistakable sexual theme running throughout his abduction experiences, many of the aliens' actions appearing consistent with those many would associate with a sexual abuser.

For example, in one hypnotic recall of the December encounter we learn that at least one visitor showed a marked interest in his penis, asking him at one point if this was "as hard as [he] could get?"[27] The reader will see immediately that this is an utterly absurd question for an alien being to put to a terrestrial one, since if they reproduce as we do they would understand the function of his penis, and if they do not, the very notion of degrees of penile hardness would be of little interest to them. Both the "love" Strieber confesses for one of his captors, and a simultaneous feeling he has of "deepest suspicion" of them—to say nothing of the admission that he even felt a kind of "sexual arousal" for one of them—make a good deal of sense if they are symbolically detached memories of a forgotten experience with a human abuser.[28] Hints of sexual abuse are also seen in the aliens' desire to put something in his mouth, and later when they insert an anal probe in his rectum. But such behavior is extremely difficult to comprehend as the actions of alien beings. As a screen memory his ambivalence toward them becomes more intelligible as well, for the affection he speaks of *is* consistent with the mixed emotions victims of sexual abuse are said to feel for a relative or family friend who abuses them.

Strieber's purpose in reviewing his past is ostensibly to show us that he likely had experiences with the visitors many years before his fateful encounter at Christmas 1985. But it becomes increasingly difficult not to question his stability. For one thing, we learn that he has experienced periods of missing time and has a number of pseudomemories of being in certain places that he knows full well he never visited. In addition to the strange situation that occurred on the train in 1957, he also recalls a period of four to six weeks in 1968 of which he claims to have absolutely no memory, even though he knows he was supposed to be traveling extensively throughout Europe at the time. Though he has a memory of being present at the University of Texas in 1966 when

Charles Whitman went on his infamous shooting spree from the clock tower, another part of him is sure he was not then on campus.[29] In all likelihood, Strieber's mind may have attempted to distance himself from the horror of such an occurrence by causing him to believe that he had not been present. Significantly enough, he makes no attempt to articulate this possibility.

Frankly, many recollections sound like nothing more than remembered nightmares. He recalls a time, for instance, when he was once frightened as a child by an appearance of a living, life-sized "Mr. Peanut" (the animated character used to advertise Planter's nuts), even though he realizes he never saw such a creature. Other "memories" are recovered of his flying with some people over the roofs of his neighborhood on a "thing like a rubber raft," and waking to find twigs in his bed; or of seeing demon-faced beings peering through the windows of his car at night. He recalls a period in 1967, when as a student in his apartment he experienced a number of blackouts several hours in duration. Significantly, despite periods of "complete perceptual chaos," he claims "There is no evidence that I suffer from any malfunction of the brain," although there is no evidence that he sought any form of medical help or professional consultation at that time which could have confirmed this statement.[30]

For that matter, throughout *Communion* Strieber gives the impression of being quite contemptuous of medical explanations, commenting on his experiences, "There are certainly many odd [sic] incidents, *but they are too variable in their nature to suggest the symptomatic consistency of disease.*"[31] He gives virtually no weight to the more conventional neurological explanations of the abduction phenomenon. This decision to ignore such possibilities may well be prompted by a desire to heighten the mystery of what was happening to him and make his book more compelling reading, but it does his cause little service. It is not enough simply to inform the reader flatly that he was not in a "hypnopompic" (waking dream) state when he first saw the visitors without providing proof; or merely to tell us that the more he studied temporal lobe disorder—an explanation frequently offered by psychiatrists and others as a possible cause of the abduction experience—"the less it seemed an answer" to him.[32] Interestingly enough, the most striking characteristic of hypnopompia is that people who suffer from this condition have great difficulty distinguishing their mental experiences from reality, and temporal lobe epilepsy (as Strieber himself states elsewhere in *Communion*) is notoriously hard to diagnose. Finally, in *Transformation* he even concedes that he is tested regularly for the condition, rendering his dismissal of it here suspect.

Just as he can dismiss what many would consider indications of a serious neurological abnormality, so he can also see a great deal of importance in events that readers will consider easily amenable to more prosaic explanations. One June night in 1978 while living with his wife in New York, we are told dramatically that "something terrible happened," but without revealing precisely just what the terrible "something" was. First Strieber vaguely claims to have received "a phone call followed by a menacing visit," then says he also remembers a series of "menacing phone calls." Though the police dismissed these events as nothing serious, Strieber still maintains that "it has always seemed to me that there was more to it than that."[33] On another occasion, he tells us of a mysterious voice which began one evening to speak to him through his stereo. While this event could have been nothing more than the freak pickup by the stereo of a passing taxi radio or C.B. radio transmission, Strieber claims the voice "held a brief conversation with us [Strieber and his wife]."[34]

Nor is the reader's respect for Strieber's cogency or normality enhanced by his admission that he and his wife were close to separation or divorce—"She really thought that she might have to leave"—because of his behavior. Indeed, one of the book's weakest sections concerns Strieber's attempt to find support for his experiences through the hypnotic recollections of his wife, Anne. For her part, when hypnotized, Anne confuses the October with the December evenings and, repeating as she does the phrase "I don't remember" many times, is obviously vague on a number of details. Furthermore, as we have seen, she even contradicts many of Strieber's claims. As we would expect, this vagueness Strieber attributes to her probably having been told by the visitors "in the strongest terms" to forget such details, but of course there is no support for this contention.[35]

Understandably enough, Strieber makes much of Anne's final words while under hypnosis, that "Whitley's supposed to go. They [presumably the aliens] came for Whitley." But despite its apparent significance, her comment is made in response to one of Budd Hop-kins's more leading questions, wherein he instructed her to "have a little dream. A fantasy."[36] Such an obvious invitation to fantasize renders anything she might say in reply of dubious value.

Communion's Contribution to the Narrative

As would be expected, Strieber's experiences contain many ele-ments found in earlier narratives. The aliens' large black eyes have been seen elsewhere, as have their three-fingered hands. But for all the supernatural powers they possess, Strieber's visitors also still need to open doors (at least on some occasions) and they seem to be gendered as we are, for Strieber had "the distinct feeling" that one of them was female. Furthermore, at least one of them has no trouble understanding the aging process, for she tells Strieber she is old. Strieber's feeling of being in a position similar to that of a guinea pig, in a trap and "absolutely helpless" is, of course, by now almost an inevitable component of the abduction scenario. The lenslike object Strieber sees in the ceiling of the examining room has also been pre-viously encountered. While the explicit use of an anal probe is a more prominent part of the experiments he is subjected to (Steven Kilburn, it will be recalled, endured only "poking" in the general region of his back), the insertion of needles into various parts of the body is typical of many earlier abductions. Strieber's memory of seeing the owl after the December abduction recalls Virginia Horton's sighting of the deer in France, and the visions of world cat-astrophe recall the vague feeling of Laura Davis (Kathie's sister from *Intruders*) that the future will only be for the young and the strong.[37] Finally, although the visitors occasionally talk to him, they are far from loquacious and only rarely provide answers to his questions.

For all the weaknesses the reader can see in Strieber's abduction accounts as purported realistic documents, as creative narratives his experiences are replete with new and innovative details. Though his descriptions tend to be quite vague, Strieber distinguishes *four* spe-cific types of alien being: small robotlike creatures; short, stocky ones with wide faces and pug noses; slender and delicate black-eyed beings about five feet tall; and slightly shorter ones with round, rather than slanted, eyes. Admittedly, some of the particulars associated with Strieber's aliens do seem quirky or without evident purpose. The visitors' sartorial preferences, for instance, are as bizarre as anything previously encountered. A typical Strieber alien can wear everything from coveralls to smooth rounded hats with a brim; some kind of breastplate or armored vest; a sandwich board; or (as we saw earlier) an imitation three-piece suit, complete with handkerchief in breast pocket, but made of cardboard! Interestingly enough, when these bizarre features are viewed symbolically as part of a mythic narrative, such details do make a kind of sense, as a way of presenting the technologically sophisticated but foolish-looking and absurdly behaving aliens as distorted reflections of ourselves, grotesque imitations of what it means to be truly human.

Strieber is also the first to suggest in this regard that on the basis of their large black eyes and stiff, rapid movements, the aliens may be a species of highly evolved "hive" insect whose members possess a communal mind, void of individuality. He came to this conclusion when observing that they moved "as if every action on the part of each independent being were decided elsewhere and then transmitted to the individual."[38] Indeed, Strieber states late in the book that "our civilization is not paying enough attention to what may be the central archetypal and mythological experience of the age." His own accompanying sense that they were fearful of us—possibly because of our unpredictable (but to them fascinating) individuality—is another new element also relevant to the mythic theme. The aliens' fear of us leads to Strieber's later claim that abductees "have all been chosen —and we are all being tamed."[39]

Other alleged abductees had been in awe of their abductors, but prior to *Communion* there had been no suggestion that abductees' relationships with the aliens was multifaceted, or anything but one-sided; even Betty Andreasson's aliens, though they told her she was "special," treated her much as a team of human researchers might a chimpanzee they had earmarked for special instruction. Although Strieber's sexual arousal recalls the Villas-Boas abduction (see chapter 2), his sense that at least one of the beings knew "every vulnerable detail of [his] self" is a new development, and will be encountered more frequently in later narratives, especially in David Jacobs's *Secret Life.*[40]

New Developments

Another very important and interesting new development in the
myth is the sense that abductees' personalities and identities were
altered in the course of their alien encounters. Prior to *Communion*,
most abductees emerged badly shaken but otherwise unchanged.
They were not demonstrably the better for their experiences, and a
sense that they were regarded as special by their abductors was
only felt "occasionally." But Strieber emphasizes how in his own
situation extreme fear produced by the abduction resulted in significant physical and psychological changes within him, to the
point where he does "not think that [his] ordinary humanity survived the transition."[41] Nor was this purely a negative experience.
In the sequel to *Communion* Strieber will argue that his "transformation" comprised a major part of the visitors' overall purpose in
being here, and that the abductions may have been designed (at
least in part) to push specifically chosen abductees in the direction
of spiritual and intellectual growth. When, during the course of one
encounter, an alien touched Strieber on the forehead with a small
wand and produced those vivid mental images which he suspected
were dramatizations of his worst fears, he wondered if he were
being given, in a manner that recalls the benevolent aliens of the
1950s, "a potential that could greatly enrich [his] life" by providing
him in some way with the means of overcoming these fears.[42]

Just why he should have been picked is never made clear, but
the visitors tell him, as they did Betty Andreasson, "You are our
chosen one." Initially, Strieber rejects this claim, concluding it is "just
bullshit," but he later comes to accept it, seeing himself as "an emissary of sorts."[43] This notion that abductees are almost to be envied
for the glimpses they have had into another world is articulated by
a university teacher named "Tom" who attended one of Hopkins's
support groups, though he had not himself been abducted.

Basically, Strieber sees the visitors trying to communicate with a
select number of human beings, largely through the use of symbols
such as the triangle. As he sees it, the visitors often appear in groups
of three and wear emblems and insignia in the shape of a triangle,
or even take triangular-shaped skin samples, as they did with him.
While this is all quite ingenious, Strieber's concentration on these
symbols seems arbitrary. Many might be more inclined to see the

circle/mandala or even the phallus as more apt symbols to concentrate on, in that they appear just as central to the alien abduction experience. For that matter, Strieber's claim that the visitors travel in groups of three is not supported even by his own experience. As the reader will recall, he distinguished *four* types of alien being, and was quite vague when it came down to the actual numbers of visitors present in any given abduction. In fact, only once did three beings come to him, and even then they were immediately joined by a fourth (the one who wore the cardboard suit). Despite Strieber's claims, only three members of Hopkins's support group explicitly referred to triangles. Under hypnosis he recalled not only having had a triangular piece of skin taken from his arm, but also seeing circles and squares as well as what he was shown by his captors.

In his lengthy examination of these symbols' significance, Strieber sees the triad representing a harmonic convergence of mind, body, and heart. When humans are seen in relation to the visitors, our coming together with them "may mean the creation of a third and greater form which will supplant us as the child does his parents." While this all may make sense when viewed as a discussion of the triad's symbolic significance, readers may well see that his very argument damages the extraterrestrial hypothesis, precisely because such symbols are at once so human and so central to a Christian iconography.[44]

But more importantly, there is no more evidence that the imprinting of such symbols on our bodies represents an alien attempt at communication than there is justification in seeing an attempt to communicate by a hornet in the circular welt left on our skin after we have been stung. It is also difficult for readers not to wonder why the visitors could not have devised a less enigmatic and more direct mode of communication, if their purpose is truly our edification.

Yet again, Strieber's attempts to see in the visitors a kind of love or concern for our welfare ignores that there is not much love visible in alien behavior. Indeed, if their typical treatment of us tells us anything it is that they have little or no idea of our sense of love or compassion. In the support group, for all Strieber's inner assurance, he finds little confirmation; some simply feel used and violated, and at least one expressed considerable anger over alien insensitivity to human needs, an anger which recalls Kathie Davis's rage when the aliens allegedly took a hybrid child from her.

Strieber has a good deal of trouble trying to square this kind of alien behavior with his belief that they are a higher and more spiritual form of being, and can only argue weakly (as John Mack will later) that a process may be at work whereby somehow all the pain and discomfort abductees are put through is for a good purpose. By this reasoning, a new and presumably better human being will emerge as a consequence of having been subjected to all the experimentation and other strange experiences initiated by the aliens. Here readers may simply conclude that Strieber is grasping at straws.

Most significant, of course, is the relationship of Strieber's theory to his own Catholic background, a relationship which, to his credit, he himself acknowledges. Just as the Pentecostal Betty Andreasson spoke in tongues and received homely platitudes from her abductors that she could easily have heard every Sunday, the more sophisticated Catholic Whitley Strieber conveys his experiences in discourse unmistakably evocative of one of the most fundamental tenets of *his* faith, the central importance of the communion service as a means of attaining spiritual transformation. After all is said and done, Strieber's aliens are not much different from interstellar priests who give us the opportunity to partake of their message. Out of our communion with the visitors, so goes the argument, will come our transformation.

That he may have come to some understanding of his own fears as a result of his experiences can be granted, and the reader can also accept his word that he is "no longer terrified" of everything under the sun.[45] But to expand this personal history of psychological development into a full-scale theory involving the entire human race will strike many readers as extravagant and baseless. For every Betty Andreasson (who also saw herself as "chosen"), the vast majority appear to remain angry and frightened individuals who have no idea of the meaning or purpose behind their experiences.

Transformation

It is not surprising that *Communion* had such a significant influence on later abduction accounts. Largely because of Strieber, the symbolic and spiritual implications of the proceedings become more prominent, and this prominence represents a major development in the evolution of the narrative. Basically, the sequel, *Transformation*, continues the chronicle of Strieber's attempts to come to terms with and eventually overcome his most primitive night fears. In *Transformation*, the fears are again manifested in the form of alien visitors whom he gradually summons sufficient courage to confront by leaving his cabin one night and venturing into the woods. But in spite of his repeated attempts to convince us that there is an objective reality to the visitors, many readers will interpret them as they did before: as psychological rather than extraterrestrial in origin.

At first glance, it might seem odd that Strieber should appear to reverse himself in *Transformation* concerning the physical reality of the visitors. Because nothing occurs in *Transformation* that is qualitatively distinct from the experiences reported in *Communion* —if anything, the encounters in the sequel are even *more* dream-like—it is difficult to see why he would be led to state at the outset that the "visitors are a genuine unknown and not an outcome of hallucination or mental illness."[46] However, with fear a major theme of this work it is not surprising that Strieber should make so much of the visitors' actual existence in order that he avoid having to face the likelihood that he *was* losing his mind, by his own admission one of his deepest ongoing concerns.

Attempting to give his fear a tangible basis in the outside world, Strieber mentions that when he was young he had considerable anxiety over being kidnapped by spacemen (and in the process of this admission, he contradicts *Communion*'s claim that he knew almost nothing about UFOs, for he reveals here that he had written the National Investigations Committee on Aerial Phenomena [NICAP] when he and a friend saw a UFO). Adding that since this anxiety predated "by a number of years any *mention* of such a possibility in media that would have been available to me," he suggests that this provides strong evidence that his fear of extraterrestrial abductors must have had an objective basis in fact. But Strieber pointedly ignores the proliferation of science fiction in theaters and television throughout that decade, many of which featured abduction-type themes and to which he could have been exposed, if only indirectly.[47] Though Strieber evidently hopes that we will see his youthful preoccupation with spacemen as evidence that he had actual contact with aliens, many readers may simply see it as proof of how active his imagination has always been, to say nothing of how easily the imagination is stimulated by contemporary popular culture. His own suggestion that there was "an entirely real experience" which he and his friends interpreted "through the science-fiction mythology that was available to us," while again ingenious, seems to be a needless reversal of cause and effect.[48] It is far easier to surmise that Strieber appropriated the science fiction icons of popular culture as a means of providing himself with a vehicle whereby he could give vent to his inner fears.

Another weakness in *Transformation* stems from Strieber's claim that "many witnesses" have corroborated his experiences. In fact, such corroboration is rarely forthcoming, or it is so far-fetched as to create the opposite impression in the reader. For example, in an attempt to validate the encounter of December 26, 1985, he tells us that an anonymous individual saw a UFO within two miles of Strieber's cabin on January 1, 1986, a full week after his own abduction. Although this gives the reader nothing by way of actual verification, Strieber makes much of it, arguing that it "suggested a presence during the same week."[49] Elsewhere he refers to an unnamed "French woman" who, like him, also had a bitter taste in her mouth following an abduction. As before, no corroborating documentation is provided, and it does not help to be told that the anonymous woman's experience occurred in 1950. As if this weren't enough, late in the book he begins to speak of having recently acquired the ability to attain out-of-body experiences and in this state travel to remote locations. At one point he even claims, again without corroboration, that he traveled astrally* one night to the home of a female friend where he implanted her with information while she slept, a fact she allegedly confirmed the following day. Also late in the book Strieber describes Mr. Bruce Lee, a senior editor for his publisher, encountering in a bookstore two strange-looking individuals in the act of appraising *Communion*, while reading it "at a remarkable rate." The individuals were short and wore clothing that hid their faces, and dark glasses which covered their "large, black, almond-shaped eyes." When asked by the editor

---

*Astral travel purportedly involves the separation of a human being's conscious self from his or her physical body, allowing the self to travel to remote locations.

what they thought of the book, they glared at him in a malevolent manner he found frightening, at which point he moved away. Yet again, there is no corroboration from Mr. Lee himself.[50]

Time and again Strieber tries to force readers into the position of seeing the reality of the visitors as the only conceivable explanation, by showing how his many attempts to dismiss them as a psychological phenomenon invariably fail. Seeing some visitors on April 1, he "entertained the notion" that his unconscious had "played some sort of April Fool's joke" on him, but this idea proves impossible to maintain. Elsewhere he tells us that, although "halfway convinced" that his visitors may be nothing more than a "self-generated attempt to escape from the pressure" of modern life, try as he might to hold to this possibility, "that [opinion] was changing." When the visitors induce in him a vivid image of the exploding moon, he tries to believe it is just a vivid nightmare, but realizes inwardly "that [the nightmare explanation] wasn't the answer, and I knew it perfectly well."[51] All other explanations, so it seems, are simply the product of rationalizing on his part, but as to why such alternate possibilities should be dismissed, no particular reasons are given.

Strieber, in fact, may be so insistent because the dreamlike, inconclusive qualities we observed in the *Communion* encounters are more obvious here. His reactions to these strange events are even harder to accept at face value than they were in the previous volume. The first such experience details events of April 2, 1986, when Strieber awoke at 3:15 A.M. in his cabin to find his son Andrew missing from his bed. We are given no explanation as to why he would have taken his son to the cabin or why he himself would be there in the first place, given the events of the previous fall and winter. Behavior such as this will strike readers as especially peculiar when they recall the number of times in *Communion* Strieber acknowledged his fear that the visitors might decide to abduct the little boy.

Searching the cabin in vain, Strieber goes outside to see if Andrew had gone to spend the night in a tent Strieber had set up for him near the cabin (again, a strange thing to do given the circumstances). Once outside, he sees a large amorphous shape in the sky which hides the stars (a cloud?), and hears a voice which asks him if he requires help in going back "upstairs." A number of other bizarre things occur, following which Strieber decides inexplicably that he has only "two options: I could either turn around and walk back to the house, retaining some shred of dignity [where this dignity has been lost is not specified], or do what I felt like doing and just fall down right there on the ground."[52] It will probably come as no surprise to the reader when told that Strieber *did* return to his bed—some will doubtless wonder if he ever left it—and woke the following morning, to be greeted by his son. But it remains that he neither determined his son's whereabouts that night nor did he ask the boy the next morning if he had gone outside, which he could easily have done without upsetting him. Even more incredibly, he said nothing to his wife about their only child's disappearance either at the time the boy went missing or afterwards, even though he admits he doubted if he "would ever see [his] son again."[53] Nor is Strieber's implicit assumption that the visitors "put" him to sleep very believable, because it does not explain why they did not simply put him to sleep earlier and keep knowledge of his son's abduction completely from him.

The next day, when his son makes some precocious comments about God, Strieber is sure the comments could only have been extraterrestrially inspired, and subsequently takes him to be examined by a psychologist. Many readers, as parents themselves, will realize that precocious children are constantly amazing adults with the sophistication of their observations, and will not be as surprised by Andrew's comments as Strieber was, for there is really nothing that must be ascribed to paranormal origin in the boy's words. Further, the extent of Andrew's knowledge of what his father has been going through is as open to question as it was in *Communion*.

Readers familiar with the sensitivity of children to adult conversation will respond with skepticism when assured by Strieber that he could keep such information successfully from his son, living as they do in such close proximity to each other in an apartment and a cabin. Also, it would be difficult for a young boy not to be upset by a father who admitted in *Communion* that his personality "deteriorated" during this period; his melodramatic behavior would not be conducive to a child's equanimity, and Strieber's boast of his son's "nonchalance" is not easily sustained.

Numerous other unrealistic aspects can be found throughout

Transformation. At times, the visitors sound more like personifications of Strieber's conscience than anything else, catching him when he makes arrogant or grandiose statements and deflating him accordingly. Whatever their role, the encounters detailed in this sequel contain features that are the least realistic of all abduction narratives, which may explain why so few of them resurface in subsequent accounts. In one abduction Strieber is escorted to a room by two blue-colored beings, who, in response to Strieber's exclamation of surprise that they should be this color, tell him they "used to be like your blacks but we decided this was better." The blue beings lead him to a room full of aliens "as white as sheets" who wear clothes reminiscent of the days of the British raj; their evident leader asks him to explain, of all things, the collapse of the British Empire! After Strieber delivers the requested address, they mock him for his intellectual presumption. Later he is shown stacks of bodies "all encased in what looked like cellophane," which Strieber interprets as the beginning of a long process of "freeing [him] from fear of death," although just how such a display would have this effect he does not make clear. In support of his claim that the experience actually occurred, he cites ironically an apparent similarity he found between his experience and a fairy tale: Both he and the character in the tale wore garments of white paper![54]

Such scenes dominate *Transformation* and may well cause readers to conclude that they are witnessing neither tragedy nor epic, but comedy and farce. In one exchange the visitors warn him that his metabolism has been changed and if he continues to eat chocolate he will die. He is also told that he will die if he takes one of two possible airplane journeys to visit his mother. Significantly, he takes neither warning to heart. As luck would have it, Strieber arrives from both trips unscathed.

When he finally does respond to warnings, it is in response to an event most readers would dismiss as sheer coincidence. An elderly woman named Mrs. Sharp (the mother of an old friend) was dying of liver cancer *and*, of all things, diabetes. Shortly before her death she spoke of being lifted up to the ceiling by "little men," a story that came to Strieber's attention. Incredibly enough, he saw great significance in this, recognizing in the old lady's obvious hallucination yet another personal warning engineered by the visitors on his behalf.

If the above stories were difficult to accept, the author describes in some detail an event that occurred when he was *two*, which involved his perceiving what appeared to be "a group of big gray monkeys," behind which was "a huge disk in the afternoon sky."[55] But the greatest strain of all on the reader follows from Strieber's reading great significance into a time when he saw "black sedans" racing down the street after having witnessed "fireballs" in the sky.

In fairness, occasionally Strieber himself seems aware of how unrealistic his abduction experiences are. In an attempt to see if the notion of alien abduction made any sense whatever, he once asked a medical doctor to construct a hypothetical scenario that involved a large-scale abduction of human beings for purposes of biological and genetic research, but based on our present level of technology. The doctor concluded that it could be successfully completed over a period not greater than six months, would require only a few thousand subjects, and could be accomplished without leaving physical scars or even any memories of the experiences in the abductees' minds. Yet Strieber refrains from drawing the most obvious inference from the doctor's conclusions, preferring to speculate that the visitors must be choosing to be absurdly inefficient for some arcane reason known only to themselves.

Given Strieber's contention that the visitors' objective is to enable him to overcome his fears, he makes a good deal of his numerous attempts to muster sufficient courage to go into the night and face them directly. However, it is hard not to see that he is simply conjuring up otherworldly adversaries in order to experience the illusion of triumphing over them. There is also a distinctly histrionic note about Strieber's melodramatic fear—so obviously borrowed from his own novel *The Hunger*—that "perhaps they would kill [him] and eat [his] soul."[56] And his belief that mysterious knocking sounds can only be explained as something done by the "visitors" will likely leave the reader (seeing shades of the seance room) recoiling in disbelief at such a clumsy and preposterous method to establish their presence.

Furthermore, in acknowledging that the visitors were never encountered on that fateful evening when he ventured out to confront them in the woods, he once again unwittingly opens the door to a psychological explanation of his fear. Simply put, since *no aliens were present*, aliens have obviously not caused his fear. Once this is acknowledged the possibility also presents itself that Strieber's construction of the entire series of abduction events may be in reverse order: that is to say, the abducting visitors have never been the cause of his fears, but instead, his fears have produced the images of abducting visitors. His visitors are not really *relevant* to his narrative; on the contrary, they appear to be tacked on to the fabric of his story rather than fundamental to it.

The final experience with the visitors occurs just before Christmas 1986, and is undeniably the most dreamlike and fantastic of all. Here, Strieber even brings his cat along, an act presumably motivated by the same spirit that causes people to pinch themselves to make sure they are not dreaming. As before, very little occurs in the course of his meeting with the visitors, and it ends abruptly.

The book closes with the author moving beyond the traditional boundaries associated with the abduction phenomenon to provide us with fairly detailed descriptions of his out-of-body experiences, supposedly prompted by the visitors. As we have already seen, the effect of such a shift in emphasis is to move the abduction phenomenon increasingly in the direction of occult and New Age activity. Perhaps aware that he is straining the reader's credulity, he closes both books with reminders that he passed polygraph tests, and that even the skeptical Philip Klass does not believe that he is deliberately lying![57]

The final section of *Transformation* is quite preachy and sententious, as Strieber admonishes us to stop denying our relationship with the alternate level of reality the visitors embody. Obviously, this comment is valid enough, at least to the extent that it invites us to pay more attention to the world of the imagination and the symbols produced by it. As he says, ours *is* undoubtedly a limited and rigidly rationalistic age. If anything, his self-styled role of shaman is more obvious in *Transformation*, for by calling his experiences "visions," he of course becomes a visionary like Joan of Arc or "the shamanic aspirants of old"; plainly he sees himself in pretty exalted company.

As an element in the overall narrative, this is not new, for Betty Andreasson also saw herself in this way, but Strieber is giving it greater emphasis, and as we will see it will take on increased prominence with the passage of time. It also represents an ingenious way around the objections that abductions could not be happening literally as described. Labeling them "visions" was a means of salvaging meaning and significance both for the experience and the alleged abductee, while simultaneously acknowledging the validity of the critics' arguments. As subsequent chapters will illustrate, this will prove to be a most successful development in the narrative and one that becomes increasingly prominent in the accounts of Jacobs, Mack, and the freshly returned Raymond Fowler.

Notes

1. At one point in *Communion: A True Story* (New York: Avon, 1987, 1988) Strieber wonders if there is "another species living upon this earth, the fairies, the gnomes, the sylphs, *vampires*, goblins . . ." (251). In his *Transformation: The Breakthrough* (New York: Avon, 1988; 1989), he admits he "could not shake the idea of the [aliens as] soul predator[s]" (184), and experiences terrible fear that they "were going to eat our souls" (232). Readers will immediately see a striking parallel with Miriam Blaylock of Strieber's vampire novel *The Hunger* (New York: William Morrow, 1981), "who drank blood, and extracted from it the stuff of souls" (127); or with his *The Wolfen* (New York: William Morrow, 1978), which dealt with supernatural beings older than humankind that coexist with us.

2. See Strieber, *Communion*, 49. It is interesting to note that, while in *Communion* Strieber is labeled an "excellent" hypnotic subject, by *Transformation* hypnosis has been discarded as an investigative tool.

3. Strieber, *Communion*, i.

4. Ibid., 4.

5. Ibid., 42, 141.

6. See ibid., 30. At one point, Strieber comments of Philip Klass that he "writes for a publication I have admired, *The Skeptical Inquirer*."

7. Ibid., 112.

8. Strieber, *Transformation*, 99.

9. Strieber, *Communion*, 35.

10. Ibid., 41, 88, 51ff.

11. Ibid., 19, 83.

12. Ibid., 139–40.

13. Ibid., 138.

14. Ibid., 138, 200–201.

15. Interestingly enough, in *Transformation* Strieber appears far more certain of the visitors' physical reality, stating on numerous occasions

"that something entirely and physically real was present" (132), even though the experiences outlined in this sequel are very vague, dreamlike, and inconclusive. Strieber's position was to change again still later, in the foreword to Kenneth Ring's *The Omega Project* (New York: William Morrow, 1992). There, he expresses the opinion "that the experience represents a response to some natural phenomenon, probably of an electromagnetic nature, and that the forms it takes depend on the enculturation of the *affected* individuals" (17, my emphasis). Still later, in his most recent abduction book, *Breakthrough* (New York: HarperCollins, 1995), he seems to have returned to a belief that the visitors are real after all!

16. Strieber, *Communion*, 50, 70, 95, 226.

17. Ibid., 164–66, 210, 258.

18. Ibid., 92, 173, 228–29.

19. Ibid., 292.

20. Ibid., 294.

21. Ibid., 15.

22. Ibid., 19.

23. Strieber concludes that the light he saw could not have been the moon, and mentions that on the morning of October 4 the waning moon, "past the half," rose about 10:30 P.M. and "set in the pre-dawn hours" (187). But he forgets that this is impossible behavior for a waning moon at this stage of its cycle, which would rise late in the evening as he says, but still be in the sky in the morning. Errors like this are far from inconsequential. Here, in his zeal to establish that no natural source of light could be present in the sky that might account for the glow he observed in the cabin, Strieber removes from the sky a moon that *was* in fact there all night, just as Betty Hill ignored the presence of *two* planets near the moon on the night of her fateful encounter.

24. Incidentally, Strieber's claim that the moon was too low to have caused the light ("well below the line of the forest" [39]) is also incorrect. That night (the early morning of October 5), the moon was high in the sky in the constellation of Taurus.

25. Strieber, *Communion*, 36.

26. Ibid., 215.

27. Ibid., 77.

28. Ibid., 99. Elsewhere he claims that he "might [be able to] love this being" as he could his own "anima" (100). This possibly fruitful psychological line of inquiry is not pursued.

29. In *Transformation*, this incident at least is partly resolved, in that he realizes he *was* on campus during the shootings after all.

30. Strieber, *Communion*, 131–34.

31. Ibid., 136, my emphasis.

32. Ibid., 125.

33. Ibid., 137.

34. Ibid., 136.

35. Ibid., 181.

36. Ibid., 208, 192.

37. Here it should be noted that Kathie Davis is obviously present at the support group chaired by Hopkins that Strieber attended, for her sister's vague premonition is quoted precisely (268) by "Mary," one of the participants.

38. Strieber, *Communion*, 142.

39. Ibid., 245, 104. Other abductees make the same point concerning their fear of us, in the course of a conversation that took place during a meeting of Budd Hopkins's support group for abductees that Strieber attended, parts of which are reproduced in *Communion*, 255ff.

40. Ibid., 101. Strieber's experiencing "a sort of love" for the aliens expands comments made by Betty Andreasson, the Tujunga abductees, and even Travis Walton, all of whom felt a personal component in their relationship with the abductors.

41. Ibid., 16.

42. Ibid., 68.

43. Ibid., 76–79, 173.

44. Ibid., 283. For an examination of the significance of the number three and the triangle, see David Fontana, *The Secret Language of Symbols* (San Francisco: Chronicle Books, 1993), 54–55, 64. Fontana shows that both symbols, while not peculiar to Christianity, have been used to suggest the notion of the Trinity by Christians throughout history.

45. Strieber, *Communion*, 144.

46. Strieber, *Transformation*, ix.

47. Ibid., 98. Even a cursory look at the science fiction films of the 1950s reveals that many of Strieber's fears had been reproduced cinematically during his formative years. The following sample, for example, all dealt with the utilization of human beings by aliens for genetic, reproductive, or other purposes, and were widely distributed throughout America: *Invaders from Mars* (1953), *It Came from Outer Space* (1953), *Killers from Space* (1954), *This Island Earth* (1955), *Not of this Earth* (1957), and *I Married a Monster from Outer Space* (1958). In addition, popular television series such as *Science-Fiction Theater* routinely featured stories of this nature. Strieber had in *Communion* admitted to watching *Alfred Hitchcock Presents* and *The Twilight Zone*, and he could easily have been acquainted with *The Outer Limits*, which was an extremely popular television series throughout America in 1963–64. Of course, the influence of such material on other abductees is also a distinct possibility.

48. Strieber, *Transformation*, 95.
49. Ibid., 228.
50. Ibid., 236. How Mr. Lee was able to discern the color of their eyes through the dark glasses is not explained.
51. Ibid., 23–24, 51.
52. Ibid., 10.
53. Ibid.
54. Ibid., 26–31.
55. Ibid., 91.
56. Ibid., 126.
57. Ibid., 267.

8

THE RETURN OF RAYMOND FOWLER:
THE WATCHERS AND THE ALLAGASH ABDUCTIONS

It was no accident that Whitley Strieber was commissioned to write the foreword to Raymond Fowler's *The Watchers* (1990), yet another episode in the life of the repeatedly abducted Betty Andreasson Luca.[1] As the world's most famous abductee at the time, Strieber was in an excellent position to pronounce on other abductees' experiences and give them a stamp of approval they might not otherwise have received, although the use of Strieber's imprimatur is fraught with risk as well. If readers of *Communion* were *not* convinced by Strieber's bizarre story, then the events portrayed in *The Watchers* might well be regarded with even greater skepticism than would otherwise be the case.

Not surprisingly, Strieber's very flattering foreword to *The Watchers* says everything one would expect it to say: Betty's honesty and integrity are lauded and Fowler's credentials and approach to his subject praised. He also oversimplifies previous accounts of Betty's abductions by smoothing out the rough edges, giving them a continuity they did not have in their original form, and alluding to them as if they had been validated beyond a shadow of a doubt. For example, he informs us that Betty's father watched the aliens walk through the door of the house "as if it was made of air."[2] Readers of *The Andreasson Affair* will recall that he saw no such thing, but rather "strange" little beings (never labeled

191

specifically as extraterrestrials), and only made the statement years after it had allegedly occurred. Betty's ability to reproduce a message the extraterrestrials inexplicably gave her in Gaelic is stated as if it were an occurrence beyond debate, but Strieber pointedly ignores any other explanations for Betty's alleged glossolalia, and disregards the extent to which the actual evidence for this claim (reproduced in Fowler's appendix) is quite weak.[3]

Like Hopkins, Strieber also attempts to strengthen the case for the reality of the abduction phenomenon by taking for granted an assumption that by now has taken on virtually axiomatic proportions, that abduction reports "share subtle features, many of which have received only minimal publicity."[4] Although he does not state his source for this assertion explicitly, it probably came from Budd Hopkins, who admitted in *Intruders* to withholding certain aspects of the Kathie Davis abductions as a means of "checking the veracity of any future reports" that came his way.[5] That such subtle similarities should receive only minimal publicity, when drawing the public's attention to them would be an excellent way of strengthening their claim to being real, says much about the way abduction authors have handled their material; needless to say, Strieber does not discuss this matter critically. Of course, we only have his unsupported word for it that such "subtle features" are present.

Strieber also tries to use his own status as a novelist to validate Betty's experiences. Claiming to be "very familiar with the workings of the human imagination," he denies that Betty could herself have concocted such elaborate narratives or that they could simply be the product of a creative mind at work. By his account, the imagination is uniquely individual and curiously insulated from the shaping power of the host culture. According to him, if Betty's stories were the product of fabrication, this would mean that she possessed "one of the strongest imaginations that has ever emerged from the human species."[6] Strieber also offers on Betty's behalf the argument that "much of her strangest testimony simply cannot have been imagined because it does not come in any way from the background of human experience."[7]

But after all is said and done, as we saw in chapter 6, Betty's narratives are not terribly elaborate or intellectually complex, or even particularly original, as we have already had occasion to see. Nor do her experiences vary much from abduction to abduction. Furthermore, it is very hard to determine how Strieber can say that Betty "does not need to recast her experience in the terminology of her beliefs," since it appears that this is exactly what she *has* done, given the extensive similarities that exist between Betty's experiences with the aliens and those of biblical prophets the stories of which as a devout Christian she would have known.[8] In fact, it does not take much effort to see that when the science-fiction paraphernalia is removed from her narratives, her encounters conform closely and predictably to a plot formula, the roots of which can be easily traced to her religious background: Supernal (heavenly) beings magically appear and give her messages and warnings for the human race, just as angels appeared to the Israelites' prophets— who were also chosen because they were "special"—with ominous messages and predictions of doom. It is also hard to follow Strieber's reasoning when he concludes that Betty's Christian faith makes her an "observer par excellence." If anything, the strength of Betty's faith would be more apt to militate against her qualifications as an unbiased observer, since, committed as she is to a very specific way of viewing the world, she will be more apt to interpret that world and anything happening in it with reference to the terminology and the imagery associated with that belief system.[9]

Strieber's claim that Betty's stories have little in common with the "background of human experience" is simply incorrect. On the contrary, many of the stories' details and much of the imagery encountered therein bear an unmistakable relationship to the everyday world. Regarding the white garment that the aliens asked Betty to put on prior to embarking on one of her experiences: Strieber makes a great deal of the fact that many abductees, including himself, also recall being asked to don similar garments such as white robes. But he ignores how widespread the color white is as a symbol of purity and how frequently white robes are associated with initiation rituals of all types in our society, to say nothing of how they are also linked with angels, supernal experiences, and heaven generally, at least in popular culture. Nowhere does Strieber betray any awareness that there is an inescapable relationship between a culture's dominant values and preoccupations and the ways in which particular narratives in that culture are formed; that the stories we tell are inevitable reflections of our beliefs and concerns.

Readers may also notice that despite Strieber's ostensible support for Fowler, there is an unmistakable reluctance on his part to extend an unqualified endorsement to the book and its claims. Rather than come out wholeheartedly in support of *The Watchers*, Strieber tells us instead that Fowler has introduced a "truly innovative" theory about "*apparent* alien encounter" that provides a "*possible* hidden purpose" of the abductors, one that Strieber senses is "*in the direction* of truth"; that Fowler's theory fits "more of the *probable* facts" than any other scenario; and that "*if* one grants that the visitors are real," Fowler "*may have come very close* to discovering what they are doing."[10]

At first glance this underlying element in Strieber's response might appear strange when one considers how similar the two authors' contentions are. The reader cannot help but wonder why Strieber should wish to distance himself from a book the contents of which he is supposed to be authenticating. It is difficult not to see this as having been prompted by a nagging feeling on his part that an unequivocal endorsement of Betty's experiences might have a negative effect on his own reputation as a serious investigator of the abduction phenomenon.[11] Calling *The Watchers* "a delicious and astonishing mystery," Strieber puts it on a level with an Agatha Christie novel, which, whatever it might say about its entertainment value, does little to advance the book's claim to be a literally true chronicle of real abduction experiences.

Fowler's Approach in *The Watchers*

In terms of its structure and narrative method, *The Watchers* is virtually indistinguishable from Fowler's other Andreasson books. It consists in the main of excerpts of a number of hypnosis sessions which are interspersed with an almost "play-by-play" commentary from Fowler on the implications of the various things that happen to Betty and her husband in the course of their various encounters with aliens. The sense of immediacy created by this method is successful up to a point, for it is hard for readers not to be caught up in the drama as it appears to unfold before their eyes.

In an effort to strengthen both the credibility of Betty's ensuing testimony and his own status as a reporter of the events, Fowler again attempts to present himself as a hardboiled skeptic, at least initially—"Not too many years ago I would have placed a book like this in a section of my library reserved for the lunatic/hoaxter fringe of ufology"—who almost in spite of himself comes to believe in the reality of Betty's experiences.[12] Despite his skeptical pretensions—given his previously stated belief in Betty, any profession of skepticism here is willfully misleading—throughout the bulk of Betty's testimony Fowler presents himself as a person who has been won over completely to a belief in the literal truth of virtually all that he is hearing. As such, he interprets the record much as a fundamentalist would interpret Scripture. Entering completely into Betty's world of aliens and abductions, Fowler asks innumerable questions that arise from her testimony, such as whether "the BB-sized object that the aliens had removed through Betty's nose in 1967 really was the same object that they had implanted behind Betty's eye in 1950."[13] In fact, Fowler's portrayal of himself as an individual who simply can't wait to receive further revelations is itself a strategy designed to draw the reader into the reality of Betty's alien-infested world. But in his very attempt to crowd out vestiges of skepticism, Fowler runs the risk of lessening his personal credibility, to the extent that he is perceived as a totally gullible observer, prepared to accept virtually all the testimony he hears.

The Watchers begins with Fowler receiving a call from a distraught Betty, who had been having unusual dreams of the face of a woman whom to her knowledge she had never seen before. In hypnosis Betty recalled having seen this woman aboard a UFO; apparently Betty had been taken along to provide comfort for the frightened woman while the aliens were removing a hybrid fetus from her. Other sessions revealed other extraterrestrial experiences, some of them undeniably bizarre.

A discussion of hypnosis occurs early in the book, in which Fowler appears almost noncommittal concerning the ability of hypnosis to retrieve the truth, concluding, "If the subject is of sound mind, is a good hypnosis subject and has a strong moral character, then I believe that hypnosis will most likely be successful in retrieving true and accurate memories." Obviously, Fowler is confident readers will have no trouble concluding that he and Betty both meet these criteria. This doubtless explains his reference to his own "staunch Christian ethics [which] preclude willful lying," as well as his reminder of Betty's own "strong Christian beliefs."[14] But readers will be excused if they find Fowler's list of necessary criteria pretty arbitrary, and wonder as well if the truth might still remain hidden even if one were to satisfy these requirements.

Following in Strieber's footsteps, Fowler also attempts to fortify his case by summarizing alternate theories for the abduction experience in order to show that the extraterrestrial hypothesis remains the most compelling, if only by default. To achieve this, he portrays the arguments offered in support of these other theories as illogical, far-fetched, or otherwise deficient. Concerning the possibility of hoaxes, for example, he acknowledges that some exist before adding reasonably enough that it is unlikely they could account for all reports. Regarding the likelihood that abductees may be psychotic, he reminds us that they routinely pass tests designed to reveal such mental states. Jung's concept of the collective unconscious, that universal storehouse of symbols and motifs, is discarded as an inadequate explanation of the numerous similarities the abduction accounts presumably contain. Those who argue that abductions are nothing more than long-buried memories of the birth process (the so-called birth-trauma advocates) Fowler dismisses for a number of reasons, arguing that even if people were to retain memories of being born, there are actually very few similarities between the abduction experience and the birth process.[15] Fowler dismisses the likelihood that fantasy-prone personalities could be behind abduction scenarios by simply saying "It is a bit much to state categorically that all abductees fall into this small percentage of our population."[16] But why it should be "a bit much" to see the fantasy-prone personality as a possible cause of *some* abduction accounts is not explained. Since by his own admission over 4 percent of the population are fantasy-prone, that would mean there are well over eleven million persons in the United States and Canada alone who have this condition, hardly a "small" number of individuals.[17]

New Elements in *The Watchers*

The Watchers contains new elements of interest, some of which are assimilated from works by Hopkins and Strieber that had appeared between the Andreasson books and will become fixtures in the abduction narrative. For one, fetal extraction featured prominently in Hopkins's *Intruders* and appears here in relation to Betty for the first time. Strieber's claim that the abduction process involves a purpose far deeper than the mere gathering of biological or genetic specimens—that the visitors are here to teach and instruct a select number of human beings—has also found a sympathetic ear, for Fowler makes a great deal more of this in the present volume than he did in the previous Andreasson books. In *The Watchers*, for example, from the outset we are told some sort of revelation is at hand. To be fair, Strieber did not invent the notion of the alien as messenger or the abductee as prophet. Indeed, he may have picked it up from *her*; Betty, it will be recalled, had earlier claimed that she had been given wisdom by the aliens. But throughout the first two books Betty's learning of moral lessons comprised only an incidental part of the overall scenario; what clearly occupied center stage were Betty's encounters in what amounted to an extraterrestrial theme park. Perhaps because Strieber's two books gave this quasimystical, New Age element a legitimacy that it had not had before, Fowler and Betty treat this aspect of her experiences more openly in the third volume. Whatever the reason, the subtitle of *The Watchers* is *The Secret Design behind UFO Abduction*, and the dust jacket explicitly promises a revelation to this effect, hinting that the aliens' motive is "disturbing" (shades of Hopkins), thus deepening the sense of mystery. Given such a guarantee, it is plain that Fowler is going out on a limb, for the success or failure of *The Watchers* is going to be determined on the basis of whether it actually delivers what it promises, whether the "message" will be commensurate with what we would expect of highly evolved extraterrestrial beings.

Fowler speaks with great assurance at the outset that Betty has been shown various examples of alien technology and has been assured that she "will be allowed to describe them to mankind to fulfill alien purposes" at the "proper" time, which presumably is fast upon us. But as we proceed through the book, we are no more enlightened by any of the snippets of alien-inspired information that Betty does provide than we were when we encountered it in the first two Andreasson books. Being told that the human race will become sterile by "pollution" and by "bacteria" and the "terribler [sic] things that are on the earth" is far from enlightening and not even scientifically credible.[18] Betty hears these predictions while being forced to watch the extraction of the hybrid fetus.[19] Just why fetal extraction would have anything to do with a preservation of our genetic heritage is unclear. Since the aliens have allegedly been watching us for many centuries, it makes no sense that they would not have interceded before now, especially if they *can* see into the future, as Betty later claims in an element new to the Andreasson series but one previously featured in Strieber's *Transformation*.[20]

Other explanations Betty imparts are similarly unedifying. We are informed that the aliens must "extrapolate" and put their "protoplasma" in the "nucleus of the fetus and the paragenetic"; that when making some adjustment to their UFO, they are "purging and lining the cyclonetic trowel," or balancing "the oscillating telemeter wheels and leveling." Although Fowler bravely attempts to prop all this up by reminding us that "Betty was confronted with technological marvels that were beyond her power of description," readers will see much in her account as reminiscent of the pseudoscientific language that has always permeated third-rate science-fiction stories and films.[21] Such words could be picked up by anyone from television, and they are used by Betty precisely as one might expect of a person who is ignorant of science when encouraged under hypnosis to provide "scientific" explanations.

For that matter, as far as this technology is concerned, what is surprising is not that it is indescribable but rather how much of it *does* make sense, after a fashion. To give only two examples: The various chambers she is put in and the procedures she must undergo (prior to embarking on a journey in a UFO) are evidently to protect her from the effects of acceleration, and the cylinder in which the little hybrid is placed is obviously some kind of incubation device not noticeably different from our own.

But while a certain amount of sense can be made of specific details in Betty's account, we cannot help but wonder increasingly about the overall purpose behind Betty's journeys and the numerous demonstrations of alien technology, since they seem both inconclusive and void of any discernible meaning or purpose. Certainly no satisfactory attempt is ever made by the aliens to explain why they are showing her these things, and especially when they repeatedly tell her to forget what she has seen. Also, readers may well ask just what there is of any significance to forget, since all Betty has been exposed to are a number of visual spectacles the point of which is impossible to divine. Contradictions proliferate in *The Watchers*, all of which remain unresolved.

Betty's Experiences and Popular Culture

That a good deal of Betty's testimony in *The Watchers* is arguably tainted becomes evident early in the book when we learn that her husband, Bob (a man with no medical or psychological training), is doing much of the hypnotizing.[22] That such a situation was absolutely unprofessional is acknowledged only to the extent that Fowler admits once to being "wary" of the practice. He takes succor from the highly questionable reassurances of Fred Max, Betty's original hypnotist, who was "confident" that Bob would be able to conduct such sessions successfully. His confidence proves misplaced when Bob asks his hypnotized wife to recall an abduction by imagining that it had been videotaped and subsequently played on a television set, encouraging her to fantasize; Betty, of course, responds accordingly.

Many of the pictures* Betty drew for *The Watchers*—those that include herself—of course are drawn from a position relative to the scene being depicted that she could not possibly have occupied. As he did in *The Andreasson Affair*, Fowler proudly points to Betty's skills as an artist, claiming that she is able to produce drawings "that tally exactly with her verbal testimony." But Betty's drawings add nothing to the credibility of her account, Fowler's assurances to the contrary notwithstanding.[23] First, it goes without saying that he could never know how accurate her drawings are. But even more revealingly, Fowler seems utterly unaware that there must be

---

*Efforts were made to obtain permission to reprint some of these pictures here, but the publishers refused to allow it.

an imaginary component in any representation of experience.
Moreover, even if she had experienced such encounters exactly as
she verbally described while under hypnosis, what we are viewing
in her drawings can never be anything more than the product of an
imagined scene, for we are not being given a precise reproduction
of what Betty claims to have seen from the actual position she
occupied relative to the events in question. For example, a number
of these pictures depict herself and her alien hosts as viewed from
a position in the sky, above and at a considerable distance from
where they are shown to be standing.

Although Strieber and Fowler put great emphasis on the orig-
inality of much of Betty's testimony, many features have fairly
precise counterparts not only in the Bible, but also in the world of
film and fiction. While not necessarily deliberate fabrications,
these aspects arguably owe more to the power of popular culture
to infiltrate the memory and imagination than to the realm of
abducting aliens. For whatever reason, echoes of motion pictures
continue to abound throughout Betty's abduction narratives.
Indeed, the links between her journeys and scenes from well-
known popular films (all available in her youth) are too frequent
to be coincidental; debts to scenes from fantasy and science fiction
movies are particularly striking. As far as science fiction is concerned, the shaft of light so frequently depicted by Betty
descending from a hovering, circular UFO is a commonplace feature found in many science fiction films such as *This Island Earth*
(1955) and *Forbidden Planet* (1956), both of which appear frequently on late-night television. Many of the technological
devices Betty encounters—the console with the colored buttons
she put her fingers on, or the translucent cylinders that were used
to protect space travelers from the ravages of interstellar flight, to
name only two—appear in similar form in both of these pictures.
Alien beings made of light are found throughout science fiction
and have appeared in many popular movies such as *Cocoon* (1985)
and *The Man Who Fell to Earth* (1976). Betty's description of thin,
ethereal beings touching hands has a near equivalent in the conclusion of *Close Encounters of the Third Kind* (1977), when a group
of aliens greet the humans and welcome them aboard their space-
craft. At one point Betty informs us that the aliens have "the capa-
bility to freely move through time," that the "past, present, and

the future are the same to them."[24] This attribute recalls the Tralfamadorians, those well-meaning alien abductors from the film adaptation of Kurt Vonnegut's novel *Slaughterhouse-Five* (1972). The ability by aliens to put large groups of people to sleep is a device that also appears frequently in science fiction, and played a prominent role in the movie *Strange Invaders* (1983).

If anything, Betty's imagery draws even more from the realm of animated fantasy films. As we saw in chapter 4, even Fowler acknowledged the relationship that certain aspects of her first abduction bore to *The Wizard of Oz* (1939). Similarly, the animating of the butterflies that occurred in *The Andreasson Affair* bore a striking similarity to a scene from Disney's *Fantasia* (1940), and the tiny, perfectly formed aliens she encountered in the alien garden are similar in many respects to the waterbabies in that film as well. In *The Watchers*, one of Betty's pictures, depicting her being wrapped in ribbons, is an almost exact duplicate of Cinderella's being prepared for the ball in Disney's animated feature film of that name. Finally, the shrinking of objects by the aliens that Betty described will remind readers of various scenes where things were miniaturized in Disney's *Alice in Wonderland* (1950).

Echoes of well-known books about UFOs can also be detected. Fowler makes much of the similarities between one of Betty's experiences—where she witnesses a UFO apparently taking on water from a lake by means of a hose—and one in Canada recorded in a then widely available UFO book, *Flying Saucers: Serious Business* (1966), by Frank Edwards. Fowler overlooks that Betty could easily have read Edwards's book and forgotten this particular incident. Even the "museum of time" Betty encountered in one of her earlier journeys is traceable to a 1955 short story entitled "The Ruum" by the American science-fiction writer Arthur Porges.[25] In that story, a man is pursued by a device which had been placed on earth millions of years ago by an alien race, the function of which was to preserve all lifeforms on a planet for presumably historical or record-keeping purposes.

Surprising as it may seem, Fowler makes virtually nothing of all these links in this or *any* of the three books devoted to Betty's experiences. Even if he were ignorant of such widely circulated fantasy and science fiction films and stories, one would still think that some sort of investigation along these lines was in order (if only to discount this possibility), since her stories sound so much like the stuff of fantasy. Fowler's failure to investigate does little to advance his reputation as a writer sincerely interested in uncovering the truth, whatever that truth may be.

If certain parts of Betty's narrative demonstrated a debt, however unconscious, to the world of books and films, the reader soon sees that Fowler himself has also been influenced by other writers, including the narratives of Budd Hopkins and Whitley Strieber in particular, whose books he admits to having read. Indeed, he alludes to several of the experiences detailed in their accounts as if they were established facts. On one occasion he refers to the case in Hopkins's *Intruders* of the "confirmed pregnancy" reported by Andrea, who claimed an intact hymen. Although readers will recall that Hopkins himself admitted the claim could not be verified, Fowler discusses the story as if it had been authenticated.

It is by such patterns of accretion that the various aspects of the abduction myth slowly gain in credibility and acceptance. Here, what originally appeared as an uncorroborated story has acquired a kind of pseudoauthenticity in the course simply of being retold. Fowler does not appear aware that if *any* story is repeated with sufficient frequency and force, it will take on the status of an established fact, a tendency that has been long known and exploited by those who would manipulate public opinion, whether town gossips or political propagandists.

Given the above, *The Watchers* can be seen as a particularly good example of how one narrative may assimilate and augment material from previously published ones, or from the culture more generally. Along these lines it is of particular interest to examine the list Fowler provides of the aliens' various abilities, for it is plain that there has been a definite development in those abilities since the publication of *The Andreasson Affair* in 1979. Significantly, in addition to those Betty was already familiar with—the ability to travel interstellar distances, communicate telepathically, conduct experiments on humans, place human beings in states of suspended animation, and pass through seemingly solid objects at will—Fowler lists several other skills which Betty's aliens did not demonstrate earlier, but which did crop up in the works of Hopkins and (especially) Strieber, and which have made their way into *The Watchers* as well. The aliens now possess the ability not only to predict our future, but also to travel between different planes of existence (whatever *that* means), and to change into pure balls of energy. Betty's aliens may also be unique in being able to shrink or expand the size of objects such as UFOs and human beings. With the exception of this ability, *none* of these newly revealed skills was conspicuous in the first two Andreasson books (if they appeared at all), but *all* were present in some form in *Intruders* (1987), *Communion* (1987), and *Transformation* (1988). Concerning the aliens' alleged ability to read our minds and control our futures, Strieber's visitors also laid claim to possessing these skills, especially in *Transformation*.

The reader will also remember that Strieber speculated extensively on the likelihood that his visitors were multidimensional, possibly existing in a timeless realm. In this context it is interesting to see how Fowler too begins to assume in *The Watchers* that the aliens are linked in some way to the supernatural. Considerable emphasis is placed on what he calls their "paraphysical" natures and their relationship to the realm of the paranormal, a realm which he chooses to assume has been scientifically confirmed. At one point Betty claims that the aliens engineered an out-of-body experience (OBE), and she remembers her "other self" looking down at her physical body as it lay on a couch. Fowler defines this (rather loosely, in fact) as an instance of the *doppelganger* experience,* and remarks that it is "a rare but well-documented phenomena [*sic*] that has been reported and investigated by researchers," as if such reporting and investigating were sufficient proof in themselves of its reality.[26] Elsewhere, he makes similar claims for the established existence of telepathy, levitation, and telekinesis. But for all his efforts, discerning readers will nevertheless see through his use of buzzwords like "well-documented," "investigated," and "researchers."

Continuing in this vein, Fowler also begins to speculate that a relationship exists between abductions and out-of-body experiences—that the aliens have the ability to trigger such experiences in their subjects virtually at will. Of course, at no point does he

---

*The "doppelganger," a term German in origin, has been traditionally defined as a ghostly apparition or double of a person, especially someone not yet dead! Fowler seems to be confusing this phenomenon with the out-of-body experience, which Betty's account more closely resembles.

acknowledge that her alien-instigated OBEs are as inconclusive and seemingly without purpose as were the tours of strange lands and demonstrations of alien technology. Nor does he make anything of the fact that Bob—who supposedly accompanies her on her astral journey—does not provide the much-needed verification for this event. For that matter, just why aliens should engineer OBEs in humans is never satisfactorily explained. Fowler's own guess that it was designed to acquaint Betty with her spiritual self is absurd since, given the strength of her religious faith, she would appear to be the last person to require such a demonstration.

Finally, Fowler's claims for such alien abilities are made with great confidence (probably because of Strieber's trail-blazing), providing another example of the manner in which specific aspects of the abduction narrative take on credibility and gradually gain hold. Strieber, of course, was the first to expand the subject to include the realm of the occult, in the process redefining, and enlarging, the boundaries of the myth. The addition of this parapsychological component in abduction accounts marks a crucial point in the development of the narrative. After the publication of *Transformation* and *The Watchers*, it becomes a commonplace.

Conspicuous Silences

Fowler's refusal to confront the numerous inconsistencies that plague Betty's narrative is one of the most glaring deficiencies in *The Watchers*. Presumably, he hopes that by avoiding any mention of such inconsistencies the reader may be apt to overlook them. Unfortunately, inconsistencies speak for themselves. As we have seen throughout the literature, no time is devoted to discussing the paradoxical combination of purported alien technical sophistication with their medical clumsiness, to say nothing of their resolute refusal to learn from past experience. Allegedly able to instigate out-of-body experiences and immobilize entire communities, they remain inexplicably ignorant of the usefulness of anesthetics when extracting a fetus from a frightened woman or when performing their various operations on Betty. Any implications that arise from their apparent need to perform the same experiments on human beings time after time are likewise disregarded.

As we have seen, Betty claims that her aliens, like Strieber's, have the ability to predict the future. Yet midway through the book she informs Fowler that the aliens have "a problem in understanding the *unpredictable* free will of mankind," influenced as it is by our erratic emotional makeup. For that matter, the very word "unpredictable" should mean nothing to beings who have "control over time" as we have been told they have.[27] Instead of dealing squarely with such seemingly contradictory testimony, Fowler lapses into an extensive discussion of another issue—the various ways authorities have kept their knowledge of UFOs from the public—that the reader will see as simply an attempt to change the subject. To this end, he marshals passages from experts such as anthropologist Margaret Mead to strengthen the contention that UFOs are extraterrestrial in origin, and quotes Dr. William D. Davis, a physicist, who muses on the likelihood that telepathy might be the means whereby communication could take place between humans and aliens.[28] Though Fowler considers the physicist's comment "prophetic"—because abductees so frequently claim to have telepathic communication with aliens—he conveniently overlooks that there is no information provided about the physicist's background to suggest that he can speak at all knowledgeably about telepathy.

Fowler's reliance on expert opinion at this juncture has not been designed merely to divert our attention from inconsistencies in Betty's narrative; it is also designed to prepare us to be more favorably receptive to his theory concerning the purpose behind the alien visitations and more accepting of his ultimate personal revelation, the nature of which he has so far given us only a dim indication. He gluts the reader with theories as to the possible purpose, origin, and nature of the aliens. He begins by speculating that a race of super-beings may have been looking after us in some way for millennia, and adds that genetic manipulation may have occurred on numerous occasions over the centuries as part of their ongoing assistance to us in our evolution. Continuing, he wonders if there might even be *two* races of extraterrestrials, the first a race of virtually supernal beings who themselves created the large-headed aliens Betty and other abductees encounter, in a manner reminiscent of God's creation of guardian angels. These beings (Betty's communicants) may even be vastly evolved versions of ourselves—that is, *our* descendants from *our* future, come back to help us through difficult times. As if this weren't enough, he then goes on to add that life may well have originated elsewhere in the universe and wonders if the panspermia hypothesis* applies in the case of life on earth. Indeed, it is even possible that our own technological developments may "have been telepathically spoon-fed to us by the aliens themselves."[29]

Obviously, the reader cannot challenge any of these bizarre claims, but many may see that the purpose behind all this is simply to overwhelm his readers' resistance by saturating them with supposed proof of the paranormal. Abductions become somewhat less outlandish in a world where telepathy, telekinesis, and astral travel are commonplace.

For all his self-proclaimed Christian respect for the truth, Fowler is not beyond making assumptions about the existence of such happenings when it suits his purposes, despite the fact that unequivocal verification has never been forthcoming. Moreover, on many occasions he minimizes material or suppresses it outright when convenient to his narrative. Of course, he made no mention of Betty's Pentecostal faith until well into the Andreasson series, in all likelihood because he saw that readers might trace the purportedly alien-inspired glossolalia to her religious background rather than to an extraterrestrial source. Another fact of potential significance that was kept from us had to do with her first husband's alcoholism. As most readers will be aware, alcoholism is not self-contained, but has a widespread effect on everyone in a family. As such, it is surely too significant a part of Betty's life to have been ignored at any point in the Andreasson saga. Yet we only learn about this issue in any detail now, even though this fact must have been in Fowler's possession from the outset.[30]

Fowler probably feels comfortable mentioning it in *The Watchers* now that Betty is happily remarried and still having abduction experiences. Still, knowing about her first husband's

---

*The panspermia hypothesis proceeds from the speculation that the building blocks of life as we understand them could have had their origins elsewhere in the universe. According to this theory, primitive organisms could have drifted across interstellar space, finally entering our earthly environment, where they began to develop. Fowler takes this one step further, and speculates that alien beings may have engineered this process.

drinking problem will be apt to lead the reader in directions other than those Fowler is privileging. Since Betty had obviously been living in an unhappy environment for many years, readers might interpret her journeys to alien lands as projections of her own desire for escape from an intolerable domestic situation. After all, the aliens even tell her she has "gone through enough" and elsewhere "predict" that she would have to move.[31] We hardly need to embrace the notion of aliens with precognitive skills as the only conceivable explanation of what may be happening to her.

Nor may readers see anything unusual in other events given otherworldly explanations. In a hypnosis session conducted by Bob in 1988, Betty recalls the aliens' apparent prediction of her sons' deaths, which took place in October 1977. Fowler concludes triumphantly that "It is obvious now that the alien had actually told Betty what was going to happen," but he again pointedly ignores that the session where this was recalled took place over a decade *after* the deaths occurred.[32] As many readers will suspect, Betty could easily have been superimposing memories of events that had not actually happened at the time. What appears to be an instance of precognition on her part, of course, could be merely an example of a most unfortunate coincidence, where an attack of anxiety happened by chance to coincide in time with the accident that killed her sons. For that matter, readers may also recall that Betty was frequently in such states of anxiety and telephoned Fowler on numerous occasions to discuss them.

Fowler's Narrative Strategies

Although Fowler's wildly speculative sections seem superfluous at first glance, as narrative strategies they begin to make sense when the author finally confesses his deep personal secret in the chapter ominously titled "Branded." Reminding readers that he has "built up a solid reputation" as a UFO investigator, he goes on to say that he recognizes he is risking this reputation by what he is about to tell us.[33] Shrewdly painting a picture of himself as a man willing to risk his reputation and that of his family in the interests of the truth, the implication here can only be that what he is about to tell us *must* be true. (The reader will now see as well the relevance of the comment he made at the outset of *The Watchers* concerning those Christian ethics of his, which precluded lying.) Even though most readers would probably be prepared to give him the benefit of the doubt regarding his "solid" reputation, there is no necessary relationship between that reputation and the truths which he is about to reveal.

At all events, it turns out that he too has very likely been visited by aliens, or so he claims. Unfortunately, the experiences from his past are far from convincing as abductions; many readers will emerge from this section having concluded that they are nothing more than vaguely remembered nightmares he had when a small boy. Throughout, he makes a great deal of personal experiences that could easily have prosaic explanations. For one thing, he sees his lifelong interest in UFOs and astronomy as a "fanaticism" so abnormal that it could only have been inspired by some sort of early encounter with extraterrestrials. While the reasons behind a specific individual's intellectual interests are indeed often difficult to pinpoint, surely most readers would consider doubtful Fowler's contention that his were extraterrestrially inspired. Fowler's use of words and phrases like "overwhelming fascination" and "near fanaticism" appear excessive, for he is using such terms to describe what many would regard as a perfectly normal preoccupation with subjects whose capacity to stimulate the mind and excite the imagination few would dispute.

Fowler's detailed descriptions of his allegedly unusual childhood experiences do nothing to increase the reader's readiness to believe that anything particularly unusual occurred. We learn that when he was five or six he had nightmares of waking up to stare at a dark figure outlined in the hall; when six, seven, or eight, he saw a small bright light moving around in his bedroom; when eight or nine, he dreamed that an entity came into his room through a window. Throughout his life, he has supposedly seen UFOs on occasion and once, as a teenager, he had a missing time experience. Finally, over the years he has occasionally encountered fleeting glimpses of mysterious apparitions.[34]

It soon becomes obvious that Fowler is no Betty Andreasson when it comes to the richness of his paranormal past. It is also very difficult not to see that virtually all the events he has described are quite ordinary. Fear of the bogey-man and the vivid nightmares that many children occasionally experience can easily account for the lights, shapes, and entities he mentions, and many people have witnessed anomalous lights and shapes in the sky. Obviously, it remains an open question what the peculiar figures he saw standing in the snow or in his cellar could possibly have to do with extraterrestrial beings and alien abductions.

Other evidence Fowler adduces is similarly unconvincing. Once, while working on the chapter of *The Watchers* entitled "Return from Oz," he received a telephone call from an abductee named Baum, which he regards as strikingly significant.[35] Again, while working on that section of the book dealing with the paraphysical aspect of the abduction problem, he received a letter reminding him not to overlook this aspect of the phenomenon; this, too, is deemed nothing short of remarkable. On another occasion, when he telephoned his former employer, the receptionist announced (to his utter astonishment) that she was an abductee; after watching a movie in a theater, a woman with the same surname as the name of the theater called to tell him of a UFO sighting, a coincidence he finds uncanny. When on vacation, his son described seeing an object in the sky which reminded him of the Goodyear blimp. Fowler suspects that this was a UFO, and wonders if someone was "watching our family."[36]

All in all, it is unlikely that Fowler's examples will have the effect on the reader that he desires; on the contrary, he emerges from this section looking not only extremely gullible but intellectually flighty (if not unstable) as well, a far cry from the "logical" and "ultraobjective" individual he has claimed to be. Reading about Travis Walton's encounter with the blond-haired alien being while aboard a UFO, only to drive by a blond man standing by the side of a road some time later, is *not* an "incredible" example of synchronicity, Fowler's assertions to the contrary notwithstanding.

Against his wife's wishes, Fowler decided to go ahead and be hypnotized. To increase the credibility of what is to come, he takes pains to remind us that many steps were taken to guard against the possibility of the hypnotist's asking leading questions. In spite of this, the reader will see numerous instances where Tony Constantino, elsewhere described as a "qualified hypnotherapist well-versed in the art of regression techniques," asked questions that were not only leading but also were based on a previously determined assumption concerning what had really happened to him that was bound to encourage Fowler to respond along predictable paths.[37] In one session, Tony asks "who" the entity was that Fowler saw in his bedroom when he was a small boy. Like all good hypnotic subjects anxious to please the hypnotist, Fowler obliges. When queried by Tony as to what Fowler and the entity "talk[ed] about," the notion that they *did* converse is implanted into Fowler's mind and prompts him to supply one. Again, when Tony asks Fowler if this being—which the reader should remember Fowler had only dimly recalled seeing years ago as a small child—was "from another world," the hypnotized Fowler is being stimulated to think of this being as an extraterrestrial. Asked if a scar he has was "caused by a physical exam," the results are bound to be similarly predictable, especially given Fowler's history of involvement with abduction scenarios.[38]

Tony also employs the same questionable technique as did Betty's husband Bob: he asks the hypnotized Fowler to imagine he is in a movie theater. Furthermore, his personal expectations also play a significant role in the results. Though we are told that "he had no experience with the UFO phenomenon," Tony's response to Fowler's account of what happened to him as a child indicates that he has a good notion of the kind of information everyone is hoping he will extract. Because Fowler's initial testimony is vague, Tony asks Fowler point-blank if he has been "programmed to forget."[39] Tony's suspicion here is one that could only be made by someone both familiar with the details of alien abduction accounts and ready to believe in them.

Even in the face of such prompting, Fowler's testimony remains imprecise. Only after considerable prodding does he respond affirmatively to Tony's question about being programmed, and even then, Fowler only says he did not *think* that his encounter with the entity in the hall was a dream. Similarly, he again only "thinks" he went through the window with the female being (a being, incidentally, whose gender and even existence he was originally unsure of).[40] Initially he suspects that the "missing time" incident is "probably nothing," but under Tony's sharply directed tutelage Fowler is soon doubting his own memory and is led to suspect that something mysterious in fact occurred. The possibility that nothing happened to Fowler that was worth remembering— surely the most likely reason for his vagueness—no one entertains.

On the contrary, Fowler eventually goes on to conclude that these childhood memories *were* "confirmed by hypnotic recall" and that he "really had an abduction experience," a "fact" that is alluded to in his fourth book, *The Allagash Abductions* (1993), as if it had been conclusively proved.[41]

Fowler's conclusions are even more surprising when one sets them against the transcripts of his actual testimony, for when he was under hypnosis he appeared quite commonsensical about his "memories." He provided alternate explanations of what may have happened, arguing that he might have simply absorbed what he heard from other abductees such as Betty over the years and superimposed these accounts onto his own past. Unfortunately, this line of inquiry is not pursued further, eclipsed as it is by his discovery of a circular scar on his lower leg, described as a *"freshly cut scoop mark."* That he has such a scar the reader must accept; that it is fresh is something he could not possibly know, and that it had "suddenly appeared overnight" is impossible to verify.[42] But oddly enough, though its discovery shocked him, he does not appear to have investigated other possible causes of the scar. Needless to say, the presence of this scar is itself a two-edged sword, for it not only provides no real proof of alien contact, but it raises once again questions concerning alien clumsiness as far as their inability to perform simple medical procedures without leaving scars is concerned. This aspect of the narrative is, of course, most damaging in terms of the effect it has on the likelihood of the story's being true, but extremely important when seen as an aspect of the myth as a whole.

The Aliens' Message

Once again reminding us that Betty believes aliens told her she had been chosen to "show the world," late in *The Watchers* Fowler announces that the time has come for the long-awaited revelation. And the message itself? It is that *"Man is not made of just flesh and blood,"* and that *"man's true essence can coexist in more than one plane, not only in this life but in the next."*[43]

Readers will be excused if they see nothing particularly profound or original in the above pronouncements; many may find them simply banal. Even more importantly, none of the truly significant questions has been answered. The motive behind the tours on which Betty was taken and the purpose and function of the devices she was shown have not been resolved; the choice of Betty, an obscure, uneducated woman, to be the recipient of such complex technological marvels, is likewise left unexplained; and the nagging business of all the operations and experiments carried out on human beings continues to be without satisfactory resolution. Despite Fowler's desperate attempt to shore up the message by pronouncing it "provocative, yet straightforward," or by theorizing that the aliens are biologically related to us as a means of justifying all the genetic tinkering supposedly going on, most readers will emerge from *The Watchers* feeling disappointed, if not also cheated.[44] For the aliens' message contains nothing that could not be found within the pages of innumerable religious tracts or heard in any number of churches, synagogues, mosques, and temples. Finally, even if all of this were literally true, alien credibility is hardly enhanced when we learn that they may have caused their own females to "have developed gynecological deficiencies requiring the use of human surrogate mothers for the reproduction of hybrid offspring."[45] Alien physician, heal thyself.

Fowler likens himself in his epilogue to a medical researcher who has inoculated himself in order to better study a disease. In fact, the analogy is not entirely apt. If anything, he is more like a person who has *caught* the very disease he was originally studying, as a consequence of which, in his illness he is not well enough to treat it successfully when encountering it in others. His final attempt to lend some credibility to the preceding events by mentioning yet again the innumerable unexplained UFO sightings must by now strike readers as simply a disingenuous attempt to buttress what in fact has been a pretty weak case for the reality of the abduction experience. By his own admission, his experiences as an abductee were inconclusive.

Why, then, did he choose to include them in the first place? The answer can only be that he thought it would give the book—and himself as narrator—additional authority and credibility. What he overlooked was that no matter who might claim the status of an abductee in this volume, nothing could satisfactorily soften or detract from the inescapable flimsiness of the aliens' messages.

The Allagash Four

In many ways *The Allagash Abductions* (1993), Fowler's next "hands-on" investigation of an abduction, follows the by-now predictable pattern established in the Andreasson books, the author employing virtually the same modus operandi as before. The Allagash story is easily summarized. During a fishing trip in 1976, four young men—identical twins Jim and Jack Weiner and their two friends, Chuck Rak and Charlie Foltz—went night-fishing and claimed to see a bright UFO above the tree line. One of them signaled it with a flashlight, at which point the object moved closer to them and shone a bright beam of light down on their canoe. The next thing the four recalled was being close to the shoreline, where they discovered to their surprise that the large fire they had built to assist them in locating their campsite from the lake had gone out.

Some years later, Jim Weiner was diagnosed as suffering from temporolimbic epilepsy (TLE), a condition which Jim's neurologist described as capable of producing many psychic symptoms, including "dissociative states with out-of-body experiences, unprovoked panic and chest pain, [and] hallucinations," and went on to add that "It is possible that Jim's reported nightmares and dreams may be TLE induced."[46] In the course of treatment he divulged a history of frightening nighttime experiences such as waking to see strange creatures looking at him, and mentioned that his brother, Jack, and the two companions who had accompanied them on the camping trip had complained of similar problems. Allegedly advised by his psychiatrist to consult a UFOlogist on the matter, Jim contacted Fowler, and in-depth studies of the four abductees eventually commenced.[47] While under hypnosis the men revealed that they had been taken aboard the UFO that night and subjected to tests, many of them of a sexual nature. Further sessions would reveal that three of the men had a history of ongoing involvement with the alien beings, in some cases going back to their childhoods.[48]

Approached by one of the abductees, Fowler's by-now predictable pattern repeats itself: An initial reluctance to get involved is replaced by a growing fascination with the story that soon evolves into a virtually complete acceptance of the entire account. Hazy or dreamlike aspects of the four men's stories are hurried over; similarities are heralded, inconsistencies ignored or minimized. In fact, so anxious is Fowler to believe this abduction that, after the first hypnosis session has taken place involving only one of the men, he is ready to exclaim confidently that "We were now dealing with the abduction of human *beings* [*sic*] by alien operators of a UFO."[49]

Of course, wherever possible evidence is interpreted in a way that reinforces the extraterrestrial hypothesis; other explanations are rarely featured and never favored. Aspects of the abduction experience that make little or no sense—an abductee's seeing aliens in his bedroom in the night, for example, and immediately going back to bed or to sleep—Fowler simply does not address. Any physical peculiarities associated with the abductees—burns, scars, or anomalous "scoopmarks"—are traced to the abductions. Scars that an abductee "suddenly" discovers on his body are assumed to have appeared in the immediate past. At one point, one of the abductees develops an unusual skin problem on his foot; although it could easily be athlete's foot or eczema, these possibilities are dismissed because he "never" gets such ailments. A mysterious man is encountered on Chuck's property with a metal detector; when asked his business, he gives a strange and unconvincing reply— that he was a road inspector. When the reply does not check out, everyone concludes that he may have been one of the Men in Black (see introduction) rather than a petty thief casing a rural area. Chuck proves difficult to hypnotize deeply; the reason given is all too familiar: There "may be much buried in his subconscious."[50] Jack's wife Mary dreamed of a deer, an event accorded great significance because of its apparent similarity to the Virginia Horton case covered by Hopkins in *Missing Time* (see chapter 6), even though Mary admits they have many deer in their rural backyard. For that matter, dreams are never seen as mere dreams but as memories of actual events which are presumably being recalled precisely as they occurred. Possibly because of his earlier emphasis on the supernatural in *The Watchers*, Fowler makes much of a poltergeist phenomenon that allegedly took place in the Weiners' home many years before when the twins were young, avoiding discussion of the weakness (not to mention the arbitrariness) of the link between extraterrestrial visitation and poltergeists.[51]

The experiences of the four Allagash abductees differ noticeably from the Andreasson abductions, even though the format and approach of the book have a familiar ring. The biggest single difference concerns the aliens' relationship to their victims; here, the abductees receive absolutely no messages from their abductors. That philosophical or moral advice is nowhere to be found may be understandable, of course, when we recall the quality of the wisdom imparted to Betty Andreasson.

The reader soon sees that we are back to the world of bug-eyed monsters with an indecipherable agenda. The experiences of the "Allagash four" (as Fowler affectionately dubs them) are more in the tradition of the abductions chronicled by Hopkins—who wrote the foreword—than Strieber (although the influence of both is apparent), suggesting that the competition for supremacy between the two distinct narrative strands that was first encountered in the late 1970s—the so-called religious or spiritual, versus the techno-logical—continues unabated.

Hopkins may well have been prompted to pen his flattering foreword by the book's contents, for they provide as precise a cor-roboration of his own abduction research as anything he could hope to find. This may be why Hopkins waxes at such length about Fowler's ability to handle interviews "without bias or slant," or to "conduct hypnotic regressions without leading the subjects" and study evidence "without censoring it to buttress our pet theories."[52] It goes without saying that anyone familiar with Fowler's previous books may have some difficulty seeing these qualities in the author. For whatever reason, the Allagash abductions closely parallel those found in *Missing Time* and *Intruders*, and take us back to a distinctly "nuts-and-bolts" approach to the issue.

Fowler's interest in the Allagash case is easy to explain. As it is the first multiple abduction case (involving identical twins, no less) that he has encountered, such a "documented corroborative abduction experience would go a long way toward demonstrating the physical reality of such experiences."[53] But readers will recog-nize that, if the four accounts do *not* corroborate each other, if they are replete with mutually exclusive elements, we may be led to precisely the opposite conclusion.

Hopkins states confidently that if the four were giving testi-mony in a trial of earthly abduction, "conviction would be a fore-gone conclusion."[54] But a case can be made that the four accounts differ significantly in precisely those areas where one would expect them to agree. Indeed, if ever there were an abduction case where we would expect all the verbal descriptions and artistic renditions of the events in question to support one another, this would be the one. For all four of the alleged abductees claim to have been involved in the same, identical abduction experience simultaneously; even more significantly, all were either trained as artists or, so we are told, are artistically inclined. While their respective treatment at the hands of the aliens could vary from person to person, we would not expect to find extensive variations in their respective physical descriptions of the same alien, for instance, or significant differences in the scientific methodology employed by the aliens from one abductee to another in the course of performing the same operation. Yet this is exactly what we do find.

Furthermore, as we will see, the differences between the Allagash aliens and those Betty Andreasson encountered could not be more striking. Gone is the benign and avuncular Quazgaa, who has been replaced by a bunch of cold and ominous technocrats. Tours of Emerald Cities and demonstrations of fabulous technology have been conspicuously deleted from the abductees' itinerary. That Fowler neither makes anything of this fact nor of the discrepancies that exist throughout the separate Allagash descriptions brings considerable discredit to his entire approach, and casts serious doubt on his conclusions.

The first major discrepancy in the Allagash testimony involves the twins' report concerning alien methods of sperm extraction. Jim Weiner states explicitly that the aliens "fiddle" with his penis in an attempt to procure an erection that is presumably a necessary prerequisite for the operation. After some effort he eventually ejaculates into a metal container. Chuck, however, is inexplicably subjected to an entirely different sperm-gathering technique. Now a black "thing" with "joints" on it flutters down "like a butterfly" and performs the extraction.[55] Notably, the other two abductees are not tampered with in this manner at all. Sperm does not appear to be taken from Jim's brother Jack (which is odd, considering their evident interest in the two as twins), but they do insert a tube into his penis which causes him to urinate.

While it might be argued that we have no right to expect any consistency in the experimental methods employed by alien beings, it is somewhat more difficult to explain away the diverse descriptions of the aliens' appearance provided by the four men.

The height of the aliens varies dramatically from observer to observer, ranging from four feet eight inches through five feet to "normal human height"; general descriptions range from "bug-like" through "Asian" to "embryonic chickens."[56] Descriptions of their clothing differ as well. Jim thought they wore blue-gray, one piece suits with gloves; Jack saw shiny, highly reflective coveralls; Charlie saw gray-white aerobic clothing and *possibly* gloves; and Chuck said they wore "dark clothing." Jim and Jack were both sure that their blackish-brown "bug-eyes" did not blink; Charlie was sure that the aliens' "Asian almond" eyes *did*, like a bird's. Jim saw no ears, but only holes; Charlie saw ears that were only "smaller" than ours but otherwise presumably similar. As far as the aliens' noses are concerned, Jim and Jack were explicit regarding the absence of one; Charlie saw a "long" and "Asian" nose and Chuck made no mention of a nose at all.[57]

It is, perhaps, just possible that such discrepancies are not beyond an explanation that could still leave the veracity of the witnesses more or less intact. But the author's refusal to confront any of these contradictions has the effect of leaving them very much alive and unresolved in the reader's mind. Of all authors, Fowler should surely take this matter up with his readership, especially considering the glaring differences in appearance between the Allagash aliens and those with whom Betty Andreasson was so familiar. Betty's aliens, it will be recalled, differed in virtually all aspects of their respective anatomies, even to their hands (Betty's had three, claw-like appendages).

Interestingly enough, the most glaring evidence of inconsistency in the aliens' appearance is visual.* While there is a strong correlation between each separate abductee's verbal description of the aliens and the picture he drew, there is little similarity from version to version. Jim described the aliens as looking like bugs and his pictorial reproduction *is* decidedly bug-like; the facial portrayals remind the reader of an insect not unlike an ant. But in Jack's drawings, on the other hand, the aliens' eyes are larger, no nostrils are visible, and there are definite protrusions where ears

---

*Unfortunately, permission was not obtained from the publisher, Wild Flower Press, to reproduce in this work the drawings made by the Allagash abductees.

should be. Strictly speaking, the aliens possess no facial features which we could ever consider similar to our own, a fact that makes Jack's later reference to the "look on their faces"—a look he interprets as "curious"—curious in itself.[58]

Charlie's aliens, while resembling Jim's in certain respects, have smaller heads and more delicate bodies than Jack's, and are the most human-looking, almost attractive in appearance. In Chuck's drawing his alien *does* resemble an "embryonic chicken" as he said, and it possesses a huge head on an impossibly tiny neck, with eyes somewhat smaller than those drawn by Jim and Jack. Chuck's various drawings of the aliens, however, are not even very consistent with each other. In one portrayal, illustrating aliens putting him back in the canoe, they bear a distinct resemblance to the cartoon figure Gumby, in no way like the being he reproduced earlier.

In the same way that many of Betty Andreasson's drawings employed a "false perspective," several of the Allagash pictures also depict scenes from positions which the abductee could not possibly have occupied, drawing more attention to the likelihood that they are imaginative constructions. For example, one drawing depicts Chuck being placed in the boat following the abduction from an imaginary point in the lake, and another depicts the operating room from a perspective neither Jim nor Jack occupied. Jack drew in detail the penis-probing instrument which, if he had been lying down as he says, would have been difficult if not impossible for him to have seen as depicted. Jack's picture of the aliens working on his own leg is also manifestly the product of his imagination, since he could not have witnessed the operation from the angle depicted, as he was lying down.

But the most interesting aspect of the drawings can be seen in the way some of them bear an uncanny resemblance to monsters from well-known science fiction films. Two drawings are remarkably like the mutant alien in the film *This Island Earth*, and the alien in a third is distinctly reminiscent of beings that appeared in a 1957 film *Invasion of the Saucer Men* as well as several episodes of *The Outer Limits*.[59] Finally, the use of a beam to spirit the four men from their canoe to the UFO is remarkably like the device employed in *Star Trek*, a resemblance even Fowler sees and comments on in passing, while remaining apparently oblivious to its implications.

That Fowler makes nothing of the above links with popular science fiction films and television programs is not really surprising. After all, he said next to nothing about Betty Andreasson's extensive indebtedness to popular culture. But even more important is the failure of the drawings to provide that corroboration which should have been forthcoming had the experience been real, since all were privy to the same events and were in a position to confirm each other's accounts visually. Fowler's silence on the subject is either the result of a blindness to the import of the visual discrepancies—surprising as it may seem, he may well believe that they *do* corroborate each other (else why include them?)—or the product of his awareness that, as they do not, the matter is best left unmentioned. If the latter is the case, his silence speaks volumes.

In an attempt to extract information from the Allagash abductees a variety of methods is employed, some of them extremely questionable. After he first heard of their case, Fowler attempted to verify that the four had indeed spoken to relatives and friends of seeing a UFO when on the camping trip immediately after their experience, and he appears to receive this corroboration. He then sent out standard questionnaires to the four men in an attempt to gather details about their experience. (That it took "several months" for them to be returned readers may consider a bit suspect in itself.)

After the matter surfaced, Fowler suggested the four men consider hypnosis, to which they agreed. Tony Constantino was once again approached in his capacity as hypnotist. Fowler characterizes him as a "neophyte" in UFO research, which is misleading when we consider the extensive work he had previously done on the Fowler's own abduction case. Fowler provides the customary assurance that "special care" was taken to avoid asking leading questions, but many of the questions asked were as leading as anything asked of Betty Andreasson and her husband. Early in the sessions, for instance, Constantino puts a proposition to Jim Weiner that cannot help but elicit a specific response. Telling Jim that "You sense that there is something you should remember," he implants the notion that something is indeed buried in his subconscious; Jim dutifully replies that he has "a sense that there is something I should remember." Somewhat later, when Fowler asks Jim "When did you see these creatures again?" he of course implants the suggestion that such creatures *were* seen again. Later, after Charlie has admitted under hypnosis that he did not think anything (other than the sighting of a UFO) out of the ordinary had happened to them, Constantino asks him "Why didn't any of you discuss what had happened?" the implication being that something *did* happen, despite Charlie's own testimony to the contrary. Then, having praised Charlie as a hypnosis subject, Constantino asks him if "somebody" told him "not to remember what happened"; Charlie of course replies in the affirmative.[60]

Manipulating the hypnotized subject's responses is not limited to the asking of loaded questions. At one point Fowler tells us, "Try as he may, Tony could not get Chuck to remember the beam reaching the canoe."[61] Finally, "in desperation," Constantino asks him to imagine he is watching a film, which as I have argued before, will strike many readers as an extremely questionable technique. Only then do they begin to get the kind of results they so obviously desire. Many readers will conclude that it is equally questionable for Constantino, who should have no interpretive preferences, to be trying so hard to extract such a specific response from a subject. Of course, Constantino is not the only one guilty of having a precise agenda. Fowler asks Chuck if he had ever seen the aliens "prior" to the experiences at Allagash, obviously inviting him to envision previous meetings. Wittingly or not, all the investigators are trying to support a thesis they have been prepared to embrace long before the actual sessions began.

Jack Weiner's wife, Mary, is openly nervous about being hypnotized. Readers will probably see nothing unusual about her nervousness, since anyone who knew they were going to be asked about what happened on a particular night in the distant past might well feel apprehension over their ability to recall such information. Doubtless for this reason, she proves impossible to hypnotize. But rather than accept this perfectly ordinary explanation for her nervousness, Constantino draws the familiar conclusion that she is probably "afraid of remembering," even though it is just as likely that she has absolutely nothing to remember, a possibility only passingly entertained by Fowler.[62]

Undaunted by this setback, the researchers then proceed to employ the services of a pendulum to extract answers from Mary, and in doing so illustrate once again how the abduction narrative is becoming increasingly replete with New Age characteristics. In this instance, the method employed involves the subject holding a pendulum—usually a small plumb bob suspended on a string. Questions are asked of the subject, and yes or no answers are determined on the basis of the direction the pendulum swings in apparent reply to each question. Here many readers may suspect that they might as well have employed the services of a Ouija board for all the credibility such a technique has. Nevertheless, out of the "answers" that emerge Fowler concludes that a dual abduction involving Jack and his wife occurred, and late in the book even alludes to the time "when [Jack] and Mary were abducted from their home" as if it had been convincingly verified.[63]

Fowler attempts bravely to convince us of the researchers' scrupulousness by mentioning that abductees like Jim were "urged" not to read UFO literature or "divulge" information of the session to the others. Here, the reader may simply regard this as yet another instance of closing the barn door after the horses have escaped, to say nothing of what it tells us about the investigators' naivete. Obviously, since over a decade has passed since the events allegedly occurred, such urgings constitute a precaution that can have little practical usefulness at this point. In fact, there is some evidence that at least three of the four *did* have some prior knowledge of UFOs. For instance, we know by his own admission that Jim has read at least one UFO-related book—notably *Communion.*[64] Charlie's signaling of the UFO with his flashlight is predicated on the assumption that they are looking at some kind of intelligently controlled craft, and is not the response one would expect of a person completely ignorant of UFOs. Finally, Chuck's reference to swamp gas when they first see the light indicates a familiarity on his part with the widely publicized incident of March 1966, when J. Allen Hynek was vilified throughout the media for suggesting that a Michigan UFO sighting could have been swamp gas mistakenly identified. Interestingly enough, Fowler never investigates the extent of the abductees' prior knowledge of UFOs; indeed, he appears to make the tacit (and unwarranted) assumptions that they neither knew much about the subject nor had they discussed the Allagash sighting among themselves over the years, a silence which does not even make sense considering the nightmares they all claimed to have had since the 1976 experience.[65]

Another distinctive aspect of the Allagash abductions concerns the aliens' particularly intense interest in the abductees' sexual organs. The Allagash aliens perform a variety of sexually oriented operations on their victims; they are stripped naked, penile and anal probes are inserted, skin scrapings are made, and enforced ejaculation occurs.[66] As readers know, the taking of sperm samples has been a part of the overall narrative for some time. Hopkins was the first, in *Missing Time* and *Intruders*, to allude explicitly to the alien interest in taking sperm and ova samples as a major feature of the abduction process, but the preoccupation with ourselves as sexual beings can be traced back to the Villas-Boas case. But nowhere in the earlier literature has there been such an obsessive and singular preoccupation with our sexual equipment. Why these four abductees should be the objects of such intense sexual curiosity does not make sense, since human sexuality is relatively simple and straightforward, the way it functions surely something the aliens could have acquired a more or less complete knowledge of decades ago with their first subjects. This preoccupation with human sexuality is duly noted, but Fowler acknowledges nothing unusual here, even though such an interest is unintelligible, were the experiences real.

More than in previous volumes on the abduction phenomenon, Fowler makes considerable use of sources of authority and expertise to strengthen his argument. In particular, he refers extensively to the work of folklorist Thomas E. Bullard's 1987 study of abductions, *UFO Abductions: The Measure of a Mystery*, by way of proving that insofar as the Allagash abductees' alleged experiences conform to Bullard's formula, so they may be considered to be descriptions of real events. What Fowler conspicuously overlooks is that the purpose of Bullard's work is to provide a detailed morphology of the abduction tale and is primarily concerned with delineating its form and structure. In the interests of his thesis, Fowler makes much of Bullard's contention concerning the consistent pattern among abduction stories, even though, as we have seen, the issue of consistency from story to story is far from established. In fact, many may suspect Fowler of manipulating Bullard's study to suit this own purposes. To say as he does that Bullard proves there are too many similarities "for them all to be hoaxes or random fantasies" is not to say that the stories must

therefore be true. The various similarities Bullard sees and catalogues are not so much indications of genuinely experienced
events—Bullard does not say that they *are*—but are just as likely
the product of an internal causality that is itself determined by narrative logic. For example, Bullard lists as a universally found feature of abduction narratives the return (that is, the abductee
always returns from the abduction experience). But surely it must
be obvious to anyone even casually familiar with the rules of narrative that all abductees *must* return from their abduction experience in order for there to be any story in the first place, other than
simply a missing person's report.

Similarly, communication with the abductors *must* either occur
or not. That some sort of medical examination of the abductee
often takes place is an element of plot that again proceeds as a
likely consequence of the fact of abduction itself, since other
motives—kidnapping for ransom, for instance—are simply ludicrous, in the circumstances. Indeed, there are very few motives
that could ever proceed from the premise of abduction by extraterrestrial beings other than the ones we have already seen, the scientific examination or other utilization of the victim or the
imparting of some form of knowledge. It is really not surprising,
then, that we would encounter these elements in virtually all the
abductions we have examined in this study. But to make this discovery is not to discover as well that the stories actually occurred.

Although Fowler deliberately refrains from any mention of the
significant differences between these abductees' experiences and
those of Betty Andreasson, the Allagash abductions bear unmistakable similarities to earlier narratives, especially those of Budd
Hopkins. While the stories add little of substance to the developing narrative, they do draw greater attention to the cold imper-
sonality of the alien technocrats, while further emphasizing the
aliens' incomprehensible gadgetry and their human victims' helplessness, fear, and passivity in the face of that gadgetry. For their
part, the aliens themselves are increasingly at the mercy of their
technology, as they monotonously go about their endlessly repeti-
tious, if not also redundant, experiments.

One element that does appear here for the first time is not
related directly to the myth itself, but rather to the attention it has
begun to receive. For the first time, academically trained individ-

uals such as Bullard are turning their attentions to the abduction phenomenon. Fowler's heavy reliance on Bullard's academic credentials is easily explained; such persons give enhanced legitimacy to the abduction phenomenon. Just as the abduction narrative gained in credibility, as stories that were originally deemed incredible acquired the texture of truth with the passage of time, in the 1990s the involvement of a small number of academics has also contributed to this process, while also making it easier for subsequent authors to treat it as being beyond the need for proof and verification, and to assume that the case for the reality of alien abductions has been made.

Notes

1. Raymond Fowler, *The Watchers* (New York: Bantam, 1990). Betty, it will be recalled from chapter 4, had divorced her first husband and later married Bob Luca.

2. Ibid., x.

3. Support for the contention that Betty spoke Gaelic can be found in Appendix 3 of Whitley Strieber's *Transformation* (New York: Avon, 1988, 1989 [271–72]), which contains lists of the words Betty spoke, together with their supposed Gaelic equivalents and an English translation. Although a few incidental phonetic similarities are present, most readers will find the overall proof far from convincing.

4. Fowler, *Watchers*, 12.

5. See Budd Hopkins, *Intruders* (New York: Ballantine, 1987), 298.

6. In this context the case of Kirk Allen is of relevance. In the course of treatment for mental illness, it emerged that Allen had invented an entire solar system of worlds complete with family dynasties, descriptions of cities, and an incredibly complex history of an empire which he claimed to rule when living in his alternate existence. The events Allen invented were so rich in detail that the psychiatrist himself came to find the fiction intrinsically fascinating. The Allen case is discussed in Dr. Robert Lindner's *Fifty-Minute Hour: A Collection of True Psychoanalytic Tales* (New York: Dell, 1986), and it is summarized in Jacques Vallee's *Revelations: Alien Contact and Human Deception* (New York: Ballantine, 1991), 127–32.

7. Fowler, *Watchers*, xi. Later in the book Fowler employs the same method by quoting a police lieutenant named Lawrence Fawcett (that he is also a UFO investigator is unmentioned), who also believes that it was

"impossible for an individual to concoct such an elaborate story and to be able to hold it together under the intensive interrogations that were conducted" (199). That intensive interrogations *were* conducted we are asked to take on faith.

8. Ibid., xiii.

9. In saying this, I am aware that strictly speaking, no one can escape from the ideological biases that we all carry with us. But it seems sensible to assume that a person with a strong fundamentalist Christian faith would be inclined to interpret something like UFOs within the framework of that faith, and be more likely to respond to the idea of extraterrestrial beings in a way that does not violate its tenets.

10. Fowler, *Watchers*, ix–x, my emphasis.

11. That Strieber's views were undergoing significant change during this period is best seen in the foreword he wrote to Kenneth Ring's *The Omega Project* (New York: William Morrow, 1992) two years later, where he explicitly deplored the domination of the extraterrestrial hypothesis over other possibilities.

12. Fowler, *Watchers*, xv.

13. Ibid., 55.

14. Ibid., xix–xx, 3.

15. Proponents argue that the abduction experience has many close resemblances to the process of birth: An initial sensation of floating is experienced, just prior to an irresistible movement toward a brightly lit operating room. Identically clad beings in gray or white surrounding the area are seen, along with medical or scientific instruments. Moments of pain are followed by peaceful sleep and comfort. The disproportionately large head of the aliens that abductees commonly encounter is distinctly similar to that of a human fetus, and is frequently cited to add strength to this theory, although critics argue convincingly that a fetus could never see itself.

16. Fowler, *Watchers*, xxi.

17. Ibid. Fowler refers to "that 4 percent of the population who have been classified as *fantasy-prone personalities*" (his emphasis). The figure 13 million (actually 13,200,000) is calculated on an estimate of the population of the United States at approximately 300 million and Canada at 30 million.

18. Ibid., 68, 48.

19. Betty's portents of doom occasioned by the sterilization of the human race as an effect of pollution is remarkably similar to the premise of Margaret Atwood's 1985 futuristic novel *The Handmaid's Tale* (Toronto: McLellan and Stuart, 1985).

20. Influence can, of course, occur in both directions. It is entirely

possible that Fowler's earlier books may well have influenced Strieber and Hopkins. Several elements from *The Andreasson Affair: Phase Two* were also found in *Communion* and *Transformation*, and include the receiving of vaguely disturbing telephone calls, the presence of mysterious helicopters hovering around abductees, and even a brief appearance of the Men in Black.

21. Fowler, *Watchers*, 48, 76–77, 89.

22. All we are told is that in the opinion of hypnotist Fred Max, Bob "had become proficient in hypnosis" (31) and that Fred "was confident" that Bob would be able to "hypnotize and interview Betty" (32). No reasons are provided in support either of the claim or Fred's confidence, other than that Fowler "deeply respected his [i.e., Fred's] professional opinion" (32). Fred, incidentally, is referred to in *The Watchers* as a "Behavioral psychologist" (5), but in *The Andreasson Affair: Phase Two* (Englewood Cliffs, N.J.: Prentice Hall, 1982), we learn that he "held a bachelor's degree in behavioral psychology" (13). As for Bob's credentials, at one point (1967), he "owned a gas station" (*The Andreasson Affair: Phase Two*, 78), and in 1987 he "was about to start work as a service manager with a local automobile dealership" (*The Watchers*, 57).

23. Ibid., 353. It is also of interest that her pictures were drawn many months *after* her hypnotic sessions (if the dates Betty affixed to them are accurate), increasing even more the likelihood that coloration by her imagination could occur.

24. Ibid., 209.

25. This story can be found in *Best Science Fiction*, ed. Edmund Crispin (London: Faber, 1955).

26. Fowler, *Watchers*, 175.

27. Ibid., 182, 209, my emphasis.

28. Interestingly, a close look at the Mead passage cited by Fowler indicates that, far from giving UFOs a blanket endorsement, she only subscribed to the notion that "something" was responsible for the sightings and acknowledged that they *might* be manifestations of extraterrestrial intelligence. The article itself is more directly concerned with the reasons many people are afraid to entertain this hypothesis. (See Fowler, *Watchers*, 192–94, 199.)

29. Fowler, *Watchers*, 237.

30. Ibid., 133.

31. Ibid., 131.

32. Ibid., 139.

33. Ibid., 240.

34. Ibid., 301–14.

35. L. Frank Baum, of course, was the author of *The Wizard of Oz*.

36. Fowler, *Watchers*, 284.

37. Raymond Fowler, *The Allagash Abductions* (Tigard, Ore.: Wild Flower Press, 1993), 35.

38. Fowler, *Watchers*, 256, 319–20. As has been shown, the persistent Tony appears again in *The Allagash Abductions* using the same intrusive methods and getting predictably similar results.

39. Fowler, *Watchers*, 241, 290.

40. Initially, in an early session, Fowler had said under hypnosis "I just really don't really [*sic*] know if they happened or not" (258), but by the time of the book's completion he lists his extraterrestrial encounters as established facts (362–63).

41. Ibid., 356.

42. Ibid., 263, 269.

43. Ibid., 244–45, italics in original.

44. Ibid., 349.

45. Ibid.

46. Fowler, *Allagash*, 276–77, quoting a September 3, 1989, letter from Bruce H. Price, M.D., to Fowler's colleague and fellow abduction investigator David Webb.

47. Ibid., 10.

48. Ibid., 227.

49. Ibid., 50, my emphasis.

50. Ibid., 230.

51. Ibid., 146–47.

52. Ibid., 2.

53. Ibid., 11.

54. Ibid., 3.

55. Ibid., 59–60, 84–85. Aliens are notoriously muddle-headed when it comes to sperm extraction and collection, and never seem to know how best to proceed. In *Intruders* Hopkins cites aliens sometimes using electric shocks or simple suction devices to trigger orgasm, while on other occasions men will be "mounted" by female aliens and a crude form of intercourse will ensue.

56. Fowler, *Allagash*, 53, 112, 136.

57. Ibid., 113.

58. Ibid., 168.

59. Readers interested in examining these and other pictorial similarities should consult Vivian Sobchack's excellent history of the science fiction film, *Screening Space: The American Science Fiction Film* (New York: Ungar, 1993), 92, 169, and passim.

60. Fowler, *Allagash*, 41, 63, 121.

61. Ibid., 128.

62. Ibid., 183.
63. Ibid., 285.
64. Ibid., 10.
65. Ibid., 11, 32, 218, 242. Of the four, Jim Weiner, Jack Weiner, and Charlie Foltz experienced nightmares of their experience, and all four experienced "nagging uneasiness" (287).
66. Ibid., 304.

9

THE 1990s:
DAVID JACOBS'S *SECRET LIFE*

The appearance of David Jacobs's *Secret Life* in 1992 marked another important step in the development of the alien abduction narrative. Jacobs's book was the first written by an individual who came to the material with an impressive set of professional credentials. Authors of previous books on the subject, knowledgeable about UFOs though they may have been, had not been trained as specialists in those research-gathering methods so necessary for the compilation of an authoritative historical record. Jacobs would appear ideally suited to this task, for he was not only an academic historian but author of a history of the UFO phenomenon, *The UFO Controversy in America* (1975).

Lavish praise is heaped both on the author and his work by the writer of the book's foreword, none other than Harvard psychiatry professor John Mack, a man who not only possessed imposing credentials of his own, but who would also soon become a member of the small but growing number of academically trained abduction researchers. Given his considerable experience and skill as a writer (he had won the Pulitzer Prize for his biography of Lawrence of Arabia), it is something of a surprise to see Mack taking his cue from his predecessors in the field, for he makes a number of statements in his foreword that are hard not to see as ill-considered, if not irresponsible. For instance, in his role of supportive authority figure, he emphasizes the sincerity and sound minds of all the thousands of abductees who have reported their stories (a figure for which he provides no support), and bolsters this contention with another unsupported (and insupportable) claim that among these multitudes, one can *never* find "personal benefit" as a motive behind abductees' decisions to go public with their disclosures. Other possible motives—public recognition and respectful attention from others, for example—Mack, like other abduction researchers before him, evidently does not consider sufficiently valid to be included.

Like Budd Hopkins and Whitley Strieber, Mack stresses the magnitude of the problem and states that in his estimation as many as a million persons or more in the United States alone could be abductees. Obviously, this figure is intended to lessen the chance of readers dismissing the issue outright as nothing more than claims made by a small minority of eccentric or disturbed persons. Presumably, anything that affects over a million people must be worthy of the consideration of reader and researcher alike. But Mack makes no attempt to verify this statistic or relate it to a particular study or information source, although it probably comes from Hopkins, who along with Jacobs and sociologist Ron Westrum conducted in 1992 a survey designed to determine such numbers.[1]

As would be expected of a foreword, Mack's comments are positively riddled with hyperbole: Jacobs's book is the result of "scrupulously conducted research"; it is "scholarly and dispassionate, yet appropriately caring," the product of "rigorous scholarship," "careful observation," and "meticulous documentation."[2] But, of course, such grandiose claims can be counterproductive if, as this chapter will show, the evidence in the text belies them. For one thing, Jacobs's summaries of earlier, well-known abductee cases contain a number of inaccuracies which might disincline readers to share John Mack's confidence. Regarding the Betty and Barney Hill abduction, Jacobs alleges that the Hills' aliens "looked very much" like others described over the years.[3] In fact, contrary to Jacobs's claim that Betty and Barney saw beings with large heads and eyes, they at no point stressed the size of their heads, and only the alien eyes drawn by Barney under hypnosis were at all large (and in his revised drawing, the eyes were less prominent). Nor is Jacobs's statement that both Hills claimed the alien leader was "larger" than their fellow abductors entirely accurate; Betty only said that the leader and the examiner were "taller" than the others.[4] As far as the nightmares Jacobs claims that both of the Hills had, only Betty experienced disturbing dreams about the abduction; Barney himself admitted to Dr. Simon that he only began to have such dreams *after* treatment had begun. Finally, contrary to Jacobs's statement that Dr. Simon was unsuccessful in his attempts to catch the Hills in contradictions concerning their respective stories, as we have seen, a number of such contradictions *can* be observed when their respective testimonies are compared.

Mack then utilizes another rhetorical device by now familiar to readers. He attempts to draw us into his circle of initiates by affirming confidently that Jacobs's book will impress "those who are open *at least* to the *possibility* that *some thing important* is happening in the lives of these individuals and countless others that cannot *readily* be explained by the theories and categories currently available to modern science."[5] Of course, Mack can speak with such confidence, since he is asking so little of readers. Defining the issue in such watered-down terms, like many before him, Mack astutely positions readers so that it will be more difficult to reject Jacobs's actual thesis in light of the evidence, because rejection has been equated at the outset with rigidity and narrow-mindedness. As will become abundantly apparent, Jacobs himself is making far greater demands of the reader than Mack suggests is the case.

It will come as no surprise to see that both Mack and Jacobs spend a good deal of time discussing what they take to be a remarkable degree of consistency from report to report among abductees, most of whom have never had the chance to communicate with one another. In his introductory note to the reader Jacobs echoes Mack, arguing that such consistency provides strong confirmation of the reality of these occurrences, bizarre though they undoubtedly are. Jacobs not only makes much of the "convergence of minute detail" among accounts, but stresses the presence of similar scars on abductees' bodies that we are told appear "immediately following an abduction."[6] Not only is there very little consistency to be found, but Jacobs repeats Fowler's mistake about abductees' scars, which neither suspects could have been noticed only long after they occurred and mistakenly linked with an abduction experience. Finally, both Mack and Jacobs overlook the fact that by the time these abduction stories came to Jacobs's attention, the core narrative had been circulating throughout North America for almost three decades. Jacobs finds it amazing that an abductee would recall events also found in Hopkins, but any readers sensitive to the complexities of narrative transmission will not consider this particularly surprising.

The Distinctive Style of *Secret Life*

As far as the content of Jacobs's book is concerned, although new elements are introduced, it does not break a great deal of new ground. What distinguishes *Secret Life* and sets it off from previous abduction books is Jacobs's narrative stance and style, products of his historical training which make the book undeniably compelling reading and seminal in the history of the developing narrative. Without question, *Secret Life* is to date the most authoritative and self-assured affirmation of the alleged reality of the abduction phenomenon. Jacobs avoids the difficulty of earlier accounts by not structuring his book around the testimony of specific individual abductees. Instead, *Secret Life* affirms a series of general statements about the abduction phenomenon in its various aspects. Specific accounts from abductees, relegated to an ancillary role, are used when they support these summaries of the phenomenon's major features. Jacobs's use of strong declarative sentences gives the impression that the various events comprising the abduction experience invariably appear with regularity and consistency, while features of the abduction process are presented as if they were facts embedded in the historical record, as indisputable as the date of an armistice or a treaty.

Jacobs's method is well illustrated by his handling of the alleged alien-induced pregnancies (despite the abductee's celibacy or scrupulous use of birth control), together with the equally mysterious sudden termination of these pregnancies. Jacobs discusses these events as if they were all frequent, independently verified facts. Asserting that in such cases an abductee's gynecologist "positively verifies" the abductee's pregnancy, he goes on to tell us that the woman "suddenly finds herself not pregnant," adding that the "Missing Fetus Syndrome" as he terms it "has happened to abductees enough times that it is now considered one of the more common effects of the abduction experience."[7] The problem here is that the only proof is in the form of the anecdotal information supplied by the alleged abductees themselves. Of course, his narrative stance—that he is dealing with established facts—allows him to ignore the possibilities of mistaken diagnoses or of miscarriages. For that matter, Jacobs does not even suggest until the book's conclusion that such alternate explanations deserve mention. Obviously, such unabashed bias in favor of the extraterrestrial explanation makes a mockery of his assertion in the opening chapter that he is "not out to convince" us that abductions are really occurring as the alleged abductees state.[8]

Evidently, Jacobs conceives of historical writing not as a narrative endeavor, but as the innocent and passive compiling, ordering, and structuring of data on which there is well-nigh universal consensus. *His* enabling fiction is that the abduction experience no longer needs to have a case made for itself, and that his own cultural values and predispositions play no role in the selections that shape his narrative. This gives great confidence to the tone of *Secret Life*, but although such assurance and authority in the narrative voice leave the reader little room for skeptical distance, such an approach is not without risks of its own. While the credibility of Jacobs's book is less reliant on the testimony of particular abductees, the credibility of Jacobs himself is very much in question. To strengthen this credibility he spends a good deal of time early in the book shoring up his credentials. He tells us how his use of hypnosis became steadily "more competent"; of how "adept" he became at distinguishing "unreliable material from what appeared to be legitimate memories"; and how his understanding of the subject became "more sophisticated" as time went on.[9] Presumably, if we accept his status as an expert on abductions, we will be more apt to accept whatever he says about them and may even tolerate his frequent decision to waive proof. But by the same token, we will not find his narrative credible or the examples he cites in support of his statements all that compelling if we are not convinced by his claims of expertise, or if we do not find his approach to the subject appropriately professional and beyond reproach.

In fact, many readers will emerge from *Secret Life* unconvinced for a number of reasons. First, as far as Jacobs's claims to competence as a hypnotist are concerned, we only have his word that such is the case; there is no evidence that he had formal training in hypnosis techniques. All we are told is that he "discussed hypnosis techniques with" Budd Hopkins, "read books about hypnosis," and "attended a hypnosis conference."[10] More important, precisely how he (or anyone else, for that matter) could become able to distinguish truth from fantasy in an abductee's testimony is similarly impossible to say. Indeed, in making such a claim he makes it difficult for the reader not to suspect that he is treating incoming data in a highly selective manner, so as to fit the overall abduction scenario *as he conceives it*.

Even more important, regardless of where they stand on the abduction issue, many readers will find the book marred by at least two related questionable assumptions: first, that all the material Jacobs presents can and should be incorporated into a coherent whole; and second, that in his role as researcher he needed to establish "hands-on" experience with actual abductees in order to study the events in question. The first of these assumptions is immediately open to question since he has already by his own admission sifted the "valid" from the "bogus." Further, his admitted desire to find such a neatly structured narrative, though it virtually guarantees that one will be forthcoming, does not mean that one is necessarily there. Jacobs's claim to having innocently discovered a coherence that inheres in the material cannot obscure how his own narrative presence constructs that coherence. Indeed, as the reader moves through *Secret Life*, many internal inconsistencies within the material *do* emerge, which cannot help but affect our readiness to accept the claim of coherence, regardless of how convincingly it has been articulated.

Jacobs's second contention is even less easily defended, based as it is on the fallacious assumption that historians should ideally be directly involved with their material. If anything, readers may conclude that he has seriously affected his ability to view the matter dispassionately by establishing such a close relationship with the abductees, and that his having come to share in the "emotionally wrenching experiences" of the individuals has lessened his ability to evaluate their stories with objectivity.[11]

In support of the supposed consistency Jacobs makes a number of statements concerning the various stages of the phenomenon, many of which are neither verified nor verifiable. Of his sixty subjects, for instance, he informs us that "all told the same stories"; that these stories fit "neatly into a pattern"; that the experiences had been locked in the abductees' memories "for many years"; and that only one of the group was "mentally disturbed."[12] Readers will see that the first two of these claims are in fact matters of opinion, while the third he has no way of verifying; the last he lacks sufficient medical expertise to state with authority.

He also argues that the descriptions of the aliens' appearance and behavior from abduction to abduction are remarkably similar, and tries to get around the undeniable differences among accounts by developing a three-tiered matrix or structure into which all the aspects of the phenomenon can be catalogued: primary experiences, involving those events which occur with greatest regularity to the largest number of people; secondary experiences, occurring less frequently but which all abductees experience in some form; and ancillary experiences, which are unusual, specialized procedures that occur only rarely. The problem with this approach is that it does not really resolve the question as to why, if they are accounts of objectively real proceedings, abduction accounts should contain so many elements that are not simply different, but mutually exclusive or otherwise self-contradictory. As we have had frequent occasion to observe, there is little correspondence even when it comes to those basics where we would expect to see some agreement—the shape and size of their eyes, hands, heads, skin color, or even clothing—to the point where the reader begins to suspect that abduction accounts are similar only to the extent that we are prepared to see consistency. Amazing as it may seem, Jacobs dismisses inconsistencies about aliens' powers to defy gravity and material reality (some can, others can't or won't) as unimportant, nothing more than the result of confusion induced by the aliens themselves. Just why aliens would go to such bizarre lengths to create confusion, he leaves for the reader to resolve.

Jacobs also seems singularly indifferent to the possibility that an alleged abductee's testimony could be contaminated by earlier abduction accounts. In the case of abductee Patti Layne, like Barney Hill, Patti's husband was dragged along rather than floated and (just like Barney) scraped the tops of his shoes in the process. One of Patti's abductors also wore a scarf as did the alien leader who apprehended the Hills, and the others sported bird insignia on their uniforms, as did Betty Andreasson's aliens. Patti's aliens are also friendly, as, for the most part, the Hill and Andreasson aliens were. Though this friendliness is seen in only a few abduction accounts, Jacobs neither draws attention to it as an atypical feature, nor does he mention the possibility that Patti could have borrowed her scenario from these other well-known abductions which she could easily have read or heard about years ago and buried in her subconscious.

Concerning implants, Jacobs makes no attempt to corroborate his statements (in the form of affidavits from appropriate medical persons, for example). We only have his word for it that odd, otherwise inexplicable holes have been found in abductees' noses; that doctors have not been able to assign prosaic causes to the nosebleeds often reported; or that implants have even been inserted in the first place, let alone retrieved. Anticipating the demand for hard evidence, Jacobs simply says that when retrieved, such objects have invariably been lost, misplaced, or "mysteriously" disappeared.[13] Such a casual attitude does little to enhance his own credibility as a historian of the phenomenon.

Similarly unfounded generalizations are made concerning the purpose behind the various experiments performed on abductees, especially female ones. Ironically enough, he invokes the stereotypically intuitive woman—"Most women *in some way* know" what is happening to them—in order to affirm confidently that aliens are "harvesting" human ova, implanting hybrid offspring, and ultimately removing the produced fetus, all the while ignoring how ludicrous is such an inefficient and needlessly time-consuming use of humans as incubators. Jacobs accepts at face value an alleged abductee's claim to know a "disgusting old hybrid embryo" was being implanted within her, and the significance of the sticky substance abductees sometimes report on their bedclothes after an abduction he similarly accepts as stated.[14]

Jacobs's Confident Style

In spite of all these weaknesses, readers accustomed to seeing the author as an authority figure could be convinced by what they are reading, for Jacobs exudes complete confidence in the reality of the abduction experience he describes. Indeed, this confidence may explain why he is so apt to gloss over vague testimony of many of his subjects. For example, his subjects, like Hopkins's, prefix responses with qualifiers such as "I think," "kind of," and "maybe." One of his abductees, recalling her experience in the so-called alien nursery, even admitted to being "very disoriented," and recalled not memories but mere "impressions." Another told him she "thinks" she walked down a hall to a point where she was "sort of" standing in the middle of rows where there were a lot of babies and, she again "thinks," also machines.[15] In another case, in a development repeated by John Mack, a woman claims that she was encouraged by her abductors to have sex with a human male, although how this could suit alien purposes is unclear, especially if their aim is a race of *hybrid* offspring. In response to Jacobs's question as to whether the man got an erection, she can only say "maybe"!

Jacobs's confidence concerning the reality of the experiences he is chronicling makes him quite insensitive on those occasions when alleged abductees respond to aspects of these experiences in inappropriate or illogical ways. Concerning this behavior, for instance, many behave more or less as one would expect any person to act under such circumstances: usually frightened and often angry. But just as often alleged abductees exhibit very unusual reactions. Barbara Archer is "not all that shocked" to see an alien in her bedroom.[16] Aliens give the seventeen-year-old Jason Howard a terrifying vision of an impending nuclear cataclysm, but he feels only "relieved" that it will not occur until he is forty (in 1999). Karen Morgan feels merely "bored" and "pissed off" (rather than curious) prior to being shown an idyllic scene of the planet to which the hybrid babies are being taken. Patti Layne actually experiences romantic feelings for an alien and is reluctant to leave, yet Jacobs makes no comment on how odd this reaction is or how atypical is her sense that she had a "really nice" time during her abduction.[17]

Other abductees report equally bizarre experiences yet display *no* emotional response, which is just as unusual. James Austino is forced to immerse himself in a pool containing a strange, slimy substance (the reason for doing this, predictably, is not given). He does as he is told and is eventually removed, but acknowledges no fear or apprehension during the course of a procedure many would find at the very least disturbing.[18] After an alleged abduction, George Kenniston floats out of a UFO back to his home and encounters his father in the doorway. In no way flushed with excitement, eager to describe this incredible experience, or otherwise visibly disturbed, he merely excuses himself and goes to bed![19] Still others report finding themselves waking up behind the steering wheels of moving cars, or of returning to consciousness many miles from where they last remembered being. Although such blackouts and their consequences would normally be intrinsically upsetting, in none of these instances do we hear of these people seeking medical help for what could be a serious neurological condition, for all they know.

The notorious lack of consistency in alien behavior Jacobs makes little of, even though the aliens' treatment of their victims and their actions continue to vary widely from case to case. For one, though Jacobs believes that secrecy seems "critically important" to the aliens, he has no difficulty with their obvious ineptitude when it comes to keeping us unaware of their presence (or at least none that he admits). Although the aliens are clumsier when it comes to clandestine activity than is the most bungling secret service of any country on earth, Jacobs sees nothing unusual in this. Nor does he find it odd that beings who can move through solid objects, travel across interstellar space, and even render themselves invisible would be simultaneously so incompetent in so many ways. As we have already seen, although their ability to pass human victims through solid panes of glass would indicate sophisticated knowledge of human nervous systems, they remain steadfastly ignorant of the causes of pain, even while apparently understanding what pain is, as evinced in their reassurances to abductees that they are not going to "hurt" them. Indeed, Jacobs is so persuaded that aliens are virtually "magical" in their capacity to control our bodies, minds, and emotions that he seems unaware of how capriciously these powers are actually used, and is apparently untroubled by the aliens' inability to learn from past mistakes in their heavy-handed and medically clumsy treatment of their subjects. Simply put, there should be no scars, bruises, or "scoopmarks." For that matter, even their choices of human subjects appear to be determined arbitrarily, if not also perversely. For example, there is no reason to employ the nonmaternal Karen

Morgan to serve as a surrogate comforter of hybrid children when another more responsive abductee (such as Kathie Davis) could do a better job. Yet they continue to use Karen repeatedly despite her admission that she does not even like babies.[20] In short, after their various activities have been looked at critically the aliens seem too stupid to have ever mastered the technology to have arrived here in the first place. In fact, about the only point where the reader *can* agree with Jacobs is when he concludes that we have no indication the aliens are brighter than we are.

For all the novelty of Jacobs's method, most of the abductions portrayed in *Secret Life* are themselves pretty standard fare, with their counterparts in earlier abduction narratives. Furthermore, those resemblances to well-known fantasy and science fiction movies which we examined in chapters 4 and 8 continue to be encountered and overlooked here as well. Some of Jacobs's subjects report being "beamed aboard" UFOs, many claim to fly in and out of their bedrooms, and a few exhibit inexplicable compulsions to drive to a specific destination where they allegedly meet aliens: All such incidents have their counterparts in such films as *This Island Earth* (1955), *Peter Pan* (1953), and *Close Encounters of the Third Kind* (1977). Other unusual aspects of the abduction process not encountered previously can also be traced to the world of the motion picture. The "breathing pool" exercise, where an abductee enters a strange pool of liquid with an alien, has a rough counterpart in *Cocoon* (1985) where a human bonded with a female extraterrestrial in a swimming pool. The infliction of pain by means of a prod or stick that one of Jacobs's abductees reported recalls the punishment inflicted on Robert Duvall in the futuristic *THX–1138* (1971). The existence of "proto-beings" or half-made humans that other abductees claim to have seen—presumably human simulacra with featureless faces not yet fully formed—recalls a central scene from *Invasion of the Body Snatchers* (1956) where Kevin McCarthy, to his horror, saw half-completed "pod-people" in the process of formation. Even the so-called staging that occurs, whereby aliens are somehow able to cause an abductee to envision and become a participant in a hypnotically induced scene that is not actually taking place, has a fictional counterpart; it is identical in nature to the brainwashing scene in *The Manchurian Candidate* (1961), where a group of captured American soldiers were led to believe they were at a garden party rather than being displayed in a medical theater by Chinese Communists.

To be fair, Jacobs's failure to mention any of these links may be because, like Fowler, he is simply unaware of them. By his own admission, he was "never attracted to science fiction."[21] Be that as it may, the links with well-known science fiction and fantasy films are as prominent a feature of these alleged abductions as they were previously and if anything, more conspicuous than in some other narratives we have examined. Leaving them unmentioned does nothing to dampen the reader's suspicions that many alleged abductees are drawing from a storehouse of long-forgotten experiences in theaters or in front of television sets.

New Elements in *Secret Life*

Although many of the experiences in *Secret Life* have their counterparts in earlier abduction narratives, like earlier studies of the phenomenon, the book contains new elements that seem almost designed to answer questions posed in older accounts, while other features from earlier narratives disappear. Conspicuously absent in Jacobs's cases is an exhortation from the aliens to the abductees to forget what happened to them, because the author finds "little evidence to suggest that the aliens specifically tell the abductee not to remember" the experience.[22] This comment is of considerable importance, for it represents Jacobs's attempt to resolve the thorny issue of the aliens' often-unsuccessful attempts to induce amnesia in their victims. By making the abductees responsible for their varying degrees of forgetfulness, he is thus able to account for inconsistent recollections in terms of human psychological factors rather than poorly executed extraterrestrial intervention. In doing so, Jacobs effectively lets the aliens off the hook, at least where this inconsistency is concerned.

Further, Jacobs makes a good deal of an apparently telepathic process which he calls "mindscan" not encountered previously to any degree (although Travis Walton and Betty Andreasson alluded to it briefly). This process supposedly involves an alien staring into the eyes of abductees in order to calm their fears, bond with them, or possibly even to extract information directly from their minds.

Likewise there is developed a sexual relationship that sometimes occurs between abductees and the so-called taller alien leader who can even induce "rapid, intense, sexual arousal and even orgasm" on occasion.[23] This new sexual component may be an elaboration of an aspect of the process encountered earlier, where abductees such as Betty Andreasson, who was told she was "special," felt she enjoyed a type of intimacy with at least some of her abductors.

Equally new are the visions presented to the abductee of worldwide cataclysm and human suffering or an idyllic pastoral scene of gardens and the like. Imaging appears with considerable frequency in *Secret Life* (as it will in John Mack's *Abduction*), and again seems to represent a refinement of an aspect of Betty Andreasson's experiences. Betty recalled having been literally taken to certain places where she saw gardens, pools, and such; more recent abduction accounts stress that the scenes presented are merely visualized and are not "real."[24]

The aliens' ability to predict the future that, of course, featured in the narratives of Betty Andreasson and Whitley Strieber, also appears in *Secret Life*, as it will in John Mack's work. But a new aspect found here involves the assigning of strange tasks to the abductee by an alien. In one case, a female abductee was asked to memorize a list of men's names because of an impending war. Jacobs concludes that such tasks may be meaningless in themselves, but are designed to enable the aliens to study various human mental functions at work. Yet to readers who recall the fairy tales and folklore of their youth, all of the above elements have a familiar ring: Fairies and witches traditionally could predict the future, and forcing a human being to perform seemingly odd tasks or enter into some activity with fabulous beings was a common feature of such encounters. Jacobs, of course, is as dismissive of such parallels as of the science fiction ones, for he is of the opinion that the stories of folklore "present only vague and general similarities" with abduction accounts.[25] It is too early to say if any of these elements will become part of the ongoing narrative, although many of them reappear in Mack's volume.

Jacobs makes little effort to examine critically aspects of the abduction such as the sexual encounters that make little sense, biological or otherwise, or the visions of universal cataclysm. It is hardly necessary, for instance, to encounter aliens in order to be made sensitive to the possibility of such catastrophes. Lynn Miller, one of Jacobs's alleged abductees, following a 1967 abduction "became convinced that a war was about to take place." Jacobs finds this amazing, since her "preoccupation with war was quite unusual for any teenage girl, but it was all the more inexplicable because Lynn had grown up as a Mennonite and . . . Mennonites are not known for their interest in war."[26] That the Vietnam War (or the Seven Days' War) was a matter of daily concern at that time; that Lynn had been born in the 1950s and grew up surrounded by all the rhetoric of the Cold War; and that Mennonite pacifism is not synonymous with indifference to war or world events, none of this is broached by Jacobs in the course of his discussion. For anyone Lynn's age to have emerged into adulthood with no knowledge or fear of nuclear destruction would have been virtually impossible, and the re-emergence of such fears needs no extraterrestrial explanation.

Readers may also be annoyed by Jacobs's steadfast refusal to consider simple explanations for some of the anomalous experiences associated with the abduction phenomenon. Referring to abductees who have "mysteriously" wakened to find themselves in a bed or room not their own or in strange sleeping positions, Jacobs ignores mundane causes: Who among us has not walked in our sleep, hurriedly put a nightgown on backwards when extremely fatigued, or become momentarily disoriented in the middle of the night and climbed into the wrong bed after a trip to the bathroom?

Rejection of Alternate Explanations

Jacobs's conclusion follows the same format as Fowler's in *The Allagash Abductions*, in that it summarizes and rejects all other possible explanations of the abduction phenomenon. But in order to do so, Jacobs, like Fowler, must oversimplify these in a way that does little to advance his preferred argument and much to detract from it. Attempting to distance alleged abductees from their earlier "contactee" ancestors, he argues that unlike the contactees, abductees only occasionally know each other and only rarely seek money or publicity. It does not follow that abductees' tales are true simply because they do *not* make similar attempts to profit. Nor is it necessary for abductees to know each other personally in order for them to be influenced by other abduction accounts. As this book has argued, we receive information in a variety of diverse and indirect ways. Finally, to imply as Jacobs does that abductees (and their authors) have not benefited financially from their stories is manifestly untrue. There is a good deal of money to be made in abduction literature. As far back as the Hills, abductees have reaped financial rewards from the publication of their accounts. Whitley Strieber and John Mack both received sizable advances for *Communion* (1987) and *Abduction* (1994) respectively, and many abduction experiences (the Hills, Travis Walton, and those chronicled by Hopkins in *Intruders*) have been made into motion pictures and "made-for-TV" movies, for which all concerned were presumably remunerated.[27]

Still, Jacobs is to be commended for addressing those who argue that the recalled abductions are themselves screen memories hiding a past history of sexual or physical abuse. Needless to say, in defiance of Kenneth Ring's discoveries he denies the likelihood of this by arguing, "Most abductees do not claim to have been sexually or physically abused."[28] One could, however, reply by pointing out that this is the whole purpose of screen memories: if the pseudomemory of an alien abduction is doing its job in successfully shielding the victim from memories of abuse by a human being, the victim naturally would not know of it. He then states that in those instances where abductees *were* abused, they can "explicitly differentiate" between memories of such abuse and those of abductions. Obviously, a point this important surely demands some form of corroborating testimony, but none is forthcoming.

In fact, Jacobs's concluding sections are replete with similarly unsubstantiated, generalized assertions. It is *not* true, as he says, that the contactees' stories were any more indebted to science fiction than are the claims of abductees; if anything, the reverse is a more likely possibility. Nor, as we have seen, is it the case that abductees do not know much about UFOs. A few were actively interested in related matters before their abductions surfaced; some had previously read books on the subject; and others become actively interested in the phenomenon after their initial experiences came to light. As readers confront Jacobs's many pronouncements, just as many questions will come to mind: Were the contactees invariably so money-hungry, as he maintains? Can children as young as two really provide accurate descriptions of their experiences? Can it be verified that not a single abduction case has been "generated" from physical or sexual abuse? Do abductees really have so little in common? Of course, even if Jacobs could answer these questions to his complete satisfaction, it would not be enough to establish the reality of abductions once and for all.

Jacobs dismisses alternate medical or psychiatric accounts of the abduction phenomenon just as casually. But, in fact, virtually every attempt to invalidate traditional scientific explanations is either based on oversimplification or falsehood. Much in the manner of Fowler, Jacobs rejects the possibility that abductees are psychotic or otherwise mentally ill, without entertaining the possibility that there could be forms of mental disturbance that medical science has not yet identified. That abductions might be recalled birth trauma is similarly rejected because people born of cesarean procedure, so he alleges, are also abductees.

According to Jacobs, Jung's vision of the collective unconscious cannot be cited as an alternate explanation, for it is itself unproven and incapable of explaining such aspects of the phenomenon as multiple abductions or physical scarring. At this point the reader may take umbrage at the historian's two-paragraph dismissal of such a prominent psychological theorist. For that matter, it does not seem to have dawned on Jacobs that the very similarities in the accounts might well constitute precisely the sort of "proof" of Jung's concept which he argues has not yet appeared. In this instance, Jung's concept of synchronicity—the belief that meaningful coincidences not only occur frequently, but are also a fundamental part of human life—might well be employed profitably as a means of explaining similarities among alleged multiple abductions and the simultaneous appearance of physical evidence as well.

Professor Michael Persinger's suggestion that temporal lobe epilepsy could be a possible cause of abduction accounts is given little weight because the population sample Persinger worked with was very small, and because his suggestion that the temporal lobe could be stimulated by geologic factors such as earthquakes is undeniably questionable. Persinger has theorized that the temporal lobe might be stimulated by "electrically charged particles in the earth's atmosphere unleashed as a result of the earth's geologic plate stress" in a manner that could "lead people to hallucinate."[29] But Jacobs also rejects Persinger's claims on the grounds that Persinger's subjects were "by and large" not abductees, and thus presumably in no position to compare the states of mind induced by Persinger with those experienced when one is abducted. Of course, this minimizes Persinger's ability to duplicate artificially, in a lab, many aspects of the alleged abduction experience that were identical to those described by abductees.

That abduction accounts might be the product of mass hysteria is ruled out because abductees are not confined to a particular geographical locale or restricted to a specific period in time. Here, the readers' readiness to accept Jacobs's argument rests entirely with how precisely terms such as "particular" or "specific" should be defined. Also as a result Jacobs fails to explore the ways in which the phenomenon changes in relation to different contexts (including social ones). Jacobs himself states later in the chapter that abduction accounts have appeared only relatively recently, and by far the greatest concentration of abductees to surface so far has been in the continental United States. Both of these facts suggest that the phenomenon arguably *does* have some specificity in place and time.[30] Hypnopompic (waking dream) states he rejects because "a large percentage" of abductions occur during the day. In fact, this claim is not verified and was recently refuted statistically by Jenny Randles, who demonstrated that the largest number of reported abductions occur at night, reaching a peak between midnight and 2:00 A.M.[31] That alleged abductions are simply fantasies or hallucinations is dismissed because as far as Jacobs is concerned the abductees' stories are neither "dreamlike or surrealistic," nor are they pleasant experiences, as Jacobs arbitrarily assumes fantasies would be. But as the reader has had ample time to see, many abductions *do* have a decidedly dreamlike or discontinuous quality about them and are far from the logical and realistic narratives Jacobs perceives.

Repudiating similarities with folklore as tenuous and "facile," Jacobs argues incredibly that, unlike folklore which is constantly changing, abduction narratives are static and consistent. Jacobs's argument is particularly surprising in light of the work of Jacques Vallee, whom he cites elsewhere, and the mass of evidence indicating that the narrative is undergoing constant change and does vary in relation to a person's "social, cultural, familial, or occupational activities."[32]

His claim that abductees are not fabricating or telling stories they had heard at some point in the past is extremely difficult to accept, given the ubiquitousness of such stories, especially in recent years. The possible influence of the hypnotist on the abductee is also rejected on the grounds that the abduction stories have a life of their own over which the hypnotist has no control. But, as we have witnessed time after time, the hypnotist often plays an active role in the proceedings (see, in particular, chapters 4 and 8). Finally, Jacobs rejects that the physical marks and scars could be similar to such psychosomatic conditions as the so-called stigmata—where an individual develops wound marks and bleeding in imitation of Christ's—simply because abductees, so we are told, develop such marks even though they are not conscious of having been abducted. Of course, that such a fact could never be known the author does not acknowledge.

In summarizing the weaknesses of these explanations, Jacobs argues that none can account for the similarities among the accounts or for the fact that abductees tell "essentially the same story" regardless of their age, race, religion, or upbringing. Yet we have seen that an abductee's background *does* have a significant effect on the kind of abduction narrative that he or she will produce: Ann Druffel's lesbian subjects, Betty Andreasson's Pentecostal faith, and Whitley Strieber's Catholicism arguably played important roles in the kind of experiences they had.

Finally, Jacobs attempts to buttress his thesis by observing that while fantasies of alien abductions have been produced, such "idiosyncratic" stories "do not match the accounts given by other abductees."[33] At this point the reader will see that he has an excellent opportunity to bolster his contention that abduction stories are real by illustrating precisely where they *do* differ from those that are openly acknowledged to be the product of imagination. But as before, Jacobs fails to provide even one example, leaving the reader to conclude that the abduction accounts are indistinguishable from those known to have been manufactured.

Despite the confidence with which Jacobs has written his book, many readers will not find *Secret Life* all that convincing; the book's most conspicuous strength is paradoxically enough also its greatest potential weakness. Although Jacobs's presentation is dramatic, its effect on many readers, though immediate, is not apt to be long lasting. After becoming used to Jacobs's forceful style, we begin to realize that the statements he makes with such assurance are far from axiomatic and more open to question than he ever admits them to be. It is also evident that, since everything in the book is resting on Jacobs's narrative shoulders, this may simply be too much responsibility for one individual. Not only has he done all the interpreting of extremely controversial material, but he frequently gives the impression of handling evidence very selectively, especially in his citation of direct testimony. Finally, his assumption that *all* the evidence, no matter how bizarre, is equally valid becomes increasingly suspect as readers encounter testimony—sexual intercourse with humans and aliens, for example—that is extremely hard to ingest. The very power of Jacobs's utterances consists in his disregard of any information that might force him to soften them.

This is not to say that novice readers coming to the abduction phenomenon for the first time will not find Jacobs's uncompromising treatment of alien abductions strong and compelling, and doubtless the power of his narrative has helped shape the developing myth. But for those readers more prepared to see that all narrative is the product of various techniques and strategies within specific social and cultural settings, *Secret Life*'s nonstop tendency to overstatement and generalization makes it ultimately less than satisfying, more of a polemic than the sober history of the phenomenon that it attempts to be.

Notes

1. See B. Hopkins, D. M. Jacobs, and R. Westrum, *Unusual Personal Experiences: An Analysis of the Data from Three National Surveys* (Las Vegas: Bigelow Holding Corporation, 1992). For a dissenting analysis of this experiment, see Lloyd Stires, "3.7 Million Americans Kidnapped by Aliens?" *Skeptical Inquirer* 17 (Winter 1993): 142–44.

2. David Jacobs, *Secret Life: Firsthand Documented Accounts of UFO Abductions* (New York: Simon & Schuster, 1992), 10–11.

3. Ibid., 20.

4. John Fuller, *The Interrupted Journey* (New York: Dell, 1966; 1987), 191.

5. Jacobs, *Secret Life*, 10, my emphasis.

6. Ibid., 25.

7. Ibid., 246.

8. Ibid., 29.

9. Ibid., 26–28.

10. Ibid., 23.

11. Ibid., 25.

12. Ibid., 24–28.

13. Ibid., 96, 240.

14. Ibid., 107–10, my emphasis.

15. Ibid., 163–65.

16. Ibid., 53.

17. Ibid., 142, 195, 210.

18. Ibid., 189–91.

19. Ibid., 212.

20. Ibid., 276–78.

21. Ibid., 19.

22. Ibid., 215.

23. Ibid., 106. Jacobs finds this and other alien-induced sexual activity "confusing" (198), but accepts that it is occurring as stated.

24. The reader may also find it interesting that this "imaging" has a close fictional counterpart in John Fowles's 1985 novel *A Maggot*. In that work, a mysterious young man in the eighteenth century travels to a remote part of England. There, he and his companions encounter in a cave miraculous beings who, before spiriting the man away, present the entire company with visions both of calamity and supernal beauty.

25. Jacobs, *Secret Life*, 298.

26. Ibid., 140.

27. In *UFO Abductions: A Dangerous Game* (Amherst, N.Y.: Prometheus Books, 1989), Philip J. Klass states that Whitley Strieber received a "$1 million cash advance" (141) for *Communion; Publishers Weekly* magazine, April 18, 1994, mentions that John Mack received a $250,000 advance from Scribner's for *Abduction* (40).

28. Ibid., 285. Although Kenneth Ring's *The Omega Project* was not published in book form until 1992, his research had appeared in the *Journal of UFO Studies* in 1990; see K. Ring and C. J. Rosing, "The Omega Project: A psychological survey of persons reporting abductions and other UFO encounters," *Journal of UFO Studies* 2(1990): 59–90.

29. Jacobs, *Secret Life*, 296.

30. Ibid., 300. See also Klass, *UFO Abductions*, 213.

31. See Jenny Randles, *UFO Study* (London: Robert Hale, 1981); reprinted in Jacques Vallee, *Revelations: Alien Contact and Human Deception* (New York: Ballantine, 1993), 269.

32. Jacobs, *Secret Life*, 302.

33. Ibid., 290.

10

JOHN MACK'S
A B D U C T I O N

If historian David Jacobs's credentials were impressive, those of Harvard psychiatrist John Mack, author of *Abduction* (1994), are (as we have seen in the previous chapter) impeccable. On balance, Mack does present as fair-minded an account as has been encountered to date, at least as these abduction narratives go. Mack appears to make a sincere attempt to be faithful to the often-conflicting bodies of information that comprise the abduction experience, while not forcing the reader to accept every aspect of it. For this reason alone, *Abduction* is less likely than other works on the subject to stretch belief beyond the breaking point.

Mack's narrative approach is different in certain respects from that employed by his predecessors. He has clearly learned to avoid many of the pitfalls incurred by previous writers. Where Jacobs's tone exuded confidence at times to the point of arrogance, Mack's is almost diffident; where Fowler's response to the subject matter was one of uncritical acceptance, Mack's is discriminating. This is not meant to imply that the narrative approach he employs is problem-free or that his attitude is noncommittal. But the author is sufficiently confident of his contents that *Abduction* is the first of its kind not to feature the customary expert's foreword, even though it is evident that one could easily have been obtained. The book, however, derives authority from its dedication to Budd Hopkins and the acknowledgment page, which reads like a "Who's Who" of abduction researchers.

Mack's narrative style is novel to the extent that we do not encounter the broad overstatements found in Jacobs, nor that readiness to believe in the literal truth of virtually every statement an alleged abductee makes that was so characteristic of Fowler and Hopkins. By openly admitting that there are degrees of plausibility where the evidence is concerned, and conceding as well that he does not "believe literally everything an abductee says," Mack makes it more difficult for the reader to dismiss the abduction experience in toto.[1] When there is no corroborating proof for a given aspect of the phenomenon, more often than not Mack reminds us of this deficiency. When certain aspects of his abductees' experiences are not encountered in other research or when their behavior is particularly idiosyncratic, he will, on occasion, comment on it. Most importantly, when an aspect of a case appears weak or amenable to an alternate explanation he actually concedes as much. For instance, concerning the frequently made assertion that alleged abductees have been noted missing by others or even observed while in the process of being abducted, Mack admits that this is "relatively rare and limited." Indeed, he may be unique in his readiness to acknowledge that, even when abductees are noticed by others to be missing, "there is no firm proof that abduction was the cause of their absence." Concerning the so-called corroborating evidence, Mack also stands alone in admitting that, however persuasive it may be, it is also "maddeningly subtle and difficult to corroborate with as much supporting data as firm proof would require."[2]

Mack is similarly forthright about the scars and scoopmarks earlier authors found so compelling, finding them "usually too trivial by themselves to be medically significant." Regarding the "missing fetus" syndrome, he observes there is "not yet a case where a physician has documented that a fetus has disappeared in relation to an abduction." As far as he is concerned, it is "almost impossible to prove" that an abductee has caused appliances to malfunction, "or even that [such events] have occurred at all."[3] Similarly, in his opinion, the much-ballyhooed implants will probably never provide the proof of alien existence that other authors such as Hopkins were so confident would be forthcoming, because such objects as have been examined are composed of familiar compounds and elements readily available on earth. As he observes, since clever and techno-logically sophisticated aliens could easily manufacture such devices in a manner that disguised their actual origin and purpose, we will probably never be able to determine anything from those objects alleged to be implants taken from an abductee's body. Mack even checks anecdotal evidence when possible, and he informs the reader on those occasions when he has spoken to relatives or friends to cor-roborate some part of an abductee's story that allegedly involved them. Most importantly, because of his willingness to make signifi-cant concessions when the occasions appear to warrant it, Mack draws far more attention to those features which cannot be dis-missed as readily. Furthermore, those statements he *does* offer in support of the phenomenon appear, as a result, more convincing, adding significantly to the book's credibility.

Mack's main reasons for rejecting a conventional psychiatric explanation, he tells us, stemmed from his recognition that what was occurring was unique, like nothing he had encountered before in his practice (in what manner it was unique he does not specify); furthermore, he was simply unable to trace the abduction experi-ence to any known form of neurological disorder. Combined with this was his own observation that the accounts were accompanied by displays of intense energy and emotion on the part of the alleged abductees unlike anything he had previously witnessed. It goes without saying that, given Mack's scientific credentials, such re-marks are bound to carry considerable weight with many readers.

For a number of reasons he was led to speculate that the abduc-tion phenomenon could be in the tradition of the visionary experi-ences of old, a possibility he considers entirely likely and one which his book maintains throughout. In support of this view he cites other instances throughout history where individuals have seemingly attained higher levels of awareness, the existence of which he believes poses an effective challenge to the prevailing materialistic worldview. Much like the shamans of old, these individuals make what he calls a spiritual "pilgrimage" during which they are initiated into an altered state of consciousness and being, receiving new knowledge from a paranormal source similar to that allegedly obtained in mystical or out-of-body experiences. He also speculates on the possible relationship between the supposed visitations of alien creatures and the traditional encounters between human beings and ghosts, witches, fairies, and the like, which he believes may indeed represent a legitimate form of contact with supranormal intelligences that has played a prominent role in many human cultures, but which our scientific age has chosen to ignore or otherwise regard contemptuously.[4] Prior to Mack, only Whitley Strieber had taken seriously the possibility that his abductors might have an ethereal essence while not being "real" in the normal sense of the word, but his claims were based only on his own experiences and therefore of limited usefulness when applied to the phenomenon as a whole.[5]

When he began his study, Mack sought advice from the almost legendary philosopher of science, Thomas Kuhn, on how best to proceed. Kuhn, author of the landmark *The Structure of Scientific Revolutions* (1962), told him to begin by assuming that the present way of thinking about the nature of reality was far too narrow, having taken on "the rigidity of a theology," and that this narrowness was reflected in a similarly rigid language, best seen in the way we reduce everything around us to simple dichotomies: Things are either "real" or "unreal," they either "exist" or "do not," and they occur either "objectively" or "subjectively."

Armed with these liberating notions, Mack attempted to suspend such restricting language forms and conceptual categories from his vocabulary and tried merely to listen to the raw data he was collecting. He soon realized that as yet, we do not really know what an "abduction experience" actually is. On the one hand there are simply too many physical elements alleged to be an integral part of the phenomenon—rashes, cuts, "scoopmarks," etc.—to allow it to be comfortably reduced to the status of a subjective experience alone. At the same time, there are just as many aspects of the accounts—abductees moving through windows and ceilings, for instance—that violate our traditional conceptions of physical reality as well. Mack goes on to argue that the only proper response to the abduction phenomenon is to admit that some enlargement or expansion of our view of reality is necessary; that only when we accept the need to broaden our consciousness may these mysterious happenings be properly understood. Presumably, this entails moving beyond dichotomous thinking in order that those aspects of the abduction experience traditionally termed "subjective" in nature will be looked at from a fresh perspective. Only when that happens will they be given enhanced status, not necessarily as hard events taking place in the traditional sense, but as phenomena that have a substance beyond the merely psychological.

Errors in *Abduction*

For all the book's virtues, like many other researchers Mack can be careless on matters of detail. His summary of the Hill case is over-simplified and he makes numerous assumptions that are simply not accurate, however entrenched a part of the Hills' legend they have in the process of transmission become. Although he implies that the abduction experience was the cause of all their anxiety, we recall that Barney Hill's health problems had been with him for some time before that event occurred; nor was there evidence in *The Interrupted Journey* that the Hills consulted Dr. Simon "reluctantly" as Mack claims.[6] And he says nothing about the fact that Betty and Barney Hill returned from their experiences with no visions for humanity; they learned very little, if anything, from their abductors. Mack also accepts several of Jacobs's uncorroborated statements on faith, and in the process participates in the process whereby features of that abduction myth became solidified. When he refers to a sperm sample being taken from Barney Hill, for instance, he cites Jacobs's *Secret Life* as his source, even though Jacobs himself provided no source in support of this fact.[7]

There are a few other problems in Mack's introductory sections. For one, his contention that abduction accounts conform to no obvious symbolic pattern is highly debatable, as we will explore further in the conclusion. Second, the values of Mack's abductees—concerning, for example, their sensitivity to environmental issues and to the rampant greed and waste behind many of the world's evils—are remarkably similar to his own (a point which he openly acknowledges). While concerns for the environment and contempt for unregulated industrial expansion are both valid and admirable, there is no particular reason why so many of the alleged abductees Mack studies should have any values and concerns in common with him. That they do cannot help but suggest that his abductees may on some level be giving him what they think he wants to hear, and that he is playing a more active role in the creation of the narrative than he realizes.

Mack's sense that there is a coherent pattern in the abduction phenomenon causes him, like Jacobs, to be less mindful of inconsistencies than he might otherwise have been. We first observe this refusal to take such variations more seriously in the abduction "overview" that occurs early in the book. Because of this, the pattern that the overview presents does not do justice to the total picture in all its incongruous complexity because it attributes a uniformity to the abduction experience that is simply not found when one examines even the narratives Mack himself has picked for inclusion in the book. This is actually quite surprising, because late in *Abduction* Mack admits candidly that he does "not know what a typical case would be, or even that there is such a thing as a typical case."[8]

Finally, his dismissal of the possibility that abductions may be traceable to a past of sexual or other forms of abuse mirrors Jacobs, and is not altogether convincing. Mack simply assumes as proven Jacobs's claim that there is not a single abduction case that has turned out to be a screen memory for sexual abuse or other trauma. Presumably an expert on such matters, Mack adds his own authority to the discussions and observes that his efforts either failed to uncover a history of abuse or that when abuse was found, the abductee could make a clear distinction between the two memories. Hence, there is not "a single abduction in [his] experience . . . that has turned out to have masked a history of sexual abuse."[9] Understandably, Mack assumes that what sexual dysfunction they display is traceable to their abduction experiences, the reality of which he accepts.

But, like earlier researchers, Mack ignores the possibility that some screen memories may be so firmly entrenched that it is beyond the power of present-day psychiatric techniques to expose or uproot them. In short, the limitations of psychiatry may be the source of his failure; after all, the science is arguably still in its infancy. Finally, it is even possible that the abuse in question might be something other than sexual abuse. After all, adults can subject their children to many kinds of abuse, not all of which is physical or sexual. Such considerations surely deserve to be discussed at length. That they are not indicates that even a writer as concerned to be scrupulous as Mack will at times deal selectively with evidence when that poses a threat to the thesis he favors. In this regard, he does not do justice to the work of researcher Kenneth

Ring, who did not simply argue that there was such a thing as an "encounter-prone" personality, or that there was a tendency in certain persons who had been affected by odd experiences to be "more open to them" in future.[10] Mack simply does not acknowledge that in *The Omega Project* (1992) Ring demonstrated that abductees had a statistically higher incidence of sexual or other forms of abuse than a control group given the same questionnaire.

In support of his contention that abductees are for the most part normal men and women from average backgrounds, Mack observes that he could find no particular link between his abductees and family dysfunction, and argues that many of his abductees came from intact, well-functioning families. Yet many of the alleged abductees featured in *Abduction* have a definite history of family troubles or some form of sexual or other dysfunction, in some cases serious enough to cause us to question Mack's judgment. For example, the mother of Sheila, one of Mack's subjects, had been sexually abused by her father, Sheila's own marriage was unhappy, and as an adult she is sexually dysfunctional. One childhood dream, involving a "figure" who came out of her closet, could possibly have been an adult who was lurking in wait for her. An obviously troubled individual whose fear of sexual intimacy is such that she refuses even to sleep in the same bed as her husband, Sheila described an unpleasant abduction experience involving "needles" which were stuck into her head and leg while she was naked.[11]

For his part, Scott had a history of severe neurological disorders going back to infancy, involving headaches, seizures, and hallucinations. Scott's sister Lee, sexually dysfunctional like Sheila, believed her fear of sex could be traced to past abuse by her father or someone else. Hypnosis revealed an alleged abduction experience that involved the insertion of a "probing instrument" in her vagina. Mack obviously favors the possibility that Lee's fear of sex was a consequence of having been abducted, but the other possibility remains strong.[12]

Jerry's parents were divorced and her first husband sexually abused their children. Though married again, she, too, has an aversion to sexual intimacy which Mack traces to an early abduction memory involving sexual activity with an alien. Although neither Catherine nor her mother believes that she was sexually abused by anyone in her family, she does have a memory of being inappropriately touched at the age of four when a family friend put his hand between her legs.[13]

Mack's other subjects reveal similar trauma in their pasts. Catherine's father was also an abusive alcoholic. Joe, a psychotherapist himself, admits that his family was cold and dysfunctional and offered him little in the way of emotional nurturing. Sara's family was similarly unhappy; her parents fought frequently and her father physically and verbally abused her. Paul's parents were alcoholics and he also believes that he was sexually abused by a family member (his grandmother, of all people).[14] Though no such memory was uncovered, one cannot help but wonder again how such a clearly unpleasant notion could take hold in an individual's mind in the first place. Paul's stepfather, himself a victim of sexual abuse, was a cruel man who beat Paul and may also have abused Paul's younger sister. Eva too had a problematic relationship with her "cold" father and seems far from close to her husband, David, for she admits that the very thought of telling him of her abduction experiences is for her "the most difficult challenge of all," presumably even more difficult than the abductions themselves. When she finally does break the news, we are told that her husband, incredibly enough, "didn't show much interest."[15] Peter's marriage also appears precarious, for his wife confided to Mack that she was afraid he would leave her. A battery of psychological tests indicated to the presiding psychologist that there was a possibility of sexual abuse in Peter's past as well.[16] It remains conceivable, then, that these recalled abductions could have been screen memories, and many readers will think it is something that should be investigated more thoroughly.

Mack's Theory

Mack must be given credit for acknowledging openly the difficulty of his endeavor to fit the types of evidence that surround alleged abduction accounts into a coherent theory. Prior to producing such a theory, he establishes a tripartite division similar to Jacobs's, whereby the various aspects of the abduction process can be classified, based not on the frequency of an event's occurrence but rather on its degree of strangeness. In the first category, he places obviously physical events such as the arrival of the UFO, the escorting of the abductee aboard the craft, and the conducting of the experiments themselves. If one is prepared to entertain the possibility that alien beings could be studying us, presumably none of the happenings in this category would be particularly difficult to accept. In the second group, Mack includes all those claimed alien capabilities that we cannot presently emulate ourselves, but could conceivably reach in the future. The ability to float around or pass through solid material falls into this grouping. Third, he lists those experiences that appear frankly transcendent, mystical, or otherwise paranormal, and involve the alleged abductee's claims of being initiated into higher states of being (in some instances into a dual human/alien identity) or experiencing memories of relationships with aliens in previous incarnations. Here, the aliens function as purely spiritual entities and are more reminiscent of angels than technologists. As we will see, this last contention gives him the most trouble.

Mack has plainly recognized that from its beginnings the abduction narrative contained two distinct strains of information: one that does not absolutely violate our understanding of the physical universe and one that does. On the one hand was the experience of the abduction, the characteristics of which did not pose too dramatic a challenge to our sense of how the universe operates. While specific alien motives remain unknown, much of what occurs is not qualitatively different from the way human scientists might use experimental animals, and alien actions remain largely at the mercy of the same laws that restrict us.

On the other hand, the second and third of Mack's types cannot be explained within present ontological parameters. Within the frankly mystical component of abduction cases, the alien beings seem capable of moving beyond mere corporeal status, assuming roles similar to that of angels or even gods, and expanding the consciousness of abductees in their concern for our future as a species. This causes Mack trouble in two respects. Not only does the existence of supernatural creatures fly in the face of scientific knowledge, but tales of aliens as unequivocally callous and indifferent, obsessed exclusively with their own scientific agenda, cannot be squared with the loving and concerned spiritual beings many abductees claim to have encountered. What made this contradiction particularly difficult to comprehend was that at times the same aliens were assuming both roles, and even within the same abduction.

To his credit, Mack is the first investigator to try to incorporate these seemingly contradictory features into a comprehensive theory. To this end, he traces the belief in higher or alternate states of reality, citing folklorists and mythologists to support his belief that abductees are participating in a legitimate phenomenon with roots in the earliest human societies. In the course of this section some readers will experience qualms regarding Mack's theory, qualms which the book may not ultimately be able to resolve. For one thing, many may suspect that the abduction experience is not as similar to the ordeal of the shaman or mystic as Mack contends.[17] Citing only the most obvious difference, while shamans' experiences are for the most part positive, the vast majority of alleged abductees are quite reluctant to embark on their journeys; and the extent to which they could be said to enjoy any special social status as a consequence of their experiences is highly debatable. For another, shamans or mystics return equipped with wisdom which they often share with others; many abductees have gained absolutely nothing of benefit. For every Betty Andreasson there are many Barney Hills who are at a loss to see any personal or other meaning in their abductions.

But even if we grant Mack's theory for the sake of argument, there is still a problem concerning his underlying assumption that the intensity of the experience which abductees endure gives it a kind of ipso facto authenticity that lifts it above and beyond the level of the purely subjective. To argue in this manner is hazardous because it can be applied to *any* traumatic incident an individual claims to have endured, and would essentially force us to believe in the literal reality of demonic possession, for example.

The Spiritual Dimension

Mack's contention that the abduction experience is primarily spiritual and educational is central to his study, and is based on many abductees' sense that, like the shaman or mystic, they have undergone spiritual growth and have been entrusted with a personal mission to educate and enlighten others. Though this is not a new element in the abduction narrative, but rather an expansion of the role assigned to Betty Andreasson by her mentor Quazgaa, Mack's deliberate emphasis on this factor is the distinguishing feature of *Abduction*. In his opinion, this claim is itself proof that something more than mere hallucination or fantasizing is occurring. As he says, he was prompted to give it more attention for three reasons: first, this aspect of the phenomenon "has either been neglected or has been viewed as incompatible with the traumatic dimension of an abduction"; second, as a "largely unresearched area [it] is of considerable significance"; and finally, he seems "to receive more information of this kind" than do other investigators.[18]

There is no doubt that many of Mack's alleged abductees make such claims, and testify to an intense intimacy with the beings who have supposedly abducted them. Given their family histories, it is not surprising that some also feel they received more nurturing from the aliens than they ever did from their parents. Joe found such emotional nourishment that he did not wish to return to earth, and considered the aliens " 'midwives' helping him stay connected with his divinity."[19] Believing he possessed a dual alien/human identity, Joe also maintained that the soul of his infant son Mark was alien in origin and was implanted in its human body before birth. Sara described her mentor as "family," while Paul also considers aliens his friends, and was told he had been " 'kind of like a spy,' put on earth for a purpose" almost as an emissary. Eva, who sees herself as a "Superwoman" ready to embark on a " 'global mission' " as a "communicator" between humanity and the aliens, is frank in her expression of "love" for them, who she assures us "mean us no harm [and] are here to help." Dave also met a friendly female alien who served as a mentor, and he believes the aliens are concerned with "the development of our soul[s]" as they accompany us (presumably everyone) through a number of lifetimes.[20] Peter and Carlos, both of whom claim dual alien/human identities, see the aliens as guardian angels or "earth gardeners" who out of tremendous compassion are "trying to arrest our destructive behavior." Convinced that as a physical infant he died very young, Carlos believes that as an alien he took over the dead body. He also suspects aliens may have cured him both of pneumonia and cancer, and suggests that the rectal examinations he and so many other male abductees are subjected to may be part of a healing process as well, at least in his own case. Finally, Arthur's aliens were uniquely described as "cute," "like bunnies" who "don't want to harm anybody."[21]

Ed was told repeatedly how sensitive he was by friendly aliens who also made him aware of the importance of environmental responsibility, advising him to "listen to the earth," for he has the ability hear the "wailing cries of the imbalances." But despite his claims that the wisdom is alien-inspired, readers may catch many echoes of the biblical book of Revelation in Ed's apocalyptic vision. For example, Ed tells of "dark, gray, malignant forms" working in opposition to other good spirits; an end of the world is prophesied, following which the few who survive will engage in a "reconstitution" of the planet. Though universal cataclysm is an inevitability, the good " 'spirits of the earth' [or 'angels of the Lord'?] will 'make safe havens' for those who will survive." Whereas Mack surprisingly sees nothing of relevance in Ed's "traditional Roman Catholic upbringing," the reader may suspect that Ed could have acquired much of this apocalyptic vision in the course of the religious instruction he would have received during the four years he spent in parochial school.[22]

Indeed, for all Mack's emphasis on the abductees having received consciousness-raising dollops of wisdom, predictions of doomsday occur with greater frequency in *Abduction* than anywhere else in the narrative literature. In this connection two points need to be raised. First, readers may see a connection between the increasing frequency of such dire prophecies and the approach of the millennium. But many will also wonder exactly how, if nothing can be done to forestall or prevent such catastrophe, Ed could ever be "used for something worthwhile," as he was told.[23] The same inconsistency also crops up in Scott's case. Scott, another self-proclaimed example of dual identity, was sure the "wisdomful" [*sic*] aliens are preparing us for the future by helping us grow spiritually, but such preparation makes little sense if the world is inevitably headed for ecological catastrophe.

Even here, another problem emerges, for the precise nature of our doom is never spelled out or specified consistently, but varies from abductee to abductee. Scott sees many of us dying from diseases such as AIDS; Jerry sees global destruction through nuclear war; Catherine's aliens are preoccupied with "the damage from pollution" and develop hybrid babies in glass cases to replace their lost genetic material; and Joe believes we are in danger of destroying ourselves through " 'electromagnetic' catastrophe resulting from the 'negative' technology human beings have created."[24] Of course, given our capacity for destructive behavior *all* of these calamities could occur simultaneously. But surely if this were in the cards such a picture would itself be conveyed to all abductees in its entirety. For that matter, not all abductees assert that the aliens are passing on messages of gloom and doom, and claim instead that they have simply come here to communicate generally (Eva), or to observe us and assist in our spiritual evolution (Dave and Peter).

Even a cursory look at the alleged abductees' statements reveals that, as we have come to expect, there is little consistency in the descriptions of alien physical characteristics. In appearance they run the gamut from Ed's sexy female alien with "loving, big, sensuous eyes" and "exquisite breasts" to Scott's "big ants," Sara's "cross between a skeleton and a walking insect," Paul's "hairless, large-eyed being" whose mouth "seemed to have 'scales around it, like plates on his lips,' " Eva's " 'midgets,' about three feet tall" with "dark brown, wrinkled skin and triangular heads," Peter's "small, hooded beings," Carlos's "large, robotlike creatures with large black eyes that appeared to have reptilian and insectile facial qualities and insectile body characteristics," or Arthur's " 'little gentle things' " that were " 'luminescent' and semitransparent, with large heads and small bodies."[25]

Although Eva offers an ingenious explanation for all these discrepancies in abductees' descriptions of alien appearance, it is doubtful if many readers will find it all that satisfactory. According to her, because the aliens are not really physical entities, what specific abductees see is the product of the aliens' "biochemical energetic makeup [*sic*]" working in combination with our admittedly imperfect "perceptive devices."[26] Of course, this admittedly imaginative attempt to solve one problem raises a new one, for if they are not physical how can we explain their obsession with *our* physical (and especially our sexual) natures? Indeed, how are they able to interact with us physically at all, if they are as Eva says?

Mack's allegation that abductees undergo significant changes in their value systems ignores that such changes might be the result of experiences entirely psychological or otherwise earthbound in origin. Here, readers will also note that the transformation process he speaks of is nowhere so common as he claims, nor are the revelations so lucid as he would have us believe. It is true that, while not all of Mack's abductees are given a sense of mission, most express concern about ecological issues and other crises facing our planet. Although many see such concern as a motive behind alien behavior, the experiences of Sheila and Jerry, who find neither friendliness nor an understanding of human feelings (to say nothing of the many other accounts featured in Hopkins's and Jacobs's books) tend to weaken these claims. For that matter, it is not necessary to acquire such concerns from an extraterrestrial or transdimensional source in order for it to be meaningful. Much of the "wisdom" abductees possess is nothing they could not have acquired from popular television programs such as *Nova* or *The Nature of Things*, while what other information they convey to us is garbled or otherwise vague and indistinct; the claim that the aliens "have lost all the genetic material" is simply pseudoscientific gibberish.[27]

The problem of vagueness persists in much of this "wisdom." Ed, for example, is spoken to in "allegorical terms" concerning the "eco-spiritual, emotional instability. . . . Volcanic eruptions are a sign. . . . It's allegorical towering plumes of eruptive rage. Not ejaculations of ecstasy, but eruptions of anguish. Be careful."[28] Readers familiar with the concept of the "Gaia"—where the earth is regarded as a unified, living system capable of responding in kind when ravished or otherwise desecrated—will probably have little trouble understanding where Ed is coming from. But the fact remains that the aliens' decision to choose to speak through him in such highly symbolic language (since he admits he is "no poet") casts serious aspersions on their methodology. Even Ed questions why they ever decided to use him.

The uses the aliens make of Scott are similarly enigmatic. Scott himself speaks vaguely of the possibility that they are preparing us for "something, that there was perhaps a 'plan' of some sort, that we are not in control and 'somebody else' is running the show." His belief that they have given him "an intense jump into a spiritual realm [he was] not even ready for" is not particularly convincing, for he adds paradoxically enough that they "would not let him talk about these experiences" or convey their teachings to other human beings. Of course, Mack's more cynical readers may conclude that it is simply prudent to keep silent when it comes to the exact nature of all this wisdom, for only when it has been articulated can it be exposed to criticism (viz., Betty Andreasson). Such facts as are imparted to Scott—such as that the aliens have come from a "yellow, mostly desert" planet "closest to where we're from"—lend support to the view, for they make no sense astronomical or otherwise.[29] Mars, the only conceivable candidate in our solar system, is a desert, but red in color.

Jerry also claims to have acquired complex information as a result of her experiences with her abductors. Though Mack attests that "the sophistication and articulateness of her writings do seem beyond her educational level," little evidence is provided that would allow readers to judge for themselves. Oddly enough, in yet another instance of hard evidence disappearing, Jerry herself burned her alien-inspired notebooks. She believes that what the aliens are doing is "somehow necessary" and for the "greater good," but, as with Scott, their motives are never explained to her. All in all, it is difficult to see much support for Mack's contention that she has undergone "intense personal growth and [experienced] philosophical and spiritual opening."[30] The one extended example of Jerry's entry concerning the creative force in the universe is not particularly reassuring:

> Imagine that your essence, your soul, was part of a whole, and as part of a whole you decided to give birth, to create. You then gave birth to your thought to create and made your thought into matter. As this birth came to be solid, you then decided you would continue to create, and after some time you decided you would like to be whole again. But in order to be whole again you had to gather up all of the fragments or pieces of your whole being. In order to become whole again you must be able to then understand that you have to then create and give birth to that thought. And in order to go back to your original form you must again reverse the process.[31]

These are far from original, recalling Edgar Allan Poe and even L. Ron Hubbard, and for that matter raise as many problems as they try to solve.[32] For one thing, Jerry (or her alien instructor) reduces the creative principle in the universe to a matter of caprice and whim, where the force involved is seemingly unable to make up its cosmic mind on whether it should even exist or not. Paul claims to have learned about a "higher consciousness" which permeates all things and links entire universes, but much of what he says in the interview is barely coherent:

> [Paul, as alien]: "What is the purpose of controlling something you don't even understand in the first place? What are you controlling? . . . I don't understand. . . . You're controlling nothing," he continued. "If you look at frequency and energy, and the way it's structured itself around the form, and you start going deeper, and you start to understand evolution, the way that connects itself to molecular structure—it goes on for eons and eons! It's further than you can fathom, and it's tried to tell you that too, and you don't understand it."
>
> "What's 'it'?" I [Mack] asked.
>
> "Consciousness," he replied, "Higher forms of consciousness. . . . You're not going to understand infinity, but it's there!"[33]

Something of a parody of profundity, the passage makes it equally hard to accept that the notebooks he claims to have on alien technology are really full of "very solid" information.[34] Significantly, none of that information is included for the reader's inspection. As far as the multiple levels of being and parallel universes are concerned, these are issues that are being widely discussed in an age that is conspicuously receptive to channeling, extrasensory perception, astrology, and other manifestations of paranormal phenomena, perhaps in reaction to our technology-dominated society. The point is that even if we can accept that change of a significant nature has taken place within the minds of Mack's abductees, it does not mean that they received their inspiration from an external source, nor is it even necessary to postulate that this be so in order for their "visions" to be meaningful commentaries on our age.

Innovations in the Abduction Narrative

Abduction contains other major innovations in the evolving narrative. Apart from the more pronounced mystical elements and more multifaceted relationships with the aliens, even claims of dual identity, abductees also allege relationships between human and alien exist that extend beyond the present lifetime of the abductee. For the first time in the history of the abduction narrative many abductees are claiming to have past-life experiences, seeing themselves as having lived in a bygone era where they often enjoyed a relationship with an alien who served as a kind of ongoing guardian spirit from incarnation to incarnation.[35]

Carlos's discovery that he had lived before actually began with a visionary flashback that he had when in the Scottish Hebrides, on the Island of Iona. Standing alone on a dock by the sea, he was suddenly enveloped in a "pink haze like a bubble," whereupon he saw himself in a former existence in the sixth century.[36] There, as a child, he was protected from Viking invaders by a monk. Understandably enough, he did not at first connect this vision with the abduction phenomenon at all. Indeed, the link between his visionary experiences on Iona and his relationship with alien abductors remains tenuous throughout; Mack appears to have included it to illustrate how sensitive Carlos is to paranormal experiences generally (he also claims to have had near-death experiences).[37]

Several of Mack's other abductees make even more detailed connections between the alien presence and the transmigration of their souls. The first hint that reincarnation can play a prominent, if somewhat tangential, role in alien-human involvement occurs in Catherine's testimony. As we have seen, the presentation of scenes both pleasant and apocalyptic has in recent years become an increasingly prominent part of the abduction process. In the course of describing such a scene, a visual screening of various landscapes put on for her benefit by the aliens, Catherine realizes this was "a travelogue of [her] past lives," the display having been intended to acquaint her with reincarnation as a fact of human existence. The aliens then tell her the purpose of this demonstration is to show her that "everything's connected." As she puts it, " 'they were showing me in a former life to show that I was connected with that, and . . . [that] I can't continue to fight them [the aliens] the way I have been fighting them because I'm connected to them too.' "[38]

Though Catherine emerges with a heightened awareness of the value of love and the harmful nature of anger and hatred, it is unclear as to how the witnessing of her previous existence as a male Egyptian tomb decorator contributed to this knowledge. It is perhaps not surprising that Joe, who claims to be able to recall vivid memories going back to his own birth, should also believe that his relationship to the aliens extends back into previous incarnations. Once, so he avers, he was a British poet named Paul Desmonte who was allegedly arrested and tortured for "blaspheming" against the establishment. Shortly before he (as Paul) died in prison, the aliens "assisted" him in his dying, which he described as a passage to a higher realm, by "helping him stay connected with his divinity." Here the aliens become almost indistinguishable from those spiritual guides who appear in many religions, serving to school and assist the soul both in life and death. In his present (and quite unhappy) incarnation, the soul who is now named Joe, with the aliens' help, "chose his [particular] mother precisely because 'it would be tough.' "[39]

Sara and Paul believe that they not only have dual identity but have experienced previous lives *as aliens*. For her part, Sara is of the opinion that both humans and aliens reincarnate, and feels intuitively that her alien mentor—a being named Mengus—who she had reason to suspect had recently died, was living again in a new form. Dave's mentor is a female named Velia who loves him unconditionally and has been with him from the time of his birth.[40] He also thinks the aliens are concerned for us throughout "all our lifetimes," their job being to "help recycle souls or something." Velia assisted him some centuries ago when, as a North American Indian, Dave (or "Panther-by-the-Creek," as he was then called) died young, having been killed (and later scalped) in a battle. Incidentally, Dave does not think that the aliens are immortal, even though the evidence suggests that their primary place of residence is the plane of existence to which human souls allegedly go when they die. Eva too thinks she lived before, and believes that she can pass between dimensions as well. In a new twist, she also thinks she has been abducted in the course of various lifetimes by aliens, who have the ability "to enter into our space and time dimension or leave it any time they want."[41]

This new role of the aliens as they transform from technocratic scientists to New Age gurus represents a most significant development in the evolving narrative. As we noted previously, as the aliens become progressively less physical, they become increasingly difficult to catch or pin down and less amenable to the usual processes of verification. After all, if aliens are essentially nonphysical just as ghosts and other ethereal beings are, we will be less apt to expect them to leave physical traces or other evidence of their existence. In seeing them in this way, one major criticism against their existence has thus been effectively removed. In this sense, the shift in emphasis away from their status as physical beings is a necessary and timely narrative defensive strategy. But the problem remains that this new function is in stark conflict with the aliens' ongoing and very physical experiments with human beings. In fact, the need to square these two roles is Mack's greatest challenge, one he is arguably unable to confront successfully. Furthermore, in many ways the stories Mack's alleged abductees are telling him raise many more questions than they answer. For example, the very termination of an alien life is hard to fathom since abductees maintain that aliens are not physical as we understand the term; there would seem to be no mortal coil for them to shake off, as it were. Significantly, the reincarnation theme plays no part in accounts by Ed, Sheila, Scott, Jerry, Peter, and Arthur.

Limitations to Mack's Approach

For all his efforts to incorporate the various seemingly incompatible components of the abduction process—the endless anal and vaginal probing with the spiritual teachings—into a meaningful pattern, many will emerge from *Abduction* unpersuaded that either Mack's methodology or his theory accommodates all the evidence in a manner that is at once consistent and intelligible. Recognizing that he can never provide unequivocal proof, Mack tries to get around the question of the abductions' "literal truth" by arguing that there are simply some phenomena that transcend our mundane and materialistic worldview. On behalf of this contention he makes the point frequently that the abduction experience may manifest itself *in* our normal world, while not being *of* it in the usual sense of the word. But whenever we are exhorted to make significant alterations to our view of the universe, we have a right to expect that the reasons be pretty compelling. Realizing this, Mack devotes a good deal of time trying to establish the case that abductions can be considered "real" events. Basically, his position is that the abductees' recalled experiences constitute "a tapestry of sufficient richness" that simply cannot be dismissed as the product of hallucination or relegated to the workings of vivid imaginations. The information he provides "is of sufficient power and solidity to enable those who are open to expanding their view of possible realities to consider that the world might contain forces and intelligences of which we have hardly allowed ourselves to dream."[42]

Mack's point concerning the inadequacy of conventional therapeutic techniques to assuage his abductees' anxieties is also well made. Dogged attempts to reduce the abductees' experiences to conventional "wisdom" are, as he says, not only "procrustean," but have failed to help the abductees in any way. Finally, in support of his position Mack argues that such openness may not require us to demolish our present view of the physical universe so much as to become more flexible to additional possibilities; that "Our use of familiar words like 'happening,' 'occurred,' and 'real' will themselves have to be thought of differently, less literally perhaps."[43]

Mack's strongly held conviction—that an external intelligence of nonhuman origin is quite likely behind the experiences of the abductees—not only colors many of his assumptions and conclusions but causes him to minimize the likelihood that more conventional explanations may be possible. For instance, he considers it "surprising that abductees as a group are not more emotionally troubled than they are."[44] Ed, for example, did not find his recalled experiences or impending global cataclysm "markedly disturbing," but readers may suspect that Ed's complacency points to a different conclusion altogether: That many of the abductees are not more troubled may be because on some level they know the experiences did not happen literally, but were more in the nature of an extremely complex and upsetting dream.[45]

In this regard a number of Mack's abductees wonder themselves if they are "making it up." Ed, for one, stops in the middle of a hypnotic session to ask Mack "Am I bullshitting you?"; Catherine admits, "I still don't remember it like a real memory"; and Sara confesses, "I don't know if I believe myself."[46] Mack reassures her that "other abductees had been struggling with the same philosophical questions," but does not seem as sensitive to the implications of Sara's doubts as he might be. Even Arthur, who experienced the most trouble-free abduction with his cute and friendly aliens, believed in his experiences "intuitively" but also told Mack "I don't intellectually."[47]

Evidence that at least part of the abductees' testimony may be affected by the world of popular culture is similarly ignored. The extent of its resemblance to well-known films, as we have seen before, is at times too striking to ignore. The multicolored "cone-shaped dome" Sheila sees while in her abductors' UFO will remind the reader of the sight greeting Richard Dreyfus when he boards the UFO in *Close Encounters* (1977). Joe's fear that "he will not want to come back to the earth at all" is a sentiment made much of in the film *Cocoon* (1985), where friendly aliens offer a group of seniors what amounts to eternal life. Another echo of *Cocoon* (and of 1951's *The Day the Earth Stood Still* as well) also appears in Paul's testimony when he talks about aliens dying but being brought back to life "by the energy of the other beings," a situation also reminiscent of Tinkerbell, from *Peter Pan*, who recovered miraculously after drinking poison meant for Peter because the children believed in fairies.[48] It will be recalled that the purpose of the aliens' visit in *Cocoon* was to revive their comrades in such a manner, and the alien Klaatu "died" but was revived by energy aboard his UFO. The "interplanetary United Nations" Joe sees during one of his abductions, consisting of a variety of beings, some of them very ugly but all existing in a harmonious atmosphere, is reminiscent of the famous interstellar "cantina scene" in *Star Wars* (1977). The "reptilian" creature Sara saw that looked "almost like a sea creature" recalls "Gill-Man," the creature from the Black Lagoon from the 1954 film of that name. The being she sees on the chair or throne of metal, with an "outer orb around the head" and "skeleton face" is very similar in nature to the leader of the Martians in the 1953 film *Invaders from Mars*.[49] The "large robot-like creatures with large, black eyes that appeared to have reptilian and insectile facial qualities and insectile body characteristics" that so disconcerted Carlos also fit the description of the monster in the four *Alien* films (1979, 1986, 1992, and 1997), and the "crystalline machinery" that Carlos thinks may produce imagery of a "miniature holographic nature" is distinctly evocative of a machine designed precisely for that purpose by the mysterious Krell, the alien race that destroyed itself in *Forbidden Planet* (1956).[50]

But films are not the only possible source of abduction material. As a group, Mack's subjects appear more aware of UFO and abduction literature than were earlier abductees, which is not surprising when we consider that by the 1990s such material had been a staple of popular culture for several decades. Ed attended an annual conference of the Mutual UFO Network before seeking out Mack; Sheila, Jerry, and Catherine watched the harrowing CBS made-for-TV film *Intruders* that was based on Hopkins's books; Dave read *Communion* and Eva started to but could not finish it; and Catherine saw the film version of Strieber's book.[51] The point in this catalogue of resemblances is not to suggest that the abductees' accounts are mere fabrications, but at least partially colored by forgotten memories. To be fair, although Mack does not discuss this aspect specifically, he does seem alone in his willingness to acknowledge that many factors other than pure memory can play a role in the formation of the eventual abduction account.

In accounting for the pretensions of the aliens to spiritual gentility while not ignoring their inhumane treatment of their victims, Mack gets assistance from several of his alleged abductees. Peter believes that the aliens have a " 'vested interest' in our planet" and "wish to help us avoid what is about to transpire," presumably some natural catastrophe occasioned by our ecological foolishness.[52] Basically, Peter reasons that the feelings of helplessness, terror, and even rage that abductees experience when undergoing the physical examinations are like a gauntlet that must be run as a necessary prelude to an eventual acceptance of the aliens' reality and the importance of their message:

> The physical aspect of the experience, Peter continued, is essential to the shifts of consciousness involved. "You have to experience it in the physical before you can accept it in the psychological," he said. "A person holds the experience in their body. They have the physical sensation of the experiences actually happening, and then it becomes part of the reality. Just accepting reality does not do it. . . . They need us to expand our accepted reality for them to be able to communicate with us, for them to be able to come here," Peter added. "It's an evolution of consciousness."[53]

Here again, the reader will doubtless have some trouble sympathizing with this line of reasoning simply because the ongoing alien experimentation still appears a needless part of the process, with no clear benefit to anyone, human or alien alike. Even after Peter tells us that abductees experience a "stretching of consciousness" as a consequence of "the terrifying physical experiences" they must endure, it will still strike many readers as neither very logical nor practical as a pedagogical procedure.[54] Surely the more positive and equally successful instructional programs enjoyed by Ed, Eva, or Arthur could be employed more widely. Arthur, after all, firmly believed that the aliens were "afraid of making us afraid," for "if they make us afraid then we'll be ineffective" as emissaries.[55]

For obvious reasons, Mack finds the above explanation very much to his liking, seeing this aspect of the abduction process as similar in nature and purpose to those shamanistic initiation rituals which were also frequently unpleasant and painful, at least initially. Once fully aware—having been cleansed by their pain, so the argument runs—abductees begin to see their abductors not as enemies but as intermediaries or messengers, existing between themselves and "the primal source of creation" and this realm as their true home.[56] Mack even invokes various instances where novices must undergo various painful ordeals before achieving higher status. But in doing so, he ignores that the "shock treatment methods" employed by Zen Buddhists on novices or the self-purification processes of the yogi or ascetic are all part of clearly defined programs understood by the participants.

Mack also ignores that the lasting bitterness and resentment many of his abductees carry with them as a result of their experiences suggest that, even if personal growth may have taken place, it is heavily contaminated by persistent negative feelings. Ed "hate[s] being in this position of no control," while Sheila is "embarrassed to have no clothes on" as aliens gaze at her. Scott "lay terrified and paralyzed on a table in a UFO," and is overwhelmed by shame.[57] Mack speaks at length about Catherine's growth but says relatively little about her sense of having been "totally violated" even though that feeling persists as well, together with her anger that they have "ruined my life." When Catherine later claims to have learned from the aliens "that certain emotions, like 'love, caring, helpfulness, compassion' are 'the key,' " the reader can only wonder why her teachers would not practice what they preach.[58] Peter, though he likens his experience to that of "a woman who goes through the pain of labor," also sees it as straightforward abuse and felt outrage over being treated "like a tagged animal."[59]

In short, it is difficult to be as sanguine or philosophical as Mack about the indignities to which abductees are allegedly subjected. Mack finds that for him "there is no inconsistency here, unless one reserves spirituality for realms of the sublime that are free of pain and struggle."[60] If anything, it is much easier to see the aliens' behavior, when set against their supposed wisdom, as proof only of their hypocrisy, a hypocrisy which only makes sense when examined thematically, in relation to the developing mythic narrative, as the next chapters will demonstrate.

Mack's Awareness of His Role

To his credit, Mack observes that the transmission of information is a fairly lengthy and problematic process to which participants contribute willy-nilly. It begins with "the aliens, or whatever they represent, to the experiencer" (or alleged abductee), moves "from the experiencer to the person selected to report the information," and from there to the reader. Significantly, Mack recognizes that "the reporter [himself] selects and interprets among the various data, stressing some bits of information over others, which is itself a kind of interpretation." With admirable candor, he adds, "It may be argued that it is my own mind that has created this coherence, and that I have shaped and interpreted the data in line with a structure that I already have in mind."[61]

Carlos, too, recognizes that he had recalled certain things "awkwardly" and that many of his experiences were not part of a continuous narrative, but consisted of images that could only be roughly approximated through the medium of language. Mack even admits that Carlos's original testimony while hypnotized was not "always altogether coherent when he describes these complex processes," and adds that he is unable to "separate cleanly the dimensions of [Carlos's] narrative that are metaphoric and mythic from those that occur in, or are of, our, or any literal, physical world."[62] Though Mack ascribes this to being overwhelmed by the sheer force and vividness of the images that have impinged upon Carlos, the reader may suspect that turning the chaotic and disjointed original body of information into a coherent narrative has effectively altered it, and that the coherence present in the finished product was created after the fact, where little or none was originally present. Such suspicions are further reinforced in the excerpt Mack provides of a taped monologue delivered by Carlos in the course of a hypnotic session:

> I'm examined, and the examining . . . and the healings . . . are pushing and probing of the discovery of my changes in the molecular body. Metamorphoses . . . diffusion . . . is the process that I have to undergo mentally/physically . . . in the fleshness . . . of a physical being, in order for the directions we're taking to go through . . . the processes . . . as natural . . . and not dissolve into an unnatural process that is too rational or too nonrational, or too irrational.[63]

Even though Mack must be given credit for acknowledging the extent to which the final version of the narrative is a creative effort, even a joint one, in raising the issue of the author's role in the narrative process, he encourages the reader to speculate on how other authors of abduction narratives may have imposed a logic of their own on what were originally disparate fragments of information. At the same time, the reader will understand why more direct transcripts of abductees' statements are not featured in *Abduction*, if Carlos's testimony is typical of what Mack has had to work with. Plainly, one could make virtually anything of such snippets, and the reader is left wondering how many accounts were similarly unintelligible when Mack first heard them.

Mack's concessions help explain why we see certain types of abductees clustered around certain authors, and reinforce one of this book's fundamental contentions: Abduction authors cannot help but move within the constraints imposed upon them by their own cultural and conceptual assumptions, and as such inevitably play a crucial role in shaping and directing the finished product, no matter what the state of the abductees' original testimonies or the nature of their original experiences might have been.

What we have before us is a large body of narrative literature that continues to exert a fascination throughout society. Rich in detail and replete with relevant symbols that reflect many aspects of the human predicament, the story speaks to us about our values and concerns far more effectively and authoritatively than any work of science fiction can do. In its ability to codify and give form and structure to the present human condition, it serves an important purpose, one that will be examined in the following chapters on myth and its meaning for contemporary society.

Notes

1. John E. Mack, *Abduction: Human Encounters with Aliens* (New York: Charles Scribner's Sons), 391.

2. Ibid., 34–35.

3. Ibid., 41.

4. Ibid., 4–11.

5. In *The Tujunga Canyon Contacts* (Englewood Cliffs, N.J.: Prentice-Hall, 1980), D. Scott Rogo had made a similar suggestion in his concluding remarks, but his theory did not play an obvious role throughout the book as it does here.

6. Mack, *Abduction*, 13. In *The Interrupted Journey*, Fuller reproduces Betty's March 12, 1962, letter to Patrick J. Quirke, M.D., wherein she plainly initiates the process, stating that she and her husband "are seeking the services of a psychiatrist who uses hypnotism" (72). Later, Fuller writes that the Hills "approached the consultation [with Dr. Simon] with mingled feelings of curiosity, nervousness, and some apprehension, although these feelings were tempered with the relief that comes from taking a decisive step and action in the direction they thought would help" (79).

7. David Jacobs, *Secret Life* (New York: Simon & Schuster, 1992), 40.

8. Mack, *Abduction*, 389.

9. Ibid., 18.

10. Ibid., 17.

11. Ibid., 69–71, 82.

12. Ibid., 69, 71, 92–94.

13. Ibid., 112, 113, 119, 145.

14. Ibid., 145, 178, 217, 219, 242.

15. Ibid., 220, 242, 245, 254–56.

16. Ibid., 302, 314.

17. For a detailed look at shamanism, see M. Harner, *The Way of the Shaman* (New York: HarperCollins, 1990).

18. Mack, *Abduction*, 46.

19. Ibid., 196.

20. Ibid., 224, 245.

21. Ibid., 367, 379. Peter, however, contradicts himself elsewhere when he claims the aliens "lost much of their emotions" (313).

22. Ibid., 61–64, 53.

23. Ibid., 60.

24. Ibid., 149, 168. Joe is also told in contrast that experimentation is designed to "perpetuate the human seed" (186).

25. Ibid., 59–60, 94, 207, 223, 243, 295, 350–51, 378.

26. Ibid., 258.

27. Ibid., 165.

28. Ibid., 60–61.

29. Ibid., 97, 101–104.

30. Ibid., 112, 131, 138.

31. Ibid., 140–41.

32. In his imaginative sketch of the universe's creation, Edgar Allan Poe in *Eureka* envisioned a similar form of pure unity originally distributing itself throughout the universe in the form of matter, and ultimately coming back to its original unified state at some point in the far distant future. L. Ron Hubbard, founder of the Church of Scientology, postulated the existence of supernal beings who, ages ago, decided to devolve into material creatures such as ourselves.

33. Mack, *Abduction*, 226.

34. Ibid., 237.

35. Ibid., 407–409.

36. Ibid., 338.

37. Ibid., 338–40.

38. Ibid., 171–73.

39. Ibid., 195, 196.

40. Here it is interesting to note that several of the aliens assisting Mack's abductees also have personal names, but none can be found in any of Hopkins's cases.

41. Mack, *Abduction*, 283, 252.

42. Ibid., 389.

43. Ibid., 405.

44. Ibid., 44.

45. See Philip Klass, "Hypnosis and UFO Abductions," *Skeptical Inquirer* 5 (Spring 1981): 16–24. Dr. Simon, of course, made this point about the Hills.

46. Mack, *Abduction*, 58, 153, 206.

47. Ibid., 214, 383.

48. Ibid., 181, 234.

49. Ibid., 212, 207. Interestingly, this film involved the kidnapping of humans by aliens.

50. Ibid., 350–53.
51. Ibid., 51, 75, 111, 145, 271, 242–43.
52. Ibid., 306–308.
53. Ibid., 308.
54. Ibid., 309.
55. Ibid., 380.
56. Ibid., 48.
57. Ibid., 58, 82, 96.
58. Ibid., 131, 154, 164.
59. Ibid., 300.
60. Ibid., 407.
61. Ibid., 353, 389.
62. Ibid., 363–66.
63. Ibid., 366.

11

THE ABDUCTION
NARRATIVE
AS A CONTEMPORARY MYTH

Even in the 1950s Carl Jung realized that the UFO phenomenon
had the potential to become part of a modern mythology. The first
to recognize the UFO as a contemporary manifestation of myth,
Jung was initially struck by the deep symbolic significance of the
flying saucer.[1] Just as the circle suggested the mandala (itself a
symbol of order, perfection, and wholeness, if not also of God), he
argued that the mandala-shaped saucers themselves "could easily
be thought of as 'gods.' " To Jung, the possibility of "order, deliverance, salvation, and wholeness" is present in the UFO as originally envisaged, and he considered it a particularly apt symbol for
the times, since it *is* technological, and "anything that looks technological goes down without difficulty with modern man."[2]

Jung's stress on the symbolic dimension of the flying saucer
paved the way for later work by making this aspect of the subject
a legitimate area of study, and in recent years a few writers have
continued his work on the UFO's mythological dimension.
Astronomer and ufologist Jacques Vallee, for one, has long maintained that although there is no convincing proof that UFOs are
extraterrestrial in origin, they do represent a form of transdimensional intelligence that periodically communicates with certain
people. As he puts it, "the UFO phenomenon is one of the ways
through which an alien form of intelligence of incredible com-

plexity is communicating with us *symbolically*."[3] In this, of course, he anticipates John Mack. But Vallee goes on to argue that the tales these people tell of their experiences become in the course of time the stuff of myth.

Vallee's work is important, because he is aware not only of the mythic component in UFOs, but of the crucial role symbols play in such narratives. As well, he is also sensitive to the importance of myth in all civilizations and cultures, seeing as he does that "mythology rules at a level of our social reality over which normal political and intellectual trends have no real power." Very much in the tradition of Jung, Vallee is of the opinion that UFOs "are constructed *both as physical craft . . . and as psychic devices*," where the appearance of the one occasions the emergence of the other, and that the very irrationality of some of the experiences may be designed to preclude rational investigation. This feature, he postulates, guarantees both the autonomy and the purity of the stories by discouraging conventional analyses, and reinforcing "the role of the rumors as secret folklore, rich in new images."[4]

It is not necessary for us to agree with every aspect of Vallee's thesis to acknowledge that he breathed new life into the Jungian assertion that the mythic element was not only of intrinsic importance, but demanded greater attention than it has hitherto received. Responding to this demand, independent scholar and journalist Keith Thompson in his *Angels and Aliens* (1991) has investigated the continuities between the unfolding UFO story and classical mythology, illustrating convincingly the number of formal elements they share. Thompson's work also follows Jung in demonstrating that much of value can be derived from the phenomenon apart from the question of its truth or falsity. Indeed, Thompson's definition of myth includes *all* occurrences that are associated with UFOs whether historical or not, and includes such well-known responses as the American Air Force's official dismissal of the phenomenon as a subject not worthy of serious attention. In considering every aspect of the UFO story as a part of an overall myth, Thompson significantly refuses to distinguish between those elements that characterize traditional views of mythology—that it must be composed of otherworldly, fantastic, or larger-than-life aspects—and those narrative structures which many consider to be merely a part of the everyday fabric of contemporary society and nothing more.

One "real-life" incident that Thompson sees as an important aspect of the UFO myth concerns the appearance on live television in 1957 by Donald Keyhoe of the National Investigations Committee on Aerial Phenomena (NICAP), when CBS "pulled" Keyhoe's microphone just as he began to depart from his prepared script and speak spontaneously about the alleged government cover-up of "the truth" about UFOs.[5] In fact, such an event caused considerable stir throughout UFO circles, and continues to reinforce another aspect of the UFO myth, the contention that governments have known both of the presence of UFOs and the abduction phenomenon as well, and have deliberately withheld this information from the public. Thompson's inclusion of such material is important for our purposes, for the suggestion that the government is in collusion with the alien abductors does emerge from time to time in abductees' testimony and figures strongly as one of the myth's thematic concerns. Betty Andreasson and her husband Bob Luca suspected they were being subjected to surveillance by unmarked helicopters, and other abductees claim to have been stalked by mysterious individuals or to have received strange telephone calls.[6]

Aspects of social history and icons from popular culture can contribute to mythic narratives as assuredly as can human encounters with supernatural beings, and Thompson is to be commended for drawing readers' attention to the extent to which the myth permeates society. An event such as the Keyhoe television appearance, for instance, has a decidedly mythic component. First, it is a modern manifestation of an American preoccupation virtually as old as the country itself, dramatizing as it does the classic confrontation between an isolated, self-reliant individual and a cold and impersonal bureaucratic institution. Furthermore, in that it raises the specter of conspiracy—Why *did* CBS pull the plug? Was it *ordered* to? If so, by *whom*? etc.—the event speaks directly to one of the twentieth century's most persistent fears: the intrusion in our lives of a sinister, unfriendly, and ubiquitous government, operating on the basis of a secret agenda all its own.

Thompson is also on firm ground when arguing that there is a resemblance between the roles played by a contactee and a prophet or seer from mythology, especially when that contactee begins to acquire legendary status with the passage of time. While it might be more difficult initially to agree with his claim that persons such as the still-living Philip Klass may also be playing what Thompson calls "mythic roles," only a cursory look at UFO litera- ture will amply demonstrate the extent to which Klass has been incorporated into the myth; many who believe in the literal reality of UFOs and abductions see him almost in a demonic light, as a witting or unwitting tool of those mysterious powers that would keep the truth from the public.

Aviation and aerospace historian Curtis Peebles, in *Watch the Skies* (1994), has also chronicled the history of what the author des- ignates the "flying saucer myth," and has provided an interesting outline of the ways in which beliefs about UFOs have changed in the years since they first came to be discussed at length in America.[7] Peebles defines myths as simple narrative constructions that spring up in society in response to social crises. According to him, turbulent social situations that produce insecurity such as the Cold War, the Bomb Scare, McCarthyism, or the Vietnam War will result in the production of myths.

Peebles's contention that a given myth may emerge in response to certain events in history is undeniable. While one might question his claim that one-line statements such as "cattle are being mutilated" or "some people are being abducted by aliens" are myths in themselves rather than the potential ingredi- ents of a myth, Peebles's recognition that myths bear an integral relationship to the culture in which they appear is beyond debate. In their original form, such assertions take the form of discrete beliefs alleged to be true. While these may not necessarily consti- tute narrative structures or make particular statements, they are certainly the building-blocks out of which myths are formed.

Peebles not only contends that the UFO myth is the product of social crises in society, but adds that as new crises occur, the myth will change, the better to accommodate and reflect society's con- cerns in the wake of such crises. Here, some readers may question his precise linking of developments in the UFO myth to specific historical occurrences such as the Cold War or the Vietnam con- flict, on the grounds that the relationship between the production of mythic narrative and social conditions is too complex to be reduced to such obvious causality. His thesis also seems somewhat ethnocentric in that he regards the phenomenon as primarily an American one, and is conspicuously silent when it comes to the worldwide interest in UFOs. Brazil and Spain, for example, did not experience national crises over the Vietnam War, nor were they directly affected by McCarthyism, yet interest in the UFO phenomenon in those countries has always been high.

Still, there is no doubt that narrative structures do not operate in a vacuum, but form and reform according to a culture's needs, desires, and concerns, as Peebles argues. Certainly, as far as the abduction myth is concerned, there is ample evidence that the narrative is undergoing constant change, and that changes in social conditions may well be playing a role in determining those changes. Furthermore, it can be demonstrated that the manifestation of UFO myths in countries such as Spain and elsewhere *are* somewhat different from those in America. Jacques Vallee, in *Revelations* (1991), for instance, provides a detailed history of the so-called UMMO phenomenon, which began when a number of strangely marked UFOs were reported to have landed near Madrid in 1966. Unusual objects were recovered from the landing sites, followed by a steady stream of surprisingly sophisticated written information which was sent in letters to various individuals throughout Europe from as far away as Australia. The letters purported to be written by beings who had arrived from a planet named Ummo. Although the entire phenomenon is without doubt an elaborate hoax, no one has yet determined who is responsible for, or capable of, orchestrating a deception of such magnitude, and some theorists have considered the possibility of a deliberately perpetrated scheme of disinformation by European governments.[8] Interestingly, despite all the publicity it acquired in Spain, France, and more recently, Argentina, it received relatively little attention in America.

All in all, Peebles's study is of considerable value, for he reminds us that there is more to UFOs than the single question of the objects' physical existence. As he assumes throughout his work, myth is invaluable, for it provides us with a way whereby some aspect of human experience can be looked at in an ordered manner, and in doing so serves a fundamental human need; as such, its importance should not be minimized as a force in our lives.

The Elements and Features of Myth

It would appear, then, that the UFO abduction narrative has acquired mythic status with the passage of time. Still, we have yet to determine precisely what factors must be present for a narrative like this to achieve such a state. In *The Many Meanings of Myth* (1984), University of Houston English scholar Martin S. Day, though advancing an extremely traditional view of myth, makes a number of points that have relevance to this concern. While Day's implicit assumption—that some cultures will not possess the requisite criteria to produce mythic thought—is simply incorrect, the criteria he cites as necessary for myth to be created are nevertheless important in themselves. The first is that "Hosts of people believe it [the mythic story] to be valid. Belief can range from fanatical insistence that the account is divine and eternal truth to 'willing suspension of disbelief,' the feeling by many readers of fiction that while imaginary the tale is wholly true to life, a genuine reading of experience."[9] As we have seen, many persons believe the abduction stories to be literally true, while others acknowledge that "something" significant is happening to the alleged abductees, and of course it is the central contention of this study that the myth is a phenomenon serious enough to be a matter worthy of society's concern.

Continuing, Day maintains that "scientifically, [a myth] cannot be proved" or "properly reconciled with phenomenological facts."[10] A myth therefore becomes impervious to scientific scrutiny, and gains a certain resilience as a consequence. In this regard, Day agrees with Jacques Vallee's observation that "mythology rules at a level of our social reality over which normal political and intellectual trends have no real power." Up to now, alleged UFO abductions have resisted all scientific efforts to validate or disprove them. The point here is that while a myth's relevance to a society has nothing to do with the extent to which its constituent parts may or may not actually be verifiable historical events, the likelihood of its gaining a foothold in society is enhanced to the degree that it eludes refutation *or* confirmation.

It used to be thought that myth was closely related to religion, that myths *had* to be about, or involve in some way, gods or other supernatural beings. Although one can always find exceptions to this requirement, it is interesting to note that the most fundamental aspect of the abduction narrative presents human beings in conflict with creatures that possess virtually supernatural powers— the ability to fly, pass through solid matter, or predict the future. In this respect the aliens are essentially indistinguishable from the gods of old.

It is also easy to challenge Day's insistence that a "sacred" element is a required component of myth, especially in light of other commentators' contentions that myth can be found everywhere. Literary critic Northrop Frye, for one, argued that myths simply combine ritual and dream to create meaningful narrative structures for society: "The union of ritual and dream in a form of verbal communication is myth."[11] As mentioned above, Keith Thompson assumed that all facets of the UFO issue are equally worthy of being considered as genuine mythological ingredients, and French literary critic and mythologist Roland Barthes believed that "since myth is a type of speech, everything can be a myth provided it is conveyed by a discourse."[12] Incidentally, Barthes was the first to see mythic messages embedded in many products of popular culture such as films, magazines, and even children's toys. Still, though Day's position can again be challenged, a supernatural element is arguably present in the abduction myth, especially in those narratives of the 1990s where abductees define the aliens in terms remarkably similar to angels on a mission primarily spiritual in purpose.

The Relevance of Myth to Society

But why is a narrative such as the abduction myth important to society and worthy of study? For one thing, mythic narratives reflect a culture's preoccupations and concerns as well as the things it fears. Myth comes into existence specifically in response to a need to account for certain aspects of the world that would otherwise remain unintelligible or objects of dread, by depicting them in narrative form. Obviously, myths do not *explain* certain aspects of the human condition in the strictest sense of the word; that is, as a scientific accounting of an event or process attempts to do. Instead, they give order and structure to events that would otherwise remain inchoate (and unintelligible) through the structured story that is created. Some might argue that, to the extent that they do this by means of language alone—rather than through the employment of scientific experimentation under controlled circumstances—they appeal to an esthetic rather than an intellectual sensibility, and have little value as sources of knowledge. Yet scientific explanations arguably spring from the same need to account for phenomena; both work toward the same goal, and both are similarly concerned with causal relationships. My point is, of course, that the myth provides information about the human condition just as valuable as can be found in treatises that emerge from the scientific or philosophical community.

Borrowing from the Greek philosopher Thales, Henry Murray described myths as narratives that captured "the interplay of personified cosmic forces."[13] Such forces and the effects they have on human beings—the subjects of myth—are frequently presented in a striking or suspenseful manner, the more vividly to illustrate the dynamics of these interactions. In this respect, as critic Harry Levin observes, myths present "symbolic answers to questions raised by man's curiosity about causes: e.g., the thunder must be the voice of Zeus."[14]

Unfortunately, some have taken such a definition to mean that this is *all* a myth does. Perhaps for this reason it has been fashionable to denigrate myths by defining them as primitive, prescientific explanations of natural and psychological phenomena, and worthless as sources of information or knowledge. It is undeniable that this very narrow conception of myth's function—that myths are little more than quaint but otherwise irrelevant stories—has affected the way they have come to be perceived, especially in the twentieth century. This contemptuous dismissal of myth is probably traceable to J. G. Frazer (1854–1941), the great anthropologist and author of the landmark study of world mythologies, *The Golden Bough*. Despite his fascination with mythology, Frazer equated myths with superstitions and saw them primarily as "primitive" man's ideas about the world; superstition he termed "applied mythology." Of course, the corollary of this last contention is that myth is nothing more than articulated superstition, interesting to the scholar and ethnologist but not to be taken seriously as a legitimate source of knowledge in its own right. To Frazer, myth "gave rise to superstitious practices and savage institutions," and was reducible to "primitive ideas minus practice . . . [representing only t]he first *incorrect* ideas suggested by the world."[15]

In spite of Frazer, more recent mythologists agree both that myths are very important aspects of a culture, and that it is really irrelevant whether they have any foundation in fiction or fact. Some have gone so far as to argue that because it has esthetic completeness, myth speaks for itself and requires no external justification for its existence. Philosopher Hans-Georg Gadamer makes this point when observing that myth is "verified by nothing else than the act of telling it. A myth which can be proved or verified by something outside of the living oral or written religious tradition is not really myth. Thus the only good definition of myth is that *myth neither requires nor includes any possible verification outside of itself.*"[16] Gadamer goes on to explain that this does not mean that some myths are not amenable to historical verification; only that they do not require such verification in order to be meaningful.

Other mythologists also regard the subject in a more kindly manner. To mythologist Joseph Campbell, far from being mere fictions, myths were essential to the psychic well-being of humankind. It was his opinion that "Man, apparently, cannot maintain himself in the universe without belief in some arrangement of the general inheritance of myth. In fact, the fullness of his life would even seem to stand in a direct ratio to the depth and range, not of his rational thought, but of his local mythology."[17] Campbell also sees myths as having an ennobling effect on human beings, sometimes providing us with a "formula for the reorientation of the human spirit—pitching it forward along the way of time, summoning man to an assumption of responsibility for the reform of the universe."[18] Neither literally true nor literally untrue, myth is essentially an artistic achievement, giving shape and form through imagery to forces that in their formlessness would remain meaningless.

For this reason, myths should not be dismissed simply because the stories they convey may not have literally happened. Indeed, the question of a literal truth at the root of a given myth or legend is usually incidental to its thematic and psychological importance to the society in which it emerged.[19] The natural forces and complex interplay of human emotions depicted in myths are no less true for their being personified. Just because thunderstorms and lightning, together with their often devastating effects, are not literally produced by gods named Zeus or Thor does not make the highly symbolic descriptions of the gods' destructive power any less relevant to the cultures in which they originated.

Many scholars share Campbell's views. Harvard anthropologist Clyde Kluckhohn speculates that "the contribution of mythology [may be] that of providing a logical model capable of overcoming contradictions in a people's view of the world and what they have deduced from their experience."[20] The American psychologist Jerome Bruner also believes myth to be an important means of linking the largely not-understood world of "preternatural forces" (i.e., those that diverge from that "everyday" natural order with which we feel safe and familiar) with the experienced facts of life, in a way that satisfies us on an emotional and conscious level simultaneously.[21]

Similarly, human passions such as love and aggressiveness, personified in gods such as Venus and Mars, become less mysterious and complex by being given recognizable human forms. In this sense, the dramas of myth are often highly complex attempts to render intelligible the effects of these emotions when they clash in various combinations. In giving an originally formless force or conflict a structure through narrative, the myth makes it somehow more manageable; still fearful, no doubt, but less dreadful, perhaps, as a result of being codified in language and symbol.

Having agreed on myth's importance, scholars are understandably less sure when it comes to determining how myths are actually made. Levin believes that *mythopoesis*—literally, "story" (*mythos*) and "making" (*poesis*)—is simply "a technical term for imagination at work."[22] Speaking of the mythmaking function, Bruner sees it as proceeding from a tendency in human beings to project or "externalize" the problem areas of life in the forms of images, symbols, and narratives, the better to observe them. Bruner also speculates that mythmaking may be similar in origin to the act of dreaming, where a human impulse is transformed into image and symbol, or "where an internal plight is converted into a story plot."[23] This, of course, recalls Northrop Frye's contention that myth enables the subjective, image-laden world of dreams to become objectified and shared. As we proceed, it will become evident that Bruner's definition of myth has considerable relevance to the abduction narrative in particular.

Exactly how myths develop in a society remains in part mysterious, but it is likely that if story-telling is an inevitable byproduct of the development of language, in any culture narratives are bound to spring up constantly and be exposed to public scrutiny, as creative individuals allow their imaginations to describe the world around them. The British classicist G. S. Kirk, for one, appears to accept this dynamic when he comments on myths:

> Their telling is subject to the rules of all traditional tales: they will be varied in some degree on virtually every occasion of telling, and the variations will be determined by the whim, the ambition or the particular thematic repertoire of the individual teller, as well as by the receptivity and special requirements of the particular audience. Themes will be suppressed, added, transposed, or replaced by other apparently equivalent themes.[24]

It also seems logical to assume that for a tale to survive the initial telling, it must be perceived to have relevance to the lives of those who hear it; that is, it must speak on some level to the concerns as well as the tastes of many human beings within a specific culture. In each retelling of such a tale, variations undoubtedly occur which are themselves the product of fallible human memories, the productivity of narrative repertoires, and the creative imaginations of other, subsequent storytellers working in combination. As new variations creep into the stories they are examined for relevance and appropriateness by every audience that receives them; if the addenda appear to pass this test, it is my contention that they will inevitably be incorporated into the core narrative.

There remains the question of why we require new myths; in particular, why was the abduction myth created in the first place? The answer to this is relatively simple: myths must be expressed in terms of imagery that is relevant to the age. No myth can ever fully transcend the particulars of time and place; the relevance of a story is intimately connected to the cultural context in which it was formed and gained currency. This is not to say that a Greek myth no longer has any meaning: only that the full import of its meaning (that which it originally had for a Greek audience) is bound to become progressively more difficult for a culture to discern as the centuries pass. The significance of concepts and characters participating in the myth, the importance of the figures of speech and the meaning of the imagery, all such elements were once readily grasped by its audiences, but they have been obscured by the social changes that occur over time.

For example, most people in contemporary society will find it difficult to become intensely involved with the well-known mythic tale of Leda and her encounter with Zeus. Zeus, it will be recalled, inflamed with desire for the beautiful Leda, assumed the form of a swan and raped her. As a result of the assault, Leda gave birth to Castor, Pollux, and most notably Helen, the original cause of the Trojan War.[25] While the fact of rape is still intrinsically shocking to us, Leda's story is rendered less dramatic and immediate by our sense of the remoteness of the event and its narrative form. In short, as the myth faded steadily into the background of time, its capacity to move us was eroded as well. This fading process presented problems for a society, if the myth's underlying truths remain relevant to the human condition and continue to need expression within the culture. In the case of Leda and Zeus, all of the elements in the original narrative are just as applicable to twentieth-century society as they were so many centuries ago. As much a vivid and terrifying portrayal of human helplessness in the face of vast, powerful, and inscrutable forces, as a statement of female subjugation and degradation by patriarchal power the story has nevertheless lost its capacity to communicate to us as directly or intensely as it once did. Hence, it is necessary to rephrase myths in terminology that *is* of relevance to the culture of the period. In our case, essentially the same scenario is presented in the abduction narrative as was present in Leda's story, but with imagery better suited for the people of our time: the imagery of technology, which, as Jung observed, has become a modern expression of godhead.

Once the reader recognizes that the abduction narrative can be regarded as a contemporary reshaping, in part, of themes present in myths such as that of Leda, its status as a myth becomes immediately evident. Where our ancestors personified as gods all those largely unintelligible forces that impinged upon them, contemporary society has its own battery of technological, governmental, and institutional forces, all of which are at once as powerful and unfathomable as were those the ancients faced. Thus, where Leda was raped by a god who inexplicably disguised himself as a swan, our age now has both men and women—purportedly thousands of them—having steel rods inserted into their navels or other orifices by extremely powerful beings, for similarly unexplained and enigmatic purposes. In fact, all of the same underlying elements of theme and plot appear in both stories: In both cases people are being violated by seemingly cold, selfish, and compassionless beings; they are experiencing primal helplessness in the face of forces they are utterly powerless to avoid, control, or even understand; and in both there is the seemingly contradictory message that there may be method in the supernatural beings' apparent madness after all.

Notes

1. C. G. Jung, "Flying Saucers: A Modern Myth of Things Seen in the Skies." *Civilization in Transition*, 2d ed., trans. R. F. C. Hull (Princeton, N.J.: Princeton University Press, 1970).

2. Ibid., 327–28.

3. Jacques Vallee, *Dimensions: A Casebook of Alien Contact* (New York: Ballantine, 1988), 257.

4. Ibid., 247–48.

5. See Thompson, *Angels and Aliens: UFOs and the Mythic Imagination* (New York: Fawcett, 1991), 247–48, for a detailed summary of this event. Keyhoe claimed that he had been censored, an accusation which the CBS Network freely admitted, since all had agreed not to depart from their previously approved scripts for security reasons.

6. See Raymond Fowler, *The Andreasson Affair: Phase Two* (Englewood Cliffs, N.J.: Prentice-Hall, 1982), 210–15; Whitley Strieber, *Communion* (New York: Avon, 1987), 137; Budd Hopkins, *Intruders* (New York: Ballantine, 1987), 295; and Raymond Fowler, *The Allagash Abductions* (Tigard, Ore.: Wild Flower Press, 1993), 312.

7. Curtis Peebles, *Watch the Skies* (Washington, D.C.: Smithsonian Institution Press, 1994).

8. Jacques Vallee, *Revelations: Alien Contact and Human Deception* (New York: Ballantine, 1991), 98–132.

9. Martin S. Day, *The Many Meanings of Myth* (Lanham, Md.: University Press of America, 1984), 10.

10. Ibid., 10–11; Vallee, *Dimensions,* 247.

11. Northrop Frye, *Anatomy of Criticism* (Princeton, N.J.: Princeton University Press, 1957), 106.

12. Roland Barthes, *Mythologies*, trans. Annette Lavers (New York: Noonday Press, 1957; 1988), 109.

13. Henry A. Murray, "The Possible Nature of a 'Mythology' to Come," from *Myth and Mythmaking*, ed. Henry A. Murray (Boston: Beacon Press, 1968), 304, my emphasis.

14. Harry Levin, "Some Meanings of Myth," from *Myth and Mythmaking*, 105.

15. Robert Ackerman, *J. G. Frazer: His Life and Work* (Cambridge: Cambridge University Press), 89.

16. Hans-Georg Gadamer, "Religious and Poetical Speaking," from *Myth, Symbol, and Reality*, ed. Alan M. Olson (Notre Dame, Ind.: University of Notre Dame Press, 1980), 92.

17. Joseph Campbell, "The Historical Development of Mythology," from *Myth and Mythmaking*, 20.

18. Ibid., 25.

19. For example, in the cases of Oedipus, Beowulf, King Arthur, and Robin Hood, that all four men may have existed historically is surely of little relevance to the appeal and significance of their narratives.

20. Clyde Kluckhohn, "Recurrent Themes in Myth and Mythmaking," from *Myth and Mythmaking*, 58. Kluckhohn is paraphrasing Claude Levi-Strauss's assessment of myth's mediating function in a culture.

21. Jerome S. Bruner, "Myth and Identity," from *Myth and Mythmaking*, 276.

22. Levin, "Some Meanings of Myth," 105.

23. Bruner, "Myth and Identity," 276.

24. G. S. Kirk, *Myth: Its Meaning and Functions in Ancient and Other Cultures* (Cambridge: Cambridge University Press), 74.

25. Many versions of the myth contend that all three of these famous personages were produced by the encounter. See Robert Graves, *The Greek Myths* (Baltimore: Penguin, 1955).

CONCLUSION:
MYTHOLOGICAL MESSAGES

There has never been much agreement concerning the influence of technology on the human condition, opinion having been split since the Industrial Revolution pretty cleanly along two lines: that the outcome has been, and will continue to be, on the whole positive; or that the benefits are far outweighed by negative consequences. Basic to the positive view is the assumption that a totally perfected technology will bring with it an accompanying liberation from all forms of toil and hardship, poverty, and disease, and that human beings, totally free for the first time in history, will make good and fruitful use of their lives in the wake of this liberation.

In keeping with this positive view, the myth of UFOs and the aliens within them initially conveyed a positive message: Another, alien race has achieved a state of technological sophistication without blowing itself up in the process; presumably, the myth tells us, so can we. Here, the UFO can be seen—and indeed, so it *was*, at least initially—in relation to this optimistic scenario as the epitome of a golden technological age. Through its capacity to move freely and effortlessly in seeming defiance of the laws of physics and momentum, the UFO also suggests we can achieve virtual godlike autonomy and all that goes with it. At the time he was writing about the subject in the mid-1950s, Jung certainly associated the UFO with such basically affirmative implications.

Although belief in the beneficence of perfected technology may make sense initially (just as the Industrial Revolution was first seen as synonymous with progress), to many, such optimism is simplistic and naive. For one thing, it is debatable that technology actually does produce the freedom from toil that its exponents so frequently argue in its defense. Moreover, to the extent that any technological device invariably imposes its own agenda on its handlers, a totally technological world may bring with it a correspondingly total subjugation to its requirements. Jacques Ellul, one of the great theorists of technology in our century, argued in *The Technological Society* that the effect of technology's presence in the Western world has been to impose entirely new, and arguably more stringent, demands on our lives:

> The machine tends not only to create a new human environment, but also to modify man's very essence. The milieu in which he lives is no longer his. He must adapt himself, as though the world were new, to a universe for which he was not created. He was made to go six kilometers an hour, and he goes a thousand. He was made to eat when he was hungry and to sleep when he was sleepy; instead, he obeys a clock.[1]

Ellul acknowledges that humankind has "been liberated little by little from physical constraints, but he is all the more the slave of abstract ones," and goes on to use the relationship between an airplane and its crew as a metaphor for such enslavement. There, the pilot becomes "immobilized in a network of tubes and ducts, [and] he is deaf, blind, and impotent" to his human needs which have been subordinated to those of the machine he must maintain.[2] All that can concern him are the relentless demands of this technological milieu epitomized in miniature by the aircraft, where attention to its demands requires the crew's total commitment of energy. Any failure on their part, any lapse from total vigilance, will result in their destruction. In Ellul's opinion, essentially the same relationship can be seen between human beings and our present, highly technological society.

It is probably no accident that the initial, positive associations attached to the UFO coincided roughly with the end of World War II and the development of atomic power, events which together exemplified the most impressive manifestations of technology the world had ever seen. In the early stages of the atom's development, predictions regarding the uses to which it could be put tended to be optimistic. But, although visions of apocalypse had been with us for millennia, with the explosion of the atomic bomb it also became apparent that for the first time in history destruction of the planet at our own hands was a distinct possibility. Because of this dramatic development, society would never again be able to ignore or dismiss those who spoke of technology's darker potential as sensationalistic fear-mongers.

In short, it became difficult for many not to view such technology with considerable ambivalence. Accordingly, negative connotations soon came to be associated with the UFO, in its capacity as a symbol of technological prowess. Just as the atom was now seen as something at once awe-inspiring but simultaneously dreadful, UFOs and their occupants also came to be regarded in a similarly problematic, if not also paradoxical, way. Our growing awareness of this dark side provides a compelling reason why the purely benevolent, golden-haired alien beings initially described by the contactees were soon replaced by a mixed bag of aliens who, though they might utter high-sounding sentiments from time to time, more often than not used us callously, treated us with indifference, and might be impelled by malevolent designs. In fact, the very contradictions in the aliens—the dramatic dichotomy between what they occasionally preached and routinely practiced—closely approximates the two responses to our technology, which at once promises us heaven on earth while all-too-frequently creating conditions more reminiscent of hell.

It should also be added that a myth that features technologically sophisticated, highly symbolic alien abductors enables us to project onto these "alien" beings human traits that we are afraid to acknowledge in ourselves. Indeed, the very word "alien" allows us the luxury of seeing them in nonhuman terms, and their characteristics—which, as I shall argue below, are little more than exaggerated versions of our own—as similarly peculiar to themselves. In thus grafting all our fears onto an external source we avoid having to face the consequences of our own irresponsible utilization of technology, or confront the need to constrain our own tendencies to misuse our newly acquired powers.

All in all, it is not difficult to see how aptly the abduction narrative presents a confused and confusing picture of the potential within our technological world for both evil and good. It depicts in a deliberately ambiguous manner the possible effects on the quality of life in a technological environment, by presenting us with beings whose power is practically magical, but who are virtual slaves to the society that has attained this state. Like Marley's ghost come to warn Scrooge, to the extent that they are so obviously at the mercy of their purely technological agenda, the aliens are living proof of the dangers of a wholesale commitment to that technology, their incongruous treatment of their human victims a reflection of the incongruity inherent in technology itself. For if the myth presents the aliens as technocrats *par excellence*, it also reveals them as beings who possess little else of meaning in their lives. In those versions where aliens take their subjects on tours of their craft, it is almost as if they can take pride *only* in their technological accomplishments, for the tours are otherwise purposeless and inconclusive; evidently, they have nothing else they could point to in their milieu such as art, music, or literature that would demonstrate an enriched state of being. Here, the myth's message is pretty obvious: If ever-increasing amounts of our energy are needed to maintain an increasingly demanding technology, in a totally technological society, *all* opportunities for the creative functions will be lost; there will simply be no room or time for the exercise of the emotions, the passions, empathetic responses, or even love.

As symbols of our own darker tendencies and potentials, it is not surprising that the UFO and its abducting occupants should become objects of fear. Given the threat that the mythic scenario poses to human self-esteem, this may account for the ongoing attempt to reduce them to comic dimensions. To this end, words and terms were designed to render the phenomenon harmless, by describing it in ludicrous language. It is surely no accident that shortly after the first postwar sightings of UFOs the term "flying saucer" was coined and immediately took hold, just as the UFOs' crewmembers were customarily described as "little green men."[3] Such naming allowed us to reduce them to manageable dimensions through language. Once cut down to the level of an animated cartoon, they cease to be so dreadful. By naming something that could otherwise be quite disconcerting in terms more appropriate to Walt Disney's animation studios (for where else but in a cartoon would we ever see saucers in flight, or green-colored men?), we gain the illusion of mastery over it, for a thing that can be laughed at has no real power over us.

Needless to say, efforts such as this to create a myth that shields us from the more disconcerting symbolic implications of the myth have largely failed.

The Appeal and Relevance of the Abduction Myth

There are, of course, many other ways to account for the public's fascination with abduction stories. First, as we have seen, as a mythic narrative UFOs are no longer seen as isolated, inexplicable images. Nor are the events associated with them random or purposeless, but have become part of a coherent and engrossing story. Public interest is also doubtless enhanced by the challenge abduction stories pose to the reasonable and commonsensical way of looking at the world encouraged by conventional society. Indeed, when we realize how so many of the constituent parts of these abduction claims are frankly at odds with the objective stance of twentieth-century science, their appropriateness for the impressionable among us is striking. Like astrology, the UFO abduction narrative is an implicit slap in the faces of those champions of conventional epistemology who would insist we believe in the triumph of rationality as manifested through science and technology.

It also goes without saying that the subject matter is intrinsically absorbing; it is hard to imagine a more vivid depiction of human powerlessness. This fear is bound to be augmented when one imagines being abducted by beings who possess the ability to invade the sanctity of anyone's personal space with impunity, including that of the reader. One may read of other paranormal occurrences—ghosts or the Loch Ness Monster, for example—secure in the knowledge that these sightings only occur sporadically, in particular or remote locales. Readers can always return to the safe world of their homes, secure in the knowledge that the phenomenon in question cannot follow. But as the abduction myth has stated almost from the outset, there is no avoiding alien abductors.

But what is most relevant in terms of the narrative's mythic function is the extent to which alien behavior might well be our own. One interesting aspect of alien life as described in the myth is that the aliens themselves appear to be at the mercy of an agenda that is as intrusive and enslaving—and perhaps also bewildering—to them as it is to their victims. In this sense, alien lives bear similarities to those in our own machine-based culture. David Jacobs, though believing in the literal truth of the abduction process, nevertheless points to an important aspect of the myth when remarking that "The evidence suggests that this [the abduction process] goes on twenty-four hours a day, month after month, year after year."[4] What could be a more appropriate metaphor of enslavement in all its unrelenting drabness than this image of continuous toil, unrelieved and monotonous, stultifying in its largely unvarying routine? On occasion, the narrative alludes to abductees asking the aliens to supply reasons for their behavior. By way of response, they are met with shrugs or unconvincing explanations that "it has to be done," both answers suggesting that the aliens themselves may be occupying niches similar to those occupied by many in the modern world who see themselves as cogs in a vast bureaucratic or corporate machine.

Alien physical features are similarly significant when viewed from a symbolic perspective. Much has been made by debunkers of the fact that, with their overly large heads, tiny necks, chins with no jaws, useless mouths and ears, to say nothing of their bodies (which never seem to require nourishment), they are anatomically absurd contradictions in terms. But the description itself is remarkably consistent when examined symbolically. Their large heads are an apt indicator not so much of great intelligence as inordinate rationality, and their disproportionately large, black, pupilless (and thus expressionless) eyes could hint of sight without insight, combined with inscrutability of purpose. Interestingly, when we exclude the oversized heads and eyes, the myth almost invariably provides descriptions of the beings in terms of what they lack, or possess only minimally: ears, pupils, eyebrows, nose, or other distinct facial features, hair, and even (for the most part) conspicuous clothing. In fact, everything about the aliens is extremely minimal. If ever a race of beings exemplified the negative consequences of rationality it is these eminently drab, boring, and virtually sexless creatures with their expressionless faces and emotionless ways. Almost inevitably they even lack genitals, and in this deficiency are precisely what we would expect products of a "perfect" technological society to be, where the inhabitants' purpose in life is exclusively utilitarian.

The symbolic importance of the lack of facial features cannot be minimized. For one, such beings are almost totally unable to reveal emotion through facial expression. They cannot smile, frown, or kiss. As the myth frequently reiterates, virtually all of them look remarkably alike, the implication here being that they lack a distinct sense of ego or self; some versions of the myth have suggested they might well be robots or automata. In repeatedly stressing this fact, the myth reminds us that individuality is incompatible with the demands of a "perfect" technological environment. While many abduction narratives stress the aliens' obsessive curiosity with our reproductive systems or neurological functions, only the occasional version has them evincing a deeper interest about our emotional lives, and none, to my knowledge, includes any instance of extensive interest on their part in our civilization and culture. Although some aliens occasionally express emotions such as surprise, annoyance, or irritation, there is nothing to indicate that they experience any such feelings at all strongly, for what feelings they may possess never interfere with their primary purpose in being here.

Almost invariably the narrative strands coalesce around one salient feature of alien life: The absence of art, music, any nonutilitarian or even remotely pleasurable objects indicates that in human terms, the aliens' technological world is indeed joyless and arid. Supporting this is the fact that color imagery plays an insignificant role throughout the narrative, and could be said to be conspicuous by its absence. Although alien shapes and sizes vary, by far the majority of alien abductors are gray-skinned, and when they wear clothing, it is usually neutrally colored. As the most drab of hues, gray has traditionally been associated not only with illness and decay, but also with gloom and monotony, indifference, and most importantly for our purposes, the absence of passion or feeling.[5] As the product of black and white, gray is indistinct, cannot be found on the spectrum, and might well be thought of as no color at all.[6]

Just as the aliens themselves are only rarely associated with color, also notable is the lack of color throughout the alien world.[7] The interior of the UFO is usually metallic white or "bluish [fluorescent] white," but other colors as we know them are only rarely encountered; metallic gray, steel blue, and variations of white dominate. All these hues have traditional symbolic connotations: Blue is frequently associated with coldness. White *can* suggest purity, perhaps hinting in this case of a pure and single-minded commitment to their agenda, but it is also commonly associated with death and decay. The dual symbolic function of this latter color hints that the aliens' dedication to their presumably scientific goals may bring with it a type of emotional enervation, seen also in the listless and feeble-looking hybrid children their experiments seem so frequently to produce. If only hinted at here, the notion persists in more recently appearing narratives that the aliens have suffered great loss as a consequence of their absorption in technology. That they may not even be able to reproduce healthy offspring, hybrid or otherwise, is a prominent theme in these accounts.

Having said all this, it would be a mistake to conclude that there is no more to the abduction myth than a mere critique of technology in itself, that no other statements are being made through the vehicle of that paradigm. The manner in which that technology is being used by those in power is also of considerable importance. In refiguring in technological clothing society's concern with power relationships in a technological age, the myth also reflects our apprehensions concerning the intrusiveness of all manifestations of such power in our lives. Practically speaking, the aliens' power bears an unmistakable resemblance to the ubiquitous tentacles of modern bureaucracy. Just as no place is safe from the intrusions of technology-assisted statecraft, so no human is beyond the reach of the aliens and their inscrutable designs. Nor is there the possibility of escape; as most versions of the myth tell us, the experiences many abductees endure are usually part of an ongoing series from which there is no deliverance or termination. The prevailing paranoia concerning a government that is at once remote and unaccountable, but ever-present in our lives, finds expression in those addenda that frequently accompany abduction narratives, and concerns the possible involvement of sinister, "unofficial" government agencies working in conjunction with the alien abductors. An abductee's house being "buzzed" by black, unmarked helicopters; unusual telephone calls made to abductees possibly by the mysterious "Men in Black"; strange automobiles being sighted in the neighborhood of an abductee; or even the numerous inexplicable reports of cattle mutilations, involvement in these occurrences is officially denied by the government, but the very denials strike a resonant chord in an age where suspicion of government is not only rampant, but in many respects under-standable. Given what we now know of the CIA's illegal use of human guinea pigs for experimental purposes, to say nothing of its involvement in the domestic affairs of foreign countries—infor-mation freely available to us all today on television—the scenario projected by programs such as *The X-Files* does not seem as bizarre today as it would have even a few decades ago. Ours is an unde-niably dark and sinister age, where there are few if any certainties to sustain us. For this reason, it would be surprising if such ele-ments had not found their way into the myth, given all the dis-concerting revelations in recent times of unquestionably under-handed government behavior.

Also running through virtually all abduction narratives is the sense that abductees have been transported to a place where vir-tually everything we deem precious has been lost. The vast majority of abductees feel, for example, completely cut off from all sources of human compassion or comfort. In keeping with the theme that modern bureaucracy is intrinsically dehumanizing, the aliens as representatives of a technocratic/bureaucratic milieu remain steadfastly insensitive to human needs, an insensitivity they never seem to overcome.

To the extent that the aliens are representatives of a faceless bureaucracy, their messages to us—be they environmental or spir-itual in nature—are also of importance to the myth. First, their spouting of high-sounding sentiments almost in the same moment as they treat us so indifferently is arguably the stuff of hypocrisy, just as government's professions of having the public good at heart so frequently strike a hollow chord. But as bureaucrats, the aliens are frequently so clumsy and inefficient that it is hard to imagine them as the intellectually superior beings their technology would suggest them to be. For all their supposed prowess, they are capable of monstrous blunders. Nor, as they go doggedly about their experiments, committing the same blatantly inefficient maneuvers again and again, do they ever seem to adapt or refine their skills or learn from previous experience that what they have been doing is a needless waste of time. Like incorrigible children, the myth reveals them as stubbornly committed to projects that make very little sense when examined closely. As Whitley Strieber discovered, we could do a much better job in a fraction of the time. Indeed, it is almost as if they are preoccupied with the very fact of intrusive knowledge-gathering for its own sake.

Another aspect portrayed in virtually all versions of the abduction myth has to do with the exercise of power. Basically, the narratives promulgate two apparently contradictory contentions: that despite the aliens' cruelties, behind the painful and degrading experiences undergone by the abductees, their abductors may be ultimately benevolent and there may be meaning to it all. Just as Leda's story hinted that she was being used for a purpose, some abduction narratives hint that alleged abductees are similarly being exploited for their own good, difficult though this may be to believe.

The implications of this element—that the abductees' suffering, as it is part of a presumably meaningful design, must be endured—are far-ranging. For one thing, it may point to that part of us that wants to believe in the beneficence of our gods, be they technological, political, or bureaucratic, despite all evidence to the contrary. But the very ease with which the myth has permeated society may also suggest that it enjoys the sanction of those in power, for to the degree that this version implicitly endorses a "grin-and-bear-it" mentality in the face of such subjugation, so does it lend a sense of valor to passive acquiescence to existing power structures. Given this, the presentation of mysterious, baffling, and fearsome aliens that purport simultaneously to be our benefactors is not surprising; indeed, it is difficult to imagine a contemporary mythology more relevant to the concerns of the age.

As the preceding chapters have demonstrated, North American civilization has been witnessing for the past several decades a narrative myth that is constantly in the making. As is the case with other forms of evolution, the basic narrative began more or less quite simply and has grown steadily in complexity and variety, putting forth an increasing number of experimental variant forms while retaining an original, rooted, narrative structure. Some of these addenda have taken hold, and become permanent fixtures of the narrative; the "New Age" material, for example, has become steadily more popular as we approach the millennium. Other elements, such as the presentation of aliens as contemporary manifestations of Old Testament angels, have declined. Indeed, the reader can predict with reasonable assurance that if the persistence of one recurring feature can be counted on, it is that the narrative will continue to re-create itself; the development of myth is an ongoing, dynamic process, bound by the rules and limitations of its own internal structure, yet open to further change as it continues to respond to the culture that engendered it. For what may be most frightening about these aliens is that they are *not* altogether alien: In many respects, be they reptilian, insectlike, or humanoid, the myth presents them deliberately as being remarkably like us in terms of behavior and motivations, members of a culture not altogether difficult to comprehend. In most respects, they are little more than exaggerated projections of ourselves; alien, *c'est nous.*

There seems to be no indication that the ongoing development of the myth is showing any signs of tapering off. Just as this book neared completion, new abduction sagas from Whitley Strieber, Raymond Fowler, Budd Hopkins, and David Jacobs have appeared; a slightly modified version of John Mack's *Abduction* was published in paperback, and two of Budd Hopkins's most famous abductees, Kathie Davis and her sister, Laura, jointly produced an updated account of their experiences. Obviously, because the abduction narrative may never be completed, and is still very much in the process of being composed, it is perhaps appropriate that this study conclude with a familiar form of open-ended closure: "To Be Continued."

Notes

1. Jacques Ellul, *The Technological Society*, trans. John Wilkinson, intro. Robert K. Merton (New York: Alfred A. Knopf, 1964), 325.

2. Ibid., 325–26.

3. And still are. An article in the July 30, 1995, issue of the London *Sunday Times* ("Film 'Proving' Aliens Visited Earth Is Hoax") reassures

readers by informing them to "RELAX. The little green men have not landed."

4. David Jacobs, *Secret Life* (New York: Simon & Schuster, 1992), 310.

5. See Tom Chetwynd, *Dictionary of Symbols* (London: Aquarian Press, 1993), who observes that the color gray calls to mind ashes, suggesting that the "fire of love" or passion has been put out.

6. It is interesting to note that in David Fontana's *The Secret Language of Symbols: A Visual Key to Their Meanings* (San Francisco: Chronicle Books, 1994), although other colors are discussed extensively for their symbolic significance, no reference is made to gray.

7. It is also interesting to compare the colorless world of the alien abductors with that of the aliens George Adamski and other contactees encountered, which was full of color and generally quite resplendent. For a more detailed look at the significance of this issue see Martin Kottmeyer, "Why Are the Grays Gray?" *MUFON UFO Journal* 319 (November 1994): 6–10. There are exceptions, of course; Betty Andreasson's alien world did feature brilliant color imagery.

SELECTED BIBLIOGRAPHY

As readers will know, the volume of UFO and abduction literature is vast. The following is a highly select sampling of the material I found most interesting and relevant to the subject at hand.

A. Abduction Narratives

Druffel, Ann, and D. Scott Rogo. *The Tujunga Canyon Contacts—Updated Edition.* New York: New American Library, 1980; 1989.

Fuller, John. *The Interrupted Journey: Two Lost Hours "Aboard a Flying Saucer."* New York: Dell, 1966; 1987.

Fowler, Raymond. *The Andreasson Affair.* Englewood Cliffs, N.J.: Prentice-Hall, 1979.

———. *The Andreasson Affair: Phase Two.* Englewood Cliffs, N.J.: Prentice-Hall, 1982.

———. *The Watchers.* New York: Bantam, 1990.

———. *The Allagash Abductions.* Tigard, Ore.: Wild Flower Press, 1993.

Hopkins, Budd. *Missing Time.* New York: Berkley, 1981; 1983.

———. *Intruders.* New York: Ballantine, 1987; 1988.

Jacobs, David. *Secret Life.* New York: Simon and Schuster, 1992.

Mack, John. *Abduction.* New York: Scribner's, 1994.

Strieber, Whitley. *Communion.* New York: Avon, 1987; 1988.

———. *Transformation.* New York: Avon, 1988; 1989.

Walton, Travis. *The Walton Experience.* New York: Berkley, 1978.

B. On Narrative Technique

Bal, Mieke. *Narratology: Introduction to the Theory of Narrative.* Toronto: University of Toronto Press, 1985.

Docherty, Thomas. *On Modern Authority: The Theory and Condition of Writing, 1500–Present.* Sussex: Harvester, 1987.

Leitch, Thomas M. *What Stories Are: Narrative Theory and Interpretation.* University Park: Penn State University Press, 1986.

Martin, Wallace. *Recent Theories of Narrative.* Ithaca, N.Y.: Cornell University Press, 1986.

Nash, Christopher, ed. *Narrative in Culture: The Uses of Storytelling in the Sciences, Philosophy, and Literature.* London and New York: Routledge, 1990.

Prince, Gerald. *Narratology: The Form and Functioning of Narrative.* Berlin: Moutin, 1982.

Propp, Vladimir. *Morphology of the Folktale.* Austin: University of Texas Press, 1968 (first English pub. 1958).

White, Hayden. *Tropics of Discourse: Essays in Cultural Criticism.* Baltimore: Johns Hopkins University Press, 1978.

C. On Myth

Ackerman, Robert. *J. G. Frazer: His Life and Work.* Cambridge: Cambridge University Press, 1990.

Bennett, L., and M. S. Feldman. *Reconstructing Reality in the Courtroom.* New Brunswick, N.J.: Rutgers University Press, 1981.

Barthes, Roland. *Mythologies,* trans. Annette Lavers. New York: Noonday Press, 1988 [1957].

Chetwynd, Tom. *Dictionary of Symbols.* London: Aquarian Press, 1982.

Cunningham, Adrian, ed. *The Theory of Myth.* London: Sheed and Ward, 1973.

Day, Martin S. *The Many Meanings of Myth.* Lanham, Md.: University Press of America, 1984.

Eliade, Mircea. *Myths, Dreams and Mysteries,* English trans. New York: Harper, 1960.

Fontana, David. *The Secret Language of Symbols.* San Francisco: Chronicle Books, 1993.

Frye, Northrop. *Anatomy of Criticism.* Princeton, N.J.: Princeton University Press, 1957.

Hamilton, Edith. *Mythology.* New York: Signet, 1969.

Jung, Carl. "Flying Saucers: A Modern Myth of Things Seen in the Skies."

From *Civilization in Transition*, vol. X. Princeton, N.J.: Princeton University Press, 1970.

Kirk, G. S. *Myth: Its Meaning and Function in Ancient and Other Cultures.* Cambridge: Cambridge University Press, 1970.

Krupp, E. C. *Beyond the Blue Horizon: Myths and Legends of the Sun, Moon, Stars, and Planets.* New York: Oxford University Press, 1991.

Lowry, Shirley Park. *Familiar Mysteries: The Truth in Myth.* New York: Oxford University Press, 1982.

Murray, Henry A., ed. *Myth and Mythmaking.* Boston: Beacon Press, 1960.

Olson, Alan M., ed. *Myth, Symbol and Reality.* Notre Dame, Ind.: University of Notre Dame Press, 1980.

Wilner, Eleanor. *Gathering the Winds: Visionary Imagination and Radical Transformation of Self and Society.* Baltimore: Johns Hopkins University Press, 1975.

D. On UFO Abductions and Related Matters

Baker, Robert A. "The Aliens among Us: Hypnotic Regression Revisited," *Skeptical Inquirer* 12, no. 2 (Winter 1987–88): 148–62.

Bowen, Charles, ed. *The Humanoids.* London: Neville Spearman, 1969.

Bullard, Thomas Eddie. "Mysteries in the Eye of the Beholder: UFOs and Their Correlates as a Folkloric Theme Past and Present." Ph.D diss., Indiana University, 1982.

———. *On Stolen Time: A Summary of a Comparative Study of the UFO Abduction Mystery.* Washington, D.C.: The Fund for UFO Research, 1987.

———. *UFO Abductions: The Measure of a Mystery.* Mount Ranier, Md.: Fund for UFO Research, 1987.

Dickinson, Terence. *The Zeta Reticuli Incident.* Milwaukee, Wisc.: Astro-Media, 1976.

Ellul, Jacques. *The Technological Society.* New York: Vintage, 1964.

Fowler, Raymond. *Casebook of a UFO Investigator: A Personal Memoir.* Englewood Cliffs, N.J.: Prentice-Hall, 1981.

Fuller, John. *Incident at Exeter: The Story of Unidentified Flying Objects over America Today.* New York: Putnam, 1966.

Good, Timothy. *Above Top Secret: The Worldwide UFO Coverup.* Toronto: Macmillan of Canada, 1988.

———. *Alien Contact: Top Secret UFO Files Revealed.* New York: William Morrow, 1993.

Harner, M. *The Way of the Shaman*. New York: HarperCollins, 1990.

Hilgard, Ernest R. "Hypnosis Gives Rise to Fantasy and Is Not a Truth Serum," *Skeptical Inquirer* 5, no. 3 (Spring 1981): 25.

Huston, Peter. "Night Terrors, Sleep Paralysis, and Devil Stricken Demonic Telephone Cords from Hell," *Skeptical Inquirer* 17, no. 1 (Fall 1992): 64–69.

Hopkins, Budd, et al. *Unusual Personal Experiences: An Analysis of the Data from Three National Surveys*. Las Vegas: Bigelow Holding Corporation, 1992.

Jacobs, David. *The UFO Controversy in America*. Bloomington, Ind.: Indiana University Press, 1975.

Klass, Philip J. "Hypnosis and UFO Abductions," *Skeptical Inquirer* 5, no. 3 (Spring 1981): 16–24.

———. *UFO Abductions: A Dangerous Game*. Amherst, N.Y.: Prometheus, 1989.

Kuhn, Thomas. *The Structure of Scientific Revolutions*. Chicago: University of Chicago Press, 1962.

Peebles, Curtis. *Watch the Skies! A Chronicle of the Flying Saucer Myth*. Washington: Smithsonian Institution Press, 1994.

Pritchard, A., et al. *Alien Discussions: Proceedings of the Abduction Study Conference*. Cambridge, Mass.: North Cambridge Press, 1994.

Randles, Jenny. *UFOs: A British Viewpoint*. London: R. Hale, 1979.

———. *Abduction: Over 200 Documented UFO Kidnappings*. London: R. Hale, 1988.

Ring, Kenneth. *The Omega Project*. New York: William Morrow, 1992.

Rogo, D. Scott, ed. *Alien Abductions: True Cases of UFO Kidnappings*. New York: New American Library, 1980.

Rosenberg, Milton. "Alien-Abduction Claims and Standards of Inquiry." (Excerpt from Rosenberg's radio interview with Charles L. Gruder, Martin Orne, and Budd Hopkins.) *Skeptical Inquirer* 12, no. 3 (Spring 1988): 270–78.

Schnabel, Jim. *Dark White: Aliens, Abductions, and the UFO Obsession*. London: Hamish Hamilton, 1994.

Thompson, Keith. *Angels and Aliens: UFOs and the Mythic Imagination*. New York: Fawcett, 1991.

Vallee, Jacques. *Dimensions: A Casebook of Alien Contact*. New York: Ballantine, 1988.

———. *Confrontations; A Scientist's Search for Alien Contact*. New York: Ballantine, 1990.

———. *Revelations: Alien Contact and Human Deception*. New York: Ballantine, 1991.

———. *Passport to Magonia*. Chicago: Contemporary Books, 1993.

Readers are also encouraged to examine the *International UFO Reporter*, published by the J. Allen Hynek Center for UFO Studies, and the Mutual UFO Network's *UFO Journal*, both of which devote attention to the abduction phenomenon, much of it written from a believer's perspective. For a more skeptical examination of the issue, the *Skeptical Inquirer*, published by the Committee for the Scientific Investigation of Claims of the Paranormal (CSICOP), routinely features articles which deal with UFOs and abductions.

INDEX

311

215, 223, 237, 241, 259, 261–62, 264, 272, 285, 295, 298, 302 (*see also* aliens, links with religion; aliens, sexual experimentation of; technology, alien); links with religion, 81, 85, 89, 91, 92–93, 96, 102, 104, 107, 215, 279, 302 (*see also* religion); origins of, 94, 166, 205; sexual experimentation of, 27, 40–42, 66, 73n5, 75n43, 102, 122, 149, 171, 174, 202, 212, 216, 222, 227n55, 236, 241, 277n24

alien powers, 26, 202–203; astral travel, 203, 206, 238, 259; beaming, 105n11, 108, 111, 126, 138, 218, 239; defying molecular structure, 26, 72, 81, 84–85, 112, 174, 202, 235, 238, 259, 285; dulling pain, 140; extrasensory perception (ESP), 124, 240; hypnosis, 26, 68, 71, 111, 239; inducing amnesia, 68, 70–71, 102, 104, 133, 140, 173, 240; inducing trances, 27, 81, 87, 153, 182, 200, 202; invisibility, 27, 142, 168, 238; levitation, 203; precognition, 198, 203, 205, 207, 241, 262, 285; shape-shifting, 123, 125, 203; telekinesis, 203, 206; telepathy, 67, 70, 71, 96, 102, 120, 202, 203, 205, 206, 240; tracking, 67–68, 104n8, 115, 122

Arnold, Kenneth, 15
Astronomy, 67
Aviation Week and Space Technology, 23

Baker, Robert, 15, 23, 24–25, 74n18
Barthes, Roland, 285
Bennett, W.L., 37
Bible, The, 35, 81, 89, 193, 200, 303
Bruner, Jerome, 288
Bullard, Thomas, 40, 41, 158n6, 222–24; *UFO Abductions: The Measure of a Mystery*, 158n16, 222–23

Campbell, Joseph, 287

Christie, Agatha, 194
Clamar, Aphrodite, 146. *See also* hypnosis
Committee for the Scientific Investigation of Claims of the Paranormal (CSICOP), 23
Condon, Edward, 131, 132; *The Condon Report*, 131, 164
Constantino, Tony, 209–10, 219–20. *See also* hypnosis
contactees, 117, 242, 243, 295; credibility of, 135; Davis, William D., 205; Meier, Billy, 105n16; purpose of, 281

Day, Martin S., 284–85; *The Many Meanings of Myth*, 284–85
doppelganger experience, 203
Druffel, Ann, 23, 107–26, 246; *The Tujunga Canyon Contacts*, 107–26. *See also* Rogo, D. Scott; geographical sightings, Tujunga Canyon

Edelstein, Harold, 86. *See also* hypnosis
Ellul, Jacques, 294; *The Technological Society*, 294
Edwards, Frank, 201; *Flying Saucers: Serious Business*, 201

Feldman, M.S., 37
film and television, 148, 179, 188n47, 200; *Alfred Hitchcock Presents*, 164, 188n47; *Alien* (and sequels), 271; *Cinderella*, 201; *Close Encounters of the Third Kind*, 200, 239, 271; *Cocoon*, 200, 239, 271; *Creature from the Black Lagoon, The*, 271; *Day the Earth Stood Still, The*, 271; *Fantasia*, 201; *Forbidden Planet*; 200, 271; *I Married a Monster from Outer Space*, 188n47; *Invaders from Mars*, 188n47, 271; *Invasion of the Body Snatchers*, 239; *Invasion of the Saucer Men*, 218; *It Came from Outer Space*, 188n47; *Killers from Space*, 188n47;